Indian Suffragettes

Female Identities and Transnational Networks

SUMITA MUKHERJEE

OXFORD
UNIVERSITY PRESS

OXFORD

UNIVERSITY PRESS

Oxford University Press is a department of the University of Oxford.
It furthers the University's objective of excellence in research, scholarship,
and education by publishing worldwide. Oxford is a registered trademark of
Oxford University Press in the UK and in certain other countries.

Published in India by
Oxford University Press
2/11 Ground Floor, Ansari Road, Daryaganj, New Delhi 110 002, India

ISBN-13 (print edition): 978-0-19-948421-8
ISBN-10 (print edition): 0-19-948421-X

ISBN-13 (eBook): 978-0-19-909370-0
ISBN-10 (eBook): 0-19-909370-9

Typeset in ScalaPro 10/13
by Tranistics Data Technologies, Kolkata 700 091
Printed in India by Replika Press Pvt. Ltd

মা ও বাবা
আমার প্রণাম ও ভালবাসা

Contents

Illustrations

Preface and Acknowledgements

The first seed of the ideas behind this book was planted in me in around 2003 with a throwaway comment by an academic who mentioned that very little had been written about the history of Indian female suffrage. I was not particularly interested in the topic at that time, so did not think much of it. There were more seeds planted by Rozina Visram, whom I first met in 2007 when I was a postdoctoral research associate at the University of Oxford, UK, researching the history of South Asians in Britain. She introduced me to the fascinating figure Sophia Duleep Singh, whom we will encounter in this book. Sophia was a woman of Indian heritage who was heavily involved in the British suffrage movement. On a research trip to New Delhi, India, in 2009, when perusing the Nehru Memorial Museum and Library Archives for Indian figures who had been to Britain, I came across the reference to a small file on a woman called Herabai Tata. Calling up this file, I was amazed by the rich material in her correspondence with her friend Jaiji Petit about her work on suffrage. I realized then that there was potential in a larger project about Indian suffrage.

My research interests have always been in mobility, migration, and networks. Having come to this through the examples of Indian suffrage activists who had travelled to or lived in Britain, I knew that any volume I wrote about Indian suffrage would have to incorporate this transnational element, and I am glad I was able to find a way of writing this book that met my interests in mobility, identity, and in women's rights. The research for this book, and the book itself, would not have been written without the award of an Arts and Humanities Research Council (AHRC) Early Career Leadership Fellowship (AH/M004236/1) in 2014. My path in applying for and being able to accept this grant felt, at times, treacherous and torturous. I should not like to dwell on the travails of my academic career but rather to emphasize my gratitude to all those people who have helped me along the way to a permanent academic post and the completion of this book. I also wish to acknowledge the financial help of the Economic History Society and the Ferguson Bequest from the University of Glasgow, Scotland, UK.

Thank you to Judith Brown and Elleke Boehmer, who nurtured and supported me in the early stages of my career. To the colleagues who helped me with my AHRC application, especially Maud Bracke, Rose Elliot, Eleanor Gordon, and colleagues in the Centre for Gender History at the University of Glasgow, UK. To the anonymous reviewers of my AHRC application, including the no-longer-anonymous Stephen Legg. To Kathryn Gleadle and Anna Snaith, who were extremely kind and helpful in reading a draft chapter each, and also Rakesh Ankit. To Daniel Grey, Jonathan Saha, and June Purvis, for their support and comments on my 2017 article, 'The All-Asian Women's Conference 1931: Indian Women and Their Leadership of a Pan-Asian Feminist Organisation' (*Women's History Review*, volume 26, issue 3), which formed the basis for the ideas in Chapter 4. To Eva Bischoff, Catherine Candy, Senia Pesata, and Mari Takayanagi, for suggestions about references. Deep thanks to Megha Harish, who gave me considerable help with transcriptions in the summer of 2016 as an undergraduate research fellow at King's College London, UK.

The help I have received from friends and colleagues not only relates to writing this book, but also my career and other writing projects more broadly. Without their support at numerous stages in my career, up until this point, I would not have been able to complete this. My list is long, but crucial supporters not already mentioned include: Rehana Ahmed, Antoinette Burton, Lucy Delap, Dave Featherstone,

Christine Ferguson, Mark Freeman, Hugo Frey, Mary Ellis Gibson, Rohini Jayatilaka, Helen Lacey, Clare Midgley, Sue Morgan, Jim Phillips, Paul Readman, Robbie Shilliam, Roona Simpson, Adam Sutcliffe, Pippa Virdee, and Rozina Visram. There are many friends and colleagues I have not mentioned here. I hope they will forgive me for not mentioning them all and know that I have appreciated all the cups of tea and all the expressions of interest in my work and career. I am also thankful to anyone who has been in the audience when I have presented work from this project, including at Albany, Canterbury, Cologne, New Delhi, Glasgow, Liverpool, London, and Oxford. I am particularly grateful to colleagues at the University of Bristol, UK, who welcomed me so kindly and have shown such interest in this project.

Thank you to the librarians and archivists at the All-India Women's Library in New Delhi, the British Library in London, especially in the Asia and Africa Reading Rooms, the John Rylands Library in Manchester, UK, the National Library of Ireland in Dublin, the Nehru Memorial Museum and Library Archives in New Delhi, India, University of Reading, Smith College in Northampton Massachusetts, US, Swarthmore College in Pennsylvania, US, the Theosophical Library in Adyar, India, the United Nations archives in Geneva, Switzerland, and the Women's Library (in Aldgate and now based at the London School of Economics), UK. I am especially grateful to the archivists who have helped me procure the images in this book.

There are some characters in this book who share a surname with me, but I am not related to any of them. I often joke that my family played no part in key historical movements in India. Although I may not have relatives who rose to prominence in either the nationalist movement or women's social reform movement, it does not mean that in their own everyday lives they did not resist and challenge political and social norms. Both my grandmothers were married young and educated little, but the opposite was the case for my mother and my aunts. In this book, I focus on the educated, wealthy, mobile Indian women who were able to network with elites around the world. For the women in my family in this period (my grandmothers and my great-grandmothers), the campaign for the vote was hardly important when they faced pressing realities of infant mortality and were forcibly prevented from inheriting property. They would probably have been happy for their husbands to vote for them, as they would have had little sense of what the vote could do for them. And yet, today, in my reality, I know that the fight for the vote was allied to and integrally related to other campaigns to improve the lives of Indian women, and women around the world. These Indian suffragettes that I write about, to whom I may not be related, opened up opportunities for my family to follow in some of the paths that they took. I am grateful to those Indian suffragettes who preserved their archives—whether in the minutes of their associations, their fragmented correspondence, or sometimes in their rose-tinted memoirs—which have enabled me to pursue this career and write this book, although I know many voices and perspectives are still missing for a complete account.

My final declaration of gratitude is for the family and friends who have created the world in which I live and am able to work. I am lucky to have a number of close friends from my school days who have supported me emotionally over the decades and are like family to me. I thank them—they know who they are. My older brother, Chiron, has been my closest friend my whole life and I am grateful for his ongoing support. But ultimate thanks go to my parents, who have supported me in the journey to complete this book in far too many ways to recall or recount here. It is they who have really allowed this project to grow and flower. This book is dedicated to them.

Abbreviations

AAWC	All-Asian Women's Conference
AIWC	All-Indian Women's Conference
BCL	British Commonwealth League
BDWCU	British Dominions Women Citizen's Union
BDWSU	British Dominions Women's Suffrage Union
ICW	International Council of Women
IFC	Indian Franchise Committee (The Lothian Committee, 1932)
IWEA	Indian Women's Education Association
IWSA	International Woman Suffrage Alliance
IAWSEC	International Alliance of Women for Suffrage and Equal Citizenship
IAW	International Alliance of Women
JPC	Joint Parliamentary Committee
NCWB	National Council of Women in Burma
NCWI	National Council of Women in India
NUSEC	National Union of Societies for Equal Citizenship
NUWSS	National Union of Women's Suffrage Societies
NWP	National Women's Party
PPWA	Pan-Pacific Women's Association
RTC	Round Table Conference

WCTU	Women's Christian Temperance Union
WFL	Women's Freedom League
WIA	Women's Indian Association
WILPF	Women's International League for Peace and Freedom
WSPU	Women's Social and Political Union
WTRL	Women's Tax Resistance League
YMCA	Young Men's Christian Association
YWCA	Young Women's Christian Association

Introduction

Indian Suffrage Networks and Identities

It is not well known, either in India or internationally, that Indian women built up a vibrant, outward-looking suffrage movement in the twentieth century. Popular depictions of suffrage campaigners in films and literature have invariably concentrated on the British suffrage movement alongside a narrative of the importance of fighting for suffrage rights as the first step in the women's rights movement. In the 1964 Disney film *Mary Poppins*, Mrs Banks is introduced wearing a 'votes for women' sash and singing 'Sister Suffragette', a song which references the militancy of the campaign and the well-known activist Emmeline Pankhurst. The 2015 film *Suffragette*, directed by Sarah Gavron, cast popular Hollywood star Meryl Streep in the role of Emmeline Pankhurst. There are also less well-known television dramas about British and American suffrage campaigners, including a 2004 American drama *Iron Jawed Angels*, starring Hilary Swank and Angelica Houston as American campaigners Alice Paul and Carrie Chapman Catt respectively. One might be forgiven, especially in the Western world, for thinking that it was only British and American women who fought for the right to vote or that women in other parts of the world did not engage in similar battles. Yet the closing credits of *Suffragette* include a time-line of female suffrage victories in other countries, which acknowledges the ways in which suffrage was a global issue. Not only did women campaign around the world, at the same time, for the vote, but suffrage campaigns were also connected internationally. India was part of this network. Indeed, from the 1910s onwards Britain and other countries were sites for Indian women to campaign for the votes for women *in India*. In my focus on Indian suffragettes in this book, I highlight not only the campaigns that took place in India, but also the intimately intertwined transnational and international nature of the women's movement and suffrage campaigns around the world in the interwar period.

The campaign for the female vote in India was a global enterprise. This book not only offers a historical analysis of Indian campaigners for the female vote and discusses their campaigns in India, but also places their campaigns and rhetoric within a transnational context. Indian women travelled to other countries and interacted with campaigning groups around the world to further their fight in India. They also engaged with and supported suffrage campaigners in other countries. Indian women were campaigning for greater participation in parliamentary structures at a time when they were still subjects under British imperial rule. Thus, much of my focus is on the relationship between Indian and British women, and also the campaigns that Indian women undertook in Britain itself for Indian suffrage. There is a common misconception that because India was subject to imperial rule there was no need or desire for a female suffrage movement. The first public demands for female suffrage were made in 1917, and Indian women were enfranchised in 1921 in the provinces of Bombay and Madras, though only if they met certain property qualifications.[1] Over stages, women in the rest of British India, who had certain property rights, were enfranchised by 1930. The franchise was widened further in 1935. After Indian independence in 1947, full adult franchise for all men and women over 21 was granted in 1950 (the age was lowered to 18 in 1988).

---

[1] Please note that throughout this book I use the names of the cities as they were known during the period I am discussing.

Indian Suffragettes focuses on how Indian women operated in various geographical spaces and how their encounter and campaigning in different places allowed them to articulate multiple political identities. It discusses, first, the imperial identity that Indian suffragettes had as British subjects and how this had an effect on their relations and interactions with British feminists around the time of the First World War. I then look at the colonial solidarity that Indian women had with the rest of the British Empire, evident in their interactions with feminists in the dominions and in the suffrage campaigns of the Indian diaspora in Africa. As I have stated, suffrage was a global issue: so I also show how Indian women presented themselves on the international stage, at international conferences, especially in Europe and America in the interwar period. In addition, Indian women had a growing sense of a regional, Asian identity, which becomes more evident in the 1930s. But throughout this period Indian men and women were involved in campaigns for greater independence from British imperial rule. Thus, Indian suffragettes also grappled with coming to terms with their national identity in India. I show how Indian women positioned themselves and were represented in these locales and invoked different identities, whether regional, national, imperial, Commonwealth, Asian, Eastern, or international, in the context of debates about the vote. In exploring these spaces, this book demonstrates that Indian suffragettes were not only nationalist campaigners but were also actively engaging with global feminist networks in the interwar period.

I describe these women as Indian 'suffragettes'. The term 'suffragette' denotes, in the widely used British context, a militant activist, whereas 'suffragist' was the term used for men and women who supported female suffrage but did so through peaceful means and actions. Despite these differences, in common (non-academic) parlance in Britain, from where I write, the term 'suffragette' has come to mean any woman who fought for female suffrage. The distinction between militant and peaceful campaigning has often been lost, although popular British imagination of suffragettes is associated with well-known militants such as Emily Wilding Davison, who was killed by the King's Horse at the Derby in 1913, or Mary Richardson, who took an axe to Velazquez's *Rokeby Venus* at the National Gallery in 1914. The Indian women I discuss in this book were not militant in their campaigns, certainly not over female suffrage. They were, though, sometimes described as suffragettes.[2] Although mindful of the difference between 'suffragette' and 'suffragist' and the dangers of using such homogenizing terminology, especially as I will later be interrogating terms that are in flux such as 'feminism' and 'citizenship', I will be labelling these women as 'suffragettes' throughout this book, and without quotation marks. This is partly for ease and familiarity, and partly because though these women were not violent, their actions and purpose were radical for the time, and often perceived as rhetorically violent.

There is no complete study of the history of the female suffrage movement in India. Geraldine Forbes, a pioneering historian of women in India, discussed suffrage in her studies from 1979 and wrote a number of articles on the campaigns headed by Indian women's organizations from 1918 to 1935.[3] Jana Matson Everett also produced a comprehensive study of the suffrage campaigns in her 1981 publication *Women and Social Change in India*.[4] Illustrated books on the history of women in India and Pakistan by Radha Kumar and Rozina Visram, both published in the early 1990s, brought more attention to the relationship suffrage campaigns had with other women's activism.[5] There have since been a handful

[2] They were described as such in 1920 in the India Home Rule League of America organ *Young India* ('Indian Suffragettes', *Young India* [August 1920], 172) and in the *West Coast Spectator*, 4 January 1919. Vijay Agnew also described these women as suffragettes in her 1979 publication *Elite Women in Indian Politics* (New Delhi: Vikas Publishing House, 1979), chapter 6.

[3] Geraldine H. Forbes, 'Votes for Women: The Demand for Women's Franchise in India 1917–1937', in *Symbols of Power: Studies on the Political Status of Women in India*, ed. Vina Mazumdar (Bombay: Allied Publishers, 1979), 3–23; Geraldine H. Forbes, 'The Indian Women's Movement: A Struggle for Women's Rights or National Liberation?', in *The Extended Family: Women and Political Participation in India and Pakistan*, ed. Gail Minault (Delhi: Chanakya Publications, 1981), 49–82; Geraldine Forbes, *Women in Modern India* (Cambridge: Cambridge University Press, 1998).

[4] Jana Matson Everett, *Women and Social Change in India* (New Delhi: Heritage, 1981).

[5] Radha Kumar, *The History of Doing: An Illustrated Account of Movements for Women's Rights and Feminism in India 1800–1990* (London: Verso, 1993);

of pieces on the topic, such as those by Mrinalini Sinha, Barbara Ramusack, Gail Pearson, and Barbara Southard (on Bengal).[6] There have also been a handful of institutional or biographical studies of Indian female suffragettes and women's organizations.[7] Literature on female suffrage in India is generally viewed through the lenses of British reformers who aided and nurtured women's groups, highlighting the roles of women such as Annie Besant, Margaret Cousins, or Eleanor Rathbone.[8] The movement has also been discussed, only briefly, in studies of global suffrage such as Jad Adams' *Women and the Vote,* or Louise Edwards and Mina Roces' volume,

---

Rozina Visram, *Women in India and Pakistan: The Struggle for Independence from British Rule* (Cambridge: Cambridge University Press, 1992).

[6] Mrinalini Sinha, 'Suffragism and Internationalism: The Enfranchisement of British and Indian Women under an Imperial State', *Indian Economic and Social History Review* 36, 4 (1999): 461–84; Barbara N. Ramusack, 'Catalysts or Helpers? British Feminists, Indian Women's Rights, and Indian Independence', in *The Extended Family: Women and Political Participation in India and Pakistan,* ed. Gail Minault (Delhi: Chanakya Publications, 1981), 109–50; Gail Pearson, 'Reserved Seats—Women and the Vote in Bombay', *Indian Economic and Social History Review* 20, 47 (1983): 47–65; Gail Pearson, 'Tradition, Law and the Female Suffrage Movement in India', in *Women's Suffrage in Asia: Gender, Nationalism and Democracy,* ed. Louise Edwards and Mina Roces (London: Routledge Curzon, 2004), 195–218; Barbara Southard, 'Colonial Politics and Women's Rights: Woman Suffrage Campaigns in Bengal, British India in the 1920s', *Modern Asian Studies* 27, 2 (1993): 397–439; Azra Asghar Ali, 'Indian Muslim Women's Suffrage Campaign: Personal Dilemma and Communal Identity 1919–47', *Journal of the Pakistan Historical Survey* 47, 2 (June 1999): 33–46; Anupama Roy, *Gendered Citizenship: Historical and Conceptual Explorations* (New Delhi: Orient Longman, 2005).

[7] Aparna Basu, ed., *The Pathfinder: Dr Muthulakshmi Reddi* (New Delhi: AIWC, 1987); Aparna Basu and Bharati Ray, *Women's Struggle: A History of the All India Women's Conference 1927–2002,* 2nd ed. (New Delhi: Manohar, 2002).

[8] Antoinette Burton has demonstrated the ways in which empire and understandings of the position of women in empire were crucial to understandings of British suffrage, for example, in *Burdens of History: British Feminists, Indian Women, and Imperial Culture, 1865–1915* (Chapel Hill: University of Carolina Press, 1994).

Women's Suffrage in Asia.[9] Yet suffrage and political representation were issues of importance to Indian women and were not merely led by Western concerns.[10]

There has not yet been any consideration of the ways in which Indian women were utilizing imperial networks to travel across the empire, and beyond, to campaign for voting rights. Louise Edwards and Mina Roces have asserted that from its inception, 'women's struggle for the vote was explicitly global'; and Ellen DuBois has explained how suffrage movements around the world had been internationalist, relying on the cooperation of women of various nations and the influence they had on each other.[11] There is need to incorporate Indian perspectives in these approaches. While there has been considerable reflection on the transnational and global organizing of women in this period, notably by Leila Rupp and, more recently, by Marie Sandell, the focus has generally been on Euro-American-centric organizations such as the International Alliance of Women (IAW) or International Council of Women (ICW), or otherwise on organizations formed along national lines.[12] June Hannam, Mrinalini Sinha,

9 Jad Adams, *Women and the Vote: A World History* (Oxford: Oxford University Press, 2014), 341–50; Louise Edwards and Mina Roces, eds, *Women's Suffrage in Asia: Gender, Nationalism and Democracy* (London: Routledge Curzon, 2004).

10 See, for example, Louise Edwards and Mina Roces, 'Introduction: Orienting the Global Women's Suffrage Movement', in *Women's Suffrage in Asia: Gender, Nationalism and Democracy*, ed. Louise Edwards and Mina Roces (London: RoutledgeCurzon, 2004), 1–23; Pearson, 'Tradition, Law and the Female Suffrage Movement'; Geraldine H. Forbes, 'Caged Tigers: "First Wave" Feminists in India', *Women's Studies International Forum* 5, 6 (1982): 525–36; Roy, *Gendered Citizenship*, chap. 4.

11 Edwards and Roces, 'Introduction', 1; Ellen DuBois, 'Woman Suffrage around the World: Three Phases of Suffragist Internationalism', in *Suffrage and Beyond: International Feminist Perspectives*, ed. Caroline Daley and Melanie Nolan (Auckland: Auckland University Press, 1994), 252–74.

12 For example, Leila J. Rupp, *Worlds of Women: The Making of an International Women's Movement* (Princeton: Princeton University Press, 1997); Leila J. Rupp, 'Constructing Internationalism: The Case of Transnational Women's Organizations, 1888–1945', *The American Historical Review* 99, 5 (1994): 1571–1600; Marie Sandell, *The Rise of Women's Transnational*

Donna Guy, and Angela Woollacott have all demanded further analysis of the international links of feminism away from these Western centres, and though this call has been heeded there are still gaps to be filled.[13] As Jacqueline deVries pointed out in 2013, suffrage history is not just about 'suffrage' or just a history about political reform; suffrage histories should engage with broader studies of political history and understandings of political processes, feminism, and regional dynamics. There still remains a need to bring together various national and imperial histories of suffrage to understand the ways in which such networks and contacts helped and inspired *each other* during the early twentieth century.[14]

Spatial Interactions, Contact Zones, and Identities

As I explore the interactions between Indian suffragettes and various other men and women in different social and political spaces, their spatial understandings and sense of place emerge as incredibly important issues. It is by locating these Indian women in different spaces that I can draw upon the ways in which their sense of citizenship and their identities shift as they engage with different transnational networks. It is in these different geographical spaces that the complex intersections of racial, gendered, class, and other social identities come to the fore in various ways. As Jennifer Anne Boittin has explained in her study of the intersections between black colonial migrants and French women in interwar Paris, locality is important

---

Activism: Identity and Sisterhood between the World Wars (London: I.B. Tauris, 2015); Francisca de Haan et al., eds, 'Introduction', in *Women's Activism: Global Perspectives from the 1890s to the Present* (London: Routledge, 2013), 1–12.

[13] June Hannam, 'International Dimensions of Women's Suffrage: "At the Crossroads of Several Interlocking Identities"', *Women's History Review* 14, 3–4 (2005): 543–60; Mrinalini Sinha, Donna J. Guy, and Angela Woollacott, 'Introduction: Why Feminisms and Internationalism?', *Gender & History* 10, 3 (1998): 345–57.

[14] Jacqueline deVries, 'Popular and Smart: Scholarship on the Women's Suffrage Movement in Britain Still Matters', *History Compass* 11, 3 (2013): 177–88.

in understanding transnational imperial history.[15] Mary John has also argued that there is a need to emphasize the local, national, and international quality of the feminisms that Asians were engaging in from the nineteenth century; the plural nature of these internationalisms; and the complex interactions and links between Asian countries in this period.[16] Specific locations, as I will discuss, have effects on the frameworks of empire and metropole, immigration and travel, race, gender, and class.

The traditional model of studying imperial relations in the British Empire has been to explore the connections between Britain and either the dominions or the colonies through the British officials who went out to live and work in distant parts of the globe. In more recent decades, new imperial histories have not only looked at non-official relations and networks, but have also studied colonial subjects who travelled to Britain. Indians had been mobile for centuries, and they did not solely travel to Britain. The interwar period may have seen a growth in transnational associations, but these connections were not newly conceived. In this book, I follow in the footsteps of Tony Ballantyne in thinking more deeply of the webbed connections of the empire, of the ways disparate parts of the empire were brought together in new relations, and of the mobility of Indian women in the early twentieth century.[17] There are multiple imperial and global connections of the early twentieth century that have yet to be explored by geographically sensitive historians. Though there have been many works looking at the relationship between mobile colonial subjects and other parts of the empire, it is my intention to draw these together by looking at Indian women who interact with the imperial and colonial spaces of Britain, as well as the white dominions and other colonies, in addition to the other international spaces of Europe, America, and Asia. In doing so, I am not merely highlighting the complex networks and

---

[15] Jennifer Anne Boittin, *Colonial Metropolis: The Urban Grounds of Anti-Imperialism and Feminism in Interwar Paris* (Lincoln: University of Nebraska Press, 2010), xx, xxii.

[16] Mary E. John, 'Women and Feminisms in Contemporary Asia: New Comparisons, New Connections?', *Interventions* 9, 2 (2007): 166.

[17] Tony Ballantyne, 'Mobility, Empire, Colonisation', *History Australia* 11, 2 (August 2014): 7–37.

travels of Indian women, but I am also paying attention to the ways in which these Indian women operated in different locales. As Alan Lester has helpfully drawn out, imperial networks are nodal and there are multiple centres of connection.[18] Further, as Ballantyne points out, these networks are neither permanent nor solid. They are constantly being constructed and are shifting, growing, and declining during the time of empire. *Indian Suffragettes* will reflect upon these changing networks.

The geographer David Featherstone has skilfully explained how solidarity can be forged by marginal groups despite uneven relations across space. He has shown how the study of historical transnational networks is important to highlight that subalterns also embraced transnational spaces. It was not just Western elites who benefitted from travel. It is in these multi-ethnic networks that Western and non-Western individuals formed solidarities and developed their ideas of internationalism and democracy.[19] There are, however, people who were not globally connected. Chris Bayly has warned that alertness to global and international connections should not create a completely homogenous picture, nor should it elide all differences.[20] Indian suffragettes were involved in globalization, global networks, and subaltern networks of resistance, using transnational and cross-national links, forming different bonds of solidarity, and expressing their identity in different ways in these spaces. We should not ignore them, but should be mindful that they do not represent all Indian women.

Featherstone has also discussed the plural forms of subaltern cosmopolitans. Satadru Sen has discussed this notion, too, in his study of the Indian prince and cricketer Kumar Shri Ranjitsinhji, who expressed his 'imperial cosmopolitanism' through his multiple

[18] Alan Lester, 'Imperial Circuits and Networks: Geographies of the British Empire', *History Compass* 4, 1 (2006): 124–41.

[19] David Featherstone, *Solidarity: Hidden Histories and Geographies of Internationalism* (London: Zed Books, 2012); David Featherstone, 'The Spatial Politics of the Past Unbound: Transnational Networks and the Making of Political Identities', *Global Networks* 7, 4 (2007): 430–52.

[20] C.A. Bayly, *The Birth of the Modern World 1780–1914. Global Connections and Comparisons* (Oxford: Blackwell, 2004), 469.

identities (or aspects of self) as both Indian and British.[21] The Indian suffragettes I discuss were cosmopolitan, moving between different spaces, and also had multiple allegiances and identities. It is through our acknowledgement of these spaces, of the networks and the marginal players in these networks, that the shifting identities and connections of the Indian suffragettes in their mobility can be understood. Further, it is through this study that we can recognize the agency of Indian women not only in their own suffrage campaigns, but also in the ways in which they influenced and shaped other women's identities and campaigns in other parts of the world. I question, however, whether Indian women were ever really 'internationalist', as so many of their concerns were nationalist or, at times, pan-Asian. Their citizenship was certainly understood through a national agenda, and their position in international spaces was certainly understood through racial lenses. While British and American women were projecting a certain form of internationalism, their definition of internationalism (alongside that of feminism) was often alienating and not the appropriate terminology for the movement, actions, and identities of Indian women.

It is through travel and migration that these cosmopolitan and shifting identities become more apparent. Indians who went abroad were able to engage in direct comparisons with other societies, which highlighted the areas that needed reform in India. Indeed, travel away from India was a chance for many Indians to learn more about India, which was so culturally, religiously, and socially diverse, and to articulate in clearer terms their own sense of 'Indianness'. Inderpal Grewal has drawn links between travels abroad in the nineteenth century and the homogenization of the image of India, in particular reference to Indian women and their link to a notion of India as 'one country'.[22] As I have discussed elsewhere, travel in the early twentieth century made Indians increasingly aware not only of their position as 'subjects', of their objectification on the international stage, but also of the political

---

[21] Satadru Sen, *Migrant Races: Empire, Identity and K.S. Ranjitsinhji* (Manchester: Manchester University Press, 2004), 128–9.

[22] Inderpal Grewal, *Home and Harem: Nation, Gender, Empire, and the Cultures of Travel* (London: Leicester University Press, 1996), 162.

and social situation in India.[23] Thus, through their travel and engagement with men and women in different countries, their sense of self was articulated with more definition and their notions of the woman's question in India and ideas of citizenship were brought to light. In different spaces, they were able to articulate their Indian position more clearly. Apart from this, they also recognized their other multiple identities and positions in imperial and transnational spaces and networks.

Indian Suffragettes and Feminism

The key framework for histories of female suffrage has been to contextualize it within an ongoing, developing 'first-wave' feminist movement. However, the definition and use of the term 'feminism', especially in the early twentieth century, has been problematic. As Lucy Delap has explained, the use of the term 'feminist' in debates about the woman question in the late nineteenth century is an anachronism. Although the first use of the term *féminisme* in French can be dated to 1837, as a perjorative term, it was more commonly used in Britain and America from 1895 where its meaning was variable and the term was often used within quotation marks. In 1933, 'feminism' was added to the Oxford English Dictionary, where it was defined as 'advocacy of women's rights'.[24] It is important to remember that 'women' is not a unitary category either, as Joan Scott has argued.[25] We need to understand these Indian women then in their relation to other social identities and fields, to multiple sites of production, and to the ways in which they constructed their selves as feminine subjects.

[23] Sumita Mukherjee, *Nationalism, Education and Migrant Identities: The England-Returned* (Abingdon: Routledge, 2010), 5–6.

[24] Lucy Delap, 'The "Woman Question" and the Origins of Feminism', in *The Cambridge History of Nineteenth Century Political Thought*, ed. Gareth Stedman Jones and Gregory Claeys (Cambridge: Cambridge University Press, 2011), 319–48, n. 1.

[25] Joan W. Scott, 'Gender: A Useful Category of Historical Analysis', *The American Historical Review* 91, 5 (1986): 1053–75.

If we appropriate (one of) the modern understandings of feminism as advocacy of women's rights and demands for legal and political equality, then the Indian suffragettes we will encounter in this book were clearly feminists. They were vocal advocates of the rights of Indian women to vote and to be represented in political bodies. However, the term 'feminism' has now, and in the past, carried connotations of aggressive dislike of men. This is not, of course, how feminism should be understood, but many of the Indian suffragettes were aware and concerned about this definition. Thus, Indian women in the interwar period were markedly averse to the term 'feminist', and were often happy to explain why they were not feminists at all, equating it with a Western struggle. Laura Bier, in her study of Egyptian feminism, has called for an expansive definition of feminism that acknowledges not only the international scope and origins but also the local iterations based on complex historical preconditions. It is in recognizing some of these specificities and complexities that one can challenge critical assertions of the cultural inauthenticity of non-Western feminisms, and also question the universalizing claims that some feminisms made at the time. Despite these differences, feminists around the world shared a sense of and belief in the importance of women and womanhood for social and political transformations in local and international settings.[26]

Indian suffragettes were energized by the woman's question and 'womanism'. They sought out female friendships and women-led organizations. It is important, therefore, to acknowledge the gendered aspect of some of the networks that these women were engaged with, across lines of cultural, racial, and political difference. Friendships across colonial borders could be individually countercultural and revolutionary, as these women learnt to navigate relationships outside fixed categories and hierarchies.[27] Friendship did not need to mean an intimate or emotional relationship. Indeed, the friendships of Indian suffragettes with other women we will see in this book were often just professional relationships, and there were moments of discord and

---

[26] Laura Bier, *Revolutionary Womanhood: Feminisms, Modernity, and the State in Nasser's Egypt* (Stanford: Stanford University Press, 2011), 8–11.

[27] See Leela Gandhi, *Affective Communities: Anticolonial Thought and the Politics of Friendship* (Delhi: Permanent Black, 2006), 9–10.

rupture in their transnational networks. Ideological differences were also apparent in these networks. We encounter the dominance of certain Western women who exhibited forms of 'imperial feminism' throughout the interwar period, which frequently created tensions. As Antoinette Burton has explained, many British (and other) women in the nineteenth century and afterwards objectified non-Western women as people who needed to be 'saved'. Despite their intentions to reform, it was through this objectification that they often exhibited imperialist tendencies of control and perpetuated hierarchies.[28] These blinkers were not unique to the nineteenth or early twentieth century. Valerie Amos and Pratibha Parmar's criticism of the ways in which ideas of racial superiority were inherent in the discourses used by British and Western feminists in 1984 applies to this earlier period, and the issues of acknowledging 'intersectionality' engage twenty-first-century feminists to this day.[29]

Although Indian women often rejected the term 'feminist', they have always engaged with feminism.[30] As Forbes has observed, Indian women in the colonial period did not call themselves feminists because it implied that they were prioritizing women's rights issues when they also faced the pressing struggle for national equality.[31] Formulating campaigns for greater representation within an imperial system, Indian suffragettes had to face two opponents: male supremacy and foreign domination. Ultimately, because they could not wage attacks on two fronts, the focus of the Indian women's movement

---

[28] Burton, *Burdens of History*; Antoinette Burton, 'The Feminist Quest for Identity: British Imperial Suffragism and "Global Sisterhood", 1900–1915', *Journal of Women's History* 3, 2 (1991): 46–73.

[29] Valerie Amos and Pratibha Parmar, 'Challenging Imperial Feminism', *Feminist Review* 17, 1 (1984): 3–19.

[30] Padma Anagol, *The Emergence of Feminism in India, 1850–1920* (Aldershot: Ashgate, 2005), chap. 1; Chandra Talpade Mohanty, 'Introduction: Cartographies of Struggle: Third World Women and the Politics of Feminism', in *Third World Women and the Politics of Feminism*, ed. Chandra Talpade Mohanty, Ann Russo, and Lourdes Torres (Bloomington: Indiana University Press, 1991), 4, 7.

[31] As discussed in Joanna Liddle and Rama Joshi, 'Gender and Imperialism in British India', *Economic and Political Weekly* 20, 43 (26 October 1985): WS77.

was to stress that imperialism was the root of inequality, as men and women faced a joint struggle for social equality, and to temper British criticisms of Indian men.[32] This dilemma was common to women fighting colonialism and demanding suffrage at the same time.[33] Thus, as we shall see, criticisms of Indian men were extremely mild, if non-existent, within the Indian suffrage movement, which has had long-lasting effects on ongoing unrealized inequalities in the Indian subcontinent today. Yet, as Chandra Talpade Mohanty has argued, there is an inescapable link between feminist and political liberation movements, and all histories of feminism are related to other struggles.[34] We see in these Indian suffragettes a complex interrelation between their feminist and nationalist anti-imperialist struggles. The Indian women's movement was dominated by middle-class women who were at odds with a paternalistic, imperial state, and also a patriarchal, middle-class nationalist movement. The movement was epitomized by tensions between progressive and conservative ideas and actions. In Mohanty's words: 'No noncontradictory or "pure" feminism is possible.'[35] Despite these contradictions, tensions, and rejections of labels, these Indian women fought for women's equality, often against fierce opposition.

The idea of the 'modern woman' (or 'modern girl') emerged in the 1920s and 1930s on the international stage, and this had a homogenizing effect on the perception of women. However, as Mrinalini Sinha has argued, the nation and nationalism had powerful salience for women, especially in anti-colonial environments. Women were not only seen as symbols of motherhood, and key to national formations, but they also increasingly portrayed themselves as 'modern' and as citizens of modern emerging or potential nation states. Although Indian women were engaging with the international feminist movement, Sinha argues that nationalism could never be separated from

[32] These terms ('male supremacy' and 'foreign domination') are used in Liddle and Joshi, 'Gender and Imperialism in British India', WS72, WS77.

[33] Susan Blackburn, 'Women's Suffrage and Democracy in Indonesia', in *Women's Suffrage in Asia*, ed. Louise Edwards and Mina Roces (London: Routledge Curzon, 2004), 98.

[34] Mohanty, 'Cartographies of Struggle', 10–12.

[35] Mohanty, 'Cartographies of Struggle', 20.

the feminist movement. In their suffrage campaigns, in particular, they demonstrated that national self-determination was a feminist issue.[36]

Women also had to deal with the intersections of gendered and racial inequality with social-class inequities, and they did so with varying degrees of success and empathy. In the early twentieth century, the British suffrage movement was not particularly racially diverse, but Britain was. Figures such as Sophia Duleep Singh or Adelaide Knight, a British member of the Canning Town Women's Social and Political Union (WSPU), who was married to a Jamaican, Donlad Adolphus Brown, were involved in the movement. However, the international suffrage associations of the interwar period were dominated by American and British white middle-class women, who perpetuated social divisions and perceptions of non-Western women. Much of their attitudes towards women of colour was characterized in debates about their responsibilities towards the 'less fortunate' and 'as preservers of racial peace'.[37] Although some African American women attended international women's conferences in this period, the lack of involvement of women from sub-Saharan Africa, or First Nations women, and the stereotypical language used to describe non-Western participants reveal the ways in which notions of racial hierarchies were prevalent within the women's movement and also how they were perpetuated by Indian women. This is particularly evident in the work of the British Commonwealth League (BCL), which we will encounter in Chapter 2.

As Leila Rupp has also shown, the participants of international women's organizations were not only generally from the middle class but they also had the means to travel.[38] The Indian women we

---

[36] Mrinalini Sinha, 'Nations in an Imperial Crucible', in *Gender and Empire*, ed. Philippa Levine (Oxford: Oxford University Press, 2004), 181–202, at 201.

[37] Elizabeth Crawford, *The Women's Suffrage Movement: A Reference Guide 1866–1928* (London: UCL Press, 1999), 325; Christine Bolt, *Sisterhood Questioned? Race, Class and Internationalism in the American and British Women's Movements, c. 1880s–1970s* (Abingdon: Routledge, 2005), 76. Sophia Duleep Singh will be discussed in Chapter 1.

[38] Rupp, *Worlds of Women.*

encounter in this book had access to wealth, which allowed them to travel and engage with women around the world. Money is rarely discussed in the archival material, but these women were sponsored by subscriptions, benefactors, donations, and their own family wealth. They were also conversant in English, educated either in India or Britain. Often because of their privileged experiences and networks, their ability to empathize with or 'speak for' lower-class and lower-caste Indian women was limited.[39] The main women's organizations in India, with which the Indian suffrage leaders were generally affiliated—the Women's Indian Association (WIA) (founded in 1917), the National Council of Women (founded in 1925), and the All-India Women's Conference (1927)—were all founded with the assistance of British or Irish women, and were dominated by middle-class educated women. However, many Indian women in these organizations insisted that they represented all women in India. This is discussed further in Chapter 5. It is as a result of the imperial situation and ways in which Indian women were portrayed by British (and other) women that they wished to assert themselves as above difference and often objected to the emphasis on international influences on the Indian women's movement. For example, Hindu men and women involved in the nationalist movement would frequently invoke the 'Golden Age' of India in the Vedic era, before successive waves of colonialism, when Indian society had supposedly endorsed female rulers and equal economic and social opportunities for men and women, to argue that ideas of gender equality were not foreign to India.

Indian women in this period have often been dismissed as inhabitants of the private, domestic sphere, whose focus was mainly on the home, whereas the nationalist movement was a male concern. As Tanika Sarkar has pointed out, Indian women were involved in various political activities in the early twentieth century, but their public political role did not mean that they were emancipated domestically. Participation in the Gandhian movement was perceived as quite respectable, even by socially conservative families, especially

---

[39] Note that, according to the 1921 census, only 12 per cent of women and girls in India were literate (J.T. Marten, *Census of India, 1921*, Volume I, Part II—Tables [Calcutta: Superintendent Government Printing, 1923], 74).

because of the traditional imagery related to religion and duty that underpinned the movement. Indians were also encouraged by the role of princesses and elite upper-class women leaders in the nationalist movement. Therefore, Indian women were able to take part in radical politics because of these traditional moorings, but this prevented challenges to other concerns about women's position in society.[40] The activities of Indian suffragettes reveal that some Indian women could get involved in radical politics and that too on the international stage, but focus on democratic citizenship meant that other women's issues such as sexual independence or even the domestic separation of spheres were rarely challenged.

Sanjam Ahluwalia has pointed out in her study of the transnational activities of Indian women activists on the issue of birth control between 1877 and 1947 that close analysis of transnational exchanges highlights the underlying inequality of power relations that determined interactions. There were also various tensions inherent within the Indian women's movement with the dominance of middle-class, upper-caste women. Forbes, Pearson, and Jayawardena have argued that the fact that Indian feminists claimed to speak on behalf of all women and were unable to do so was because of an uneasy relationship with Gandhian nationalism, as they wished to avoid confrontation with male nationalist leaders. However, Ahluwalia argues, this assumes that feminist politics was the given position for all Indian women. It is extremely difficult, as a historian, to speak for the women (rural, illiterate, of a lower class and caste) whom the Indian female leaders claimed to be speaking for without homogenizing or making colonialist assumptions about their positions. Evidently, the Indian women leaders I will be discussing felt able to and, importantly, *wished* to represent these 'other' women. It is my intention to follow Ahluwalia's example in minding the historical contexts of these relationships and yet also to not dismiss the activities of elite Indian women immediately out of hand.[41]

---

[40] Tanika Sarkar, 'Politics and Women in Bengal: The Conditions and Meaning of Participation', *Indian Economic and Social History Review* 21, 1 (1984): 91–101.

[41] Sanjam Ahluwalia, *Reproductive Restraints: Birth Control in India, 1877–1947* (Urbana: University of Illinois Press, 2008), 8–9, 15, 86.

Indian Suffragettes and Indian Politics

Campaigns for the enfranchisement of Indian women could only become an issue when Indians were allowed to participate in parliamentary bodies in India. After 1858, India was ruled by the British Crown with a viceroy who was the acting head of state in situ in India. His counterpart, the secretary of state for India, held a cabinet post in the British parliament. The viceroy had an imperial council of state, with nominated British and Indian representatives advising on all governmental matters. Indians could not elect members to this council. There were, however, democratic structures at lower levels of the government. Women in some areas could exercise their right to vote to determine local politics by voting in municipal elections and also village councils (panchayats). There were campaigns by women for representation in other political bodies. Indian women, such as Pandita Ramabai, had campaigned for greater democratic powers in organizations such as the Indian National Congress (founded in 1885), but my focus is on parliamentary franchise at provincial and national levels.

The first public demands for female suffrage in India took place in 1917 when the secretary of state and viceroy of India, Montagu and Chelmsford respectively, came to India to discuss constitutional reform. In 1919, the Government of India Act created a new Central Legislative Assembly and a new male electorate, but only 3 per cent of Indian men were enfranchised to vote for representatives to Provincial Assemblies, and only 0.06 per cent for the Central Assembly.[42] Women were slowly enfranchised after 1920, as we shall see, but it was after the First World War that nationalist sentiment and activity increased exponentially in India. The appendix to this book includes a timeline of key events in the history of India and international suffrage.

There were several points of tension over the next decades. The imagery of women murdered in the 1919 Amritsar massacre, for example, gave flame to the women's political movement as they engaged in debates and disagreements with British representation of the massacre. In 1927, the publication of the American journalist Katherine

---

[42] Liddle and Joshi, 'Gender and Imperialism in British India', WS74.

Mayo's book *Mother India* became a global moment of controversy. Her book was critical of various practices in India, but Mayo was criticized for her superficial level of research. Mrinalini Sinha has argued that this publication and the resulting controversy were instrumental in the conception of women as political subjects in India: that women were increasingly then seen as having a discrete political identity and their collective agency was increasingly galvanized to contribute to new national imaginings of Indian citizenship.[43]

Indian electoral politics was also characterized by the issue of 'communal' representation. With a Hindu majority, but a large Muslim population, the imperial government was concerned about placating different religious communities, but also fostered differences through political rule. The Muslim League was founded in 1906, following the partition of Bengal in 1905. In 1909, the Morley–Minto reforms enshrined communal difference and the principle of quotas by establishing political categories and fixed representation for Muslims, depressed classes, and landlords. In 1916, Congress and the Muslim League came to an agreement, known as the Lucknow Pact, whereby Congress accepted the principle of separate Muslim electorates. Thus, the question of female suffrage and representation in India was intertwined with these broader questions of political quotas and whether Indian women should be divided along similar lines. Although Indian suffragettes generally argued that Indian women were united as women and were above such communal divisions, these questions did exercise many Muslim women.[44]

In the 1930s, a series of negotiations over constitutional reform took place while the civil disobedience movement was also growing. Historians have neglected to mention the Indian female delegates at the Round Table Conferences (RTCs) that took place in London from 1930 to 1932, which reveals the myopic nature of the political histories of the transfer of power. These women were actively involved in the subcommittees of the conference, consistently and constantly raising the question of women's franchise during discussions of

---

[43] Mrinalini Sinha, *Specters of Mother India: The Global Restructuring of an Empire* (Durham: Duke University Press, 2006), 11–12, 14.

[44] Ali, 'Indian Muslim Women's Suffrage'.

electorates. Survey books on the political history of India might be excused for failing to mention them, but the fact that major studies by R.J. Moore, which focus specifically on constitutional negotiations and dedicate in-depth analysis to the RTCs, do not discuss the female involvement is unacceptable.[45] It is this dismissal and obfuscation of women's involvement in constitutional negotiations and their engagement with the imperial government which has led to a belief that female suffrage was not important to Indian women. Certainly, Indian women generally held auxiliary roles in the nationalist move-ment, were sidelined into specific duties by Gandhi such as spinning khadi and picketing liquor shops, and were encouraged to focus on social reform first and foremost, but they were actively engaged in the activities associated with fighting for democratic rights.[46] Intimately involved with the nationalist agenda, these women were reconfiguring perceptions about women's rights and interests. Their engagement with British and other colonial feminists in London itself demonstrates that international feminism was not merely an outward-looking movement of Western feminists, but was shaped and directed by colonized women too, actively engaging and setting their own agenda.

Although the Indian subcontinent was eventually to be divided in 1947, before 1940 these ideas had not gained much political traction. In the 1936–7 general election, the Muslim League had won only 4.4 per cent of the total Muslim votes cast. Mobilized by this poor result, the Muslim League was able to attract more support over the next few years, and in March 1940 they adopted the Lahore Resolution, in

[45] The focus of the second chapter of R.J. Moore's *Endgames of Empire: Studies of Britain's Indian Problem* (Delhi: Oxford University Press, 1988) is on the RTCs and it makes no mention the women delegates or women's issues discussed at these conferences. His *The Crisis of Indian Unity 1917–1940* (Oxford: Clarendon Press, 1974) deals even more extensively with the RTCs and only mentions in passing that Begum Shahnawaz was a delegate at the First and Third Conferences (123, 284), and that Sarojini Naidu attended the Second, seemingly unaware of Radhabai Subbarayan's contribution. It also does not discuss the demands and negotiations surrounding female fran-chise at all.

[46] See Madhu Kishwar, 'Gandhi on Women', *Economic and Political Weekly*, 20, 41 (12 October 1985), 1753–8.

which, without specifying geographical boundaries, they demanded independent Muslim states in the north-west and north-east of India. Though a federal system might have been adopted, following the 1945–6 general election where the Muslim League was successful in obtaining the vast majority of Muslim seats, and with growing 'communal' violence, the British government decided to withdraw from India and to partition the subcontinent. Partition followed in August 1947, with the creation of a new state of Pakistan, which was divided into East and West Pakistan. The focus of this book is on suffrage campaigns in British India and then in independent India, but I will discuss Pakistan and Bangladesh briefly in the epilogue.

Female suffrage campaigns in India had not just emerged in the 1930s out of civil disobedience, but had earlier origins. They were internationally engaged, but also pragmatic and reactive to domestic developments. Mrinalini Sinha has warned against falling into the provincializing trap of comparing the Indian women's movement to the modernity of European suffrage movements. In this 'global narrative of intersecting histories', in a world also beset by social and political change following the First World War, *Indian Suffragettes* demonstrates how generic European concepts could be partial and in need of contextualization, but also how 'universal' many of those concepts of womanhood, modernity, suffrage, and citizenship really were in the interwar period.[47]

The Approach to Indian Suffragettes

In 1931, there were over 170 million women living in India.[48] This book offers insight into the activities of just a minuscule proportion of that population. The appendix offers short biographies of some of the key Indian women (and a few of their other colleagues) who led and featured in the transnational networks of Indian suffrage campaigning. Their perspectives, and broader debates and discussions about Indian suffrage and spatial identities have been drawn from a range

---

[47] Sinha, *Specters of Mother India*, 15–16.

[48] According to the 1931 Census of India, there were 171,008,855 women in India (J.H. Hutton, *Census of India, 1931*, vol. 1, part 1 [Delhi: Manager of Publications, 1933], 34).

of archival sources, brought together to offer a multi-layered understanding of transnational activism in the interwar period.

Individual perspectives and voices are drawn from personal writings, from the memoirs, articles, some transcribed interviews, and the correspondence of these suffrage activists. These are all sources that have either been published or collated in archives, and thus often written with a public in mind, and also with attempts to demonstrate modernity (and a national identity) through these forms of writing. These are materials that have been deposited in known archives and so the focus may be skewed towards those who left behind records. Despite various limitations, especially as the majority of sources found were written or kept in English, these sources offer some insight into the perspectives of Indian (and other) women at the time and the ways in which they located themselves and their potential for agency.

As the focus is not merely on individuals but on the campaigning groups they were a part of or interacted with, many of the sources discussed in this book are from organizational records. One of the key types of material I use are the specialist journals and newspapers which were the organs of women's groups around the world, from *Stri Dharma* (the organ of the WIA) to *Equal Rights* (the US National Women's Party [NWP] newspaper) to *The Vote* (the Women's Freedom League [WFL] paper), among others. These international publications, edited by women, reveal the ways in which feminist associations communicated with and learnt from each other in the interwar period, and how they presented their public advocacy.[49] The minute books and records of associations, together with the private writings of women, shed light on the activities and perspectives of these women. Analysing these, we see how the terminology of the women's movement changes and how campaign strategies develop.

I also look at other newspapers and periodicals which report on the activities of Indian suffragettes. These not only include Indian newspapers, which remarkably hardly mention suffrage

---

49 For more on *Stri Dharma* as a powerful medium for Indian women activists, see Michelle Elizabeth Tusan, 'Writing Stri Dharma: International Feminism, Nationalist Politics, and Women's Press Advocacy in Late Colonial India', *Women's History Review* 12, 4 (2003): 623–49.

campaigning, but also international newspapers, including those published in the USA, Australia, New Zealand, and Britain, found in physical archives and helped by some valuable digitization projects. Unfortunately, again, this means I have been reliant on what has been preserved and has been made accessible. On the question of suffrage and political representation, Indian suffragettes were required to engage with political bodies and petition the British parliament. The India Office was compelled to engage with this issue, as were government bodies in both Britain and India, as the issue of franchise more broadly was intertwined with issues of imperial rule and national sovereignty. Thus, various government officials were involved in committees and produced reports on the issue of female franchise in India, which I read alongside government correspondence and memoranda. Reading these sources together shows how suffrage was not just handed to Indian women upon Independence; it was the result of an involved fight and discussion within imperial, national, and international contexts.

As intimated earlier, this book is divided into chapters that focus on spatial identities, but it also follows a loose chronological structure. Thus, the first chapter looks at the early networks between British suffrage organizations and Indian women in the 1910s and the ways in which Indian suffragettes positioned themselves as imperial subjects, while also being drawn to their regional identities. I look at the way in which Indian women were utilized and exoticized by British imperial feminists and how the issue of the female vote in India was first discussed. I follow the activities of Indian women from the 1917 deputation to the secretary of state and viceroy, which marked the first formal demand to the government for votes for Indian women, until the 1919 Government of India Act allowed Indian provinces the autonomy to decide to enfranchise women and the first votes were given to women in Madras and Bombay.

Moving beyond the binary imperial relationship between Britain and India, the second chapter considers the ways in which Indian women used broader networks within the British Empire in their fight for the vote and how they were able to present themselves as colonial subjects within a sisterhood of empire. With a particular focus on networks with Antipodeans, I also explore the suffrage campaigns of Indians overseas in other colonies and how the Commonwealth was understood by Indian women. While the Indian diaspora in Africa and the Indian Ocean has recently drawn considerable attention from scholars, with discussions on imperial citizenship, identity, and political representation, the position of women in these colonies has hardly been discussed. Therefore, I not only reflect on the connections the Indian women's movement had with the diaspora, but also consider broader questions of race and racial hierarchies.

Indian women attended their first international suffrage conference in 1920 in Geneva. The third chapter, therefore, explores Indian interactions with international women's conferences in the 1920s and 1930s, their engagement with the League of Nations and campaigns in the USA. This chapter looks at the ways in which Indian women started to embrace these new international networks and how Indian suffragettes were discussing feminism in international contexts. As Indian women engaged with international organizations, they soon became interested in the shift among women's organizations towards more regional associations. Chapter 4 focuses on the discrete Asian and Eastern networks that Indian women were engaging in, predominately from the 1930s onwards, with particular focus on the All-Asian Women's Conference (AAWC) of 1931. It examines the terminology used by and about Indian women as being invariably constituted of such terms as 'Eastern', 'Oriental', and 'Asian'. Indian women attempted to challenge certain tropes about submissive Indian women, but the terms 'Oriental' and 'Eastern' remained prevalent throughout this period, often used by Indian women themselves; thus, they were beset by contradictions as they used self-orientalizing language to assert their 'traditions' while wishing to make claims to public roles in Western-modelled political institutions.

The final chapter returns to consider the relationship between British and Indian feminists in the 1930s and 1940s, and a developing national and nationalist identity. It examines some key constitutional negotiations that took place in London that led to the 1935 Government of India Act, and the ways in which Indian suffragettes increasingly rejected British interventionist help. This chapter explores the divisions within the Indian suffrage movement, particularly over the extent of the franchise, reservation of seats, and the communal question. The suffrage issue was not merely about the vote, but also about political representation. But how representative was the Indian suffrage movement itself? The epilogue looks briefly at constitutional developments in India, Pakistan, and Bangladesh after 1947, as they relate to female franchise and ongoing strategies to increase the representation of women in parliamentary bodies.

This book is being published in 2018, the centenary of the (partial) award of female suffrage in the UK, where there are various national celebrations planned. The United States of America is also gearing up to celebrate their female suffrage centennial in 2020. I hope this study of transnational connections will globalize and decentre suffrage narratives, showing how suffrage victories were interlinked around the world and how various other centenary anniversaries of suffrage should be celebrated throughout the twenty-first century. This is also a book about Indian women and speaks to the ongoing Indian predicament in relation to feminist politics today. It highlights the enduring influence of colonialism on the social background of women involved in the public sphere in India, and also the boundaries of such debates, as Indian women, and their allies, continue to participate in varied campaigns for social and political equality across the Indian subcontinent and beyond.

1

Indian Suffragettes and British Imperial Connections

I n 1911 an Indian princess appeared in a London court, facing fines for her role in the British suffrage movement. Eight years later, in 1919, an Indian poet, an Indian student, and an Indian social reformer were addressing British Members of Parliament (MPs) in the House of Commons about the Indian suffrage movement. Before 1920, Indian women, of various backgrounds, who had lived in Britain for varying lengths of time were engaging with the British suffrage movement and promoting the Indian suffrage movement. They lobbied parliament, headed processions and demonstrations, gave speeches and addresses, opened fairs, wrote articles, arranged meetings and resolutions, all in Britain and all in their drive to enfranchise Indian women. For some of these suffragettes, though their visits to Britain were their first time overseas, they were visiting a space familiar to them politically and culturally. They were, after all, subjects of the British Crown, educated in systems that had not only taught them English but also British history and literature.[1]

---

[1] See Gauri Viswanathan, *Masks of Conquest: Literary Study and British Rule in India* (New York: Columbia University Press, 1989).

They were members of the British Empire at a time when, before the 1920s, most Indian nationalists were demanding dominion status within the Commonwealth and not yet forcefully for full independence. However, inspired by the development of women's reform groups within India and the international suffrage movement, especially the one centred around Britain, Indian suffragettes were mobilizing beyond the environs of India, projecting themselves into the imperial metropolis, in a fight to enfranchise Indian women and thus to allow them to have a greater public political role within an imperial system.

Indian men and women could sit on local councils in the nineteenth century, and Indian men were represented in provincial legislatures (in a very limited fashion) from 1909. In 1917, the viceroy (Lord Chelmsford) and secretary of state (Edwin Montagu) began to discuss the introduction of reforms into the viceroy's council of state and representative assemblies. It was from this time onwards that Indian men and women could (and did) start demanding greater political representation, with greater expectation of a positive outcome. But, India was still subject to the British Crown. For any political concessions Indians had to look to British officials serving in India and ultimately to the British government. Therefore, as Indian women started to demand the vote, they had to appeal to British sentiment as well as Indian opinion.

As a result of this relationship, Indian suffragettes in the 1910s positioned themselves as imperial citizens. Indian suffragettes realized that they were dependent on the favourable opinion in the imperial metropolis and directed their energies in that direction. Their campaigns relied heavily on British feminist support and they expected British women to aid them from a sense of their imperial responsibility. It was only after the 1920s, as we shall see in more detail in Chapter 5, that the suffrage question became closely allied to nationalism. Before this, as Indian national identities were still being shaped and articulated, Indian women were more likely to identify with their province or with an imperial framework. As they were imperial citizens, some Indian women were engaged with the British fight for female enfranchisement. All British women were not enfranchised until 1928; so, there was some overlap with the British and Indian suffrage movements. In this chapter, I explore these connections and overlaps in the lead-up to and immediate aftermath of the 1919 Government of India Act. While Indian women were not enfranchised by law, this Act gave Indian provinces the autonomy to decide whether they would allow Indian women to vote, and was the first concession in a long fight for female enfranchisement.

Imperial Feminism and Indian Women in Britain before 1917

Although some British women had been able to vote before the nineteenth century, the 1832 Reform Act had explicitly excluded women from the franchise. In 1866, John Stuart Mill presented a petition (with 4,000 signatures) to parliament demanding female suffrage, but to no avail. The height of militancy took place during the 1910s. However, it was the First World War that proved to be a pivotal turning point for the long-standing British female suffrage movement as the government sought to reward noticeable contributions of women on the 'Home Front'. In 1918 the parliamentary vote was granted to some British women for the first time—to those who were over 30 years old and lived on property more than £5 in value. It was only in 1928 with the Equal Franchise Act that all women over the age of 21 could vote in national elections. The 1918 Representation of the People Act enfranchised 'British subjects', which technically meant any subject of the British Empire living in Britain, who met the required residency qualifications and was registered, could vote. There was no discrimination based on race.[2] But, though there were women from around the world including China, India, the West Indies, and parts of Africa living in Britain at this time, especially in and around the port cities, the British female suffrage movement was predominately 'white'. However, as Britain was an imperial power, and as British women were demanding a franchise in the imperial parliament, British suffrage supporters had to deal with the issue of race and empire, implicitly and explicitly, in their campaigns.

---

[2] Even today, Commonwealth citizens resident in the UK can vote in elections even if they are not British nationals.

Although there is a notion that British suffragettes (and note I use this term as shorthand for British suffragists and suffragettes too) were liberal campaigners, many were particularly conservative in their attitudes towards empire. Many British suffrage campaigners were in favour of maintaining the empire and wished to strengthen the imperial mission through their participation in parliament. Antoinette Burton has showed how Indian women, in particular, were used as a symbol of concern by British suffragettes. British suffrage campaigners argued that British women would use the vote to maintain the civilizing sentiments of the imperial mission. The conviction that Indian women were a special 'feminist burden' was an expression of their 'imperial feminism'. Though these British feminists demonstrated interest in Indian women, they exhibited sympathy and protectiveness that offered little consideration for? Indian women's needs.[3]

As Burton has skilfully detailed, suffrage periodicals such as the *Women's Franchise* and *Common Cause* (the organ of the National Union of Women's Suffrage Societies [NUWSS]) often discussed Indian women and the extent of their 'degradation' in the first decades of the twentieth century.[4] The enfranchisement of Indian women was not yet a concern, as evident in an article in the *The Vote* in April 1912 which discussed the problems of purdah (veiled seclusion) and illiteracy in India.[5] The stereotype of the 'enslaved' Indian women was conveniently used by suffragettes in their arguments against the anti-suffrage lobby as they implied that anti-suffragists wanted to 'enslave' British women in the same manner. Many British suffragettes also demanded recognition that they were invested in empire and wished to promote moral and 'pure' imperialism. As a commentator, probably Helena Swanwick, wrote for the *Common Cause*, 'if it were only for the sake of India, women here in Great Britain would be bound to demand the vote' because of the 'vast multitude

[3] Antoinette Burton, *Burdens of History: British Feminists, Indian Women, and Imperial Culture, 1865–1915* (Chapel Hill: University of Carolina Press, 1994), chap. 1.

[4] Burton, *Burdens of History*, 180.

[5] C. D., 'Purdah Life in the East', *The Vote*, 20 April 1912, 13–14, from *Feminism and the Periodical Press, 1900–1918*, ed. Lucy Delap, Maria DiCenzo, and Leila Ryan (Abingdon: Routledge, 2006).

of silent and too suffering women' who were part of their imperial responsibility.[6]

This imperial feminism was also evident in the introverted focus of the British movement. Many suffrage workers in the early twentieth century believed Britain was the 'storm-centre' of the women's movement. This term was coined by the American suffrage leader Carrie Chapman Catt at the 1901 International Woman Suffrage Alliance (IWSA) meeting in Amsterdam, even though other parts of the world, including parts of America, were enfranchising women before Britain.[7] Christabel Pankhurst was adamant that British women should be enfranchised before others, especially 'Eastern' women. In 1908, she commented on political reform developments in Turkey, admitting that though Turkish women might be fit for the franchise, it was inappropriate for Turkish men or women to get the vote before British women, who are 'more fitted for political liberty' and the 'rightful heirs to constitutional liberty'.[8] Some British suffragettes then had a keen sense of who should be enfranchised and in what kind of political system.

The position of India was invoked by pro- and anti-suffragists during British debates. In 1910, MPs such as Annan Bryce and F. E. Smith told parliament that one of the reasons against passing the Women's Franchise Bill was because Indians would not like to be ruled by British women voters. Smith also argued that the 'no taxation without representation' demand made by some British suffragettes was not a valid argument as Indians paid taxes but did not vote.[9] Keir Hardie was quick to respond that Indian women could vote in elections for councils in India and that enfranchising

---

[6] Burton, *Burdens of History*, 184–7. As Megan Smitley has argued, this sentiment extended to Scottish suffragettes too. See Megan Smitley, '"Inebriates", "Heathens", Templars and Suffragists: Scotland and Imperial Feminism c.1870–1914', *Women's History Review* 11, 3 (2002): 455–80. I thank Eleanor Gordon for directing me to this work.

[7] Burton, *Burdens of History*, 200–1.

[8] Christabel Pankhurst, 'Shall this Country Lead the Way?' *Votes for Women*, 3 September 1908, quoted in Burton, *Burdens of History*, 200.

[9] Parliamentary Franchise (Women) Bill, *HC Deb* 11 July 1910, vol. 19, cc57, cc74, available at http://hansard.millbanksystems.com/commons/1910/jul/11/parliamentary-franchise-women-bill, accessed 7 August 2017; John Rylands [JR], GB133 MML5/22, newscutting (no date/title).

British women would not weaken their standing in the opinion of Indian subjects.[10] In a pamphlet Annie Besant wrote on the suffrage question in 1914, she refuted the argument by Lord Curzon (former viceroy of India) that British female enfranchisement would have a terrible effect on India because Indians would revolt over the idea of British women having a say in imperial politics. Besant explained that Indians had had no objections to Queen Victoria ruling over them, nor numerous other Indian female sovereigns. She conceded that some Indians might have concerns about the social freedoms of English women, but that they were unlikely to object to their political emancipation and would honour Britain for showing respect to their women.[11]

Indians were being evoked and objectified in the British suffrage movement then, but they were usually based on remote images of India. Yet there were a few hundred Indian women who lived in Britain and there were practical repercussions for some of these British residents. Sushama Sen, for example, was living in London in 1910, as her husband was legal advisor to the Orissa rajas. They stayed in a house in Hampstead with other Indians including Miss Joshi, who would later become a prominent Indian campaigner (Rani Rajwade). As Sen recalls:

> At this time the Women's Sufferagette [*sic*] movement who were fighting for their Votes, was at its height. In those days there were few Indian women in London. Hearing of me they sent me an invitation to join their demonstration at Picadilly [*sic*] Circus, and to march with them led by Mrs Pankhurst to the Parliament House.... It was a great experience for me, at the same time it was a novel sight for a single Indian woman amidst the procession, and I was the subject of public gaze.[12]

Sen noted the novelty of her involvement and she would have been consciously aware of her 'difference'. Having an Indian woman in a British suffrage demonstration was useful for imperial feminists

---

[10] *HC Deb* 11 July 1910, vol. 19, cc142–3.

[11] Annie Besant, *Women and Politics: The Way out of the Present Difficulty* (London: Theosophical Publishing Society, 1914), 16.

[12] Sushama Sen, *Memoirs of an Octogenarian* (Delhi: Chatterjee and Sen, 1971), 117.

to demonstrate the reach of their influence. In this extract from her autobiography, Sen may have been referring to the Black Friday march in November 1910, though there are no known reports of her involvement. However, it is known that another woman of Indian descent was involved in that procession: Princess Sophia Duleep Singh. I will come back to Duleep Singh a little later.

There were other occasions where Indian women were involved in British suffrage campaigns as symbols rather than as active campaigners. The most notable example of this is in the 1911 suffrage procession. To mark the coronation of George V, British suffrage campaigners organized a procession through London on 17 June 1911 to demand votes for women. An 'Empire Pageant' was included in the procession, with representatives from some parts of the British Empire, including at least three women from India.

Indians had already been put on 'display' in various ways in 1911. To mark the coronation of King George V in June 1911 a contingent of the Indian Army, about 700 men, was brought to Britain, and the men camped in the Home Park at Hampton Court.[13] This had followed a 'Festival of Empire' at Crystal Palace in May 1911, which had included an Indian court and re-enactment of the 1877 Delhi Durbar where Queen Victoria had been proclaimed empress of India.[14] The WSPU newspaper, *Votes for Women*, explained that suffrage campaigners were putting on a related event that would not only demand voting rights but would also celebrate Britain's imperial reach:

> At this time of Coronation, when the country is expending itself in honour and welcome to the Colonies, we Suffragists will not be behind in demonstrating our warmth of feeling for outsider lands....

[13] 'The Indian Camp at Hampton Court', *Indian Magazine and Review* (July 1911), 191; 'Officers of the Indian Contingent at the Coronation of King George V in the camp at Hampton Court, June 1911', available at http://www.nam.ac.uk/online-collection/detail.php?acc=1982-06-4-1, accessed 7 August 2017.

[14] 'The Indian Exhibition at the Crystal Palace', *Indian Magazine and Review* (July 1911), 191–3; 'Festival of Empire, 1911', available at http://www.open.ac.uk/researchprojects/makingbritain/content/festival-empire-1911, accessed 7 August 2017.

Our greetings to the Colonies are not expressed in guns and the tramp of armies, nor yet in champagne and much eating; just in roses, masses and masses of roses, festoons fluttering in the breeze, linking together the most distant parts of the world—a profusion of blossoms, out of which emerge the East and the West, enthroned together above the encircling groups, symbols of all the lands where George V is proclaimed as King.[15]

Behind English, Welsh, Scottish, and Irish contingents, the suffrage procession included women from New Zealand, Australia, Canada, South Africa, and India, bearing national emblems (fern tree, kangaroo, maple leaf, springbok, elephant).[16] New Zealand led the empire contingent, as they were the first to give women the vote. After the white dominions, the 'daughter' colonies were to follow, that is, India and, ostensibly, representatives of colonies in the West Indies and Africa, but only India had any such representation in the end. Jane Fisher Unwin was one of the founders of the WFL and daughter of the well-known Liberal Richard Cobden. She, along with representatives of the WSPU, of which she was also a member, contacted Indian women living in the UK and organized the decorations and collection of subscriptions for the elephant banner, which cost between £4 and £5. In the lead-up to the event, *Votes for Women* urged more women to take part in the India section, noting that it was not likely to be as large as the other parts of the imperial contingent.[17]

On 17 June 1911, the pageant marched along the streets of London. Sophia Duleep Singh was a part of the overall procession, but not under the 'India' flag. In the India section, three Indian women have been identified.[18] They were Mrs P. L. Roy, Mrs Bhagwati Bhola Nauth, and Mrs Mukerjea. As described in the programme for the procession in the women's newspaper *The Vote*, 'Mrs Roy, one of the most emancipated of Indian women' and 'Mrs Bhola Nauth,

---

[15] 'The Empire Pageant', *Votes for Women*, 9 June 1911, 595.

[16] 'The Empire Pageant', *Votes for Women*, 9 June 1911, 595.

[17] The initial representatives appeared only to be Mrs P. L. Roy, Mrs Fisher Unwin, and Helen B. Hanson. ('Women's Coronation Procession', *Votes for Women*, 16 June 1911, 613, 615).

[18] 'Five-Mile Procession of Suffragists', *The Observer*, 11 June 1911, 5.

Hon. Secretary of the Indian Women's Education Fund' were 'well known Indian women'.[19] Bhola Nauth had been living in Britain since at least 1908. Her husband was Major Bhola Nauth, a member of the Indian Medical Service.[20] Mrs P. L. Roy (Lolita), from Calcutta, was the wife of an Indian barrister, Piera Lal Roy, and had six children. The Roy family moved to London at the beginning of the twentieth century. Two of her sons served in the First World War. The third woman identified in the procession, Mukerjea, was Leila (Leilavati), daughter of Lolita Roy, who had married S. V. Mukerjea, a civil servant, in London in December 1910.[21]

The involvement of Indian women in this procession was remarked upon with interest by various observers. A photo of the women and the 'India' flag was printed in *Votes for Women* on 30 June (see Image 1.1). A commentator for the London paper *T. P.'s Weekly* noted this interest.

> A gentleman who was for many years governor of an Indian province was most struck by the appearance of women from that far-off, marvellous land in the international group. Perhaps he was right in thinking those women in their Oriental dress the most significant feature of the whole Procession. It showed that the Women's Question is without race, or creed, or boundary.[22]

A report in the *Bath Chronicle* also described the whole procession and remarked that 'most notable of all—and most significant—under the "Elephant" of India came a group of dusky men and women'. The commentator explained that it was notable that Indian men were

[19] 'The Women's Procession: Descriptive Programme of the Order of March', *The Vote*, 17 June 1911, 95.

[20] 'Women Doctors in India', *Indian Magazine and Review* (September 1912), 247.

[21] Among the guests to their wedding reception were Bhola Nauth and Sophia Duleep Singh ('A Brahmo Somaj Wedding in London', *Indian Magazine and Review* [January 1911]: 25–6). In 1911, Mukerjea was 22 years old, Roy was 46 (Census extract in 'The Roy Brothers: Fighting for King and Emperor', 9 October 2013, available at https://greatwarlondon.wordpress.com/2013/10/09/the-roy-brothers-fighting-for-king-and-emperor/, accessed 7 August 2017).

[22] Extract from 'Frances' in *T. P's Weekly* quoted in 'Echoes of the Procession', *Votes for Women*, 30 June 1911, 640.

THE INDIAN CONTINGENT IN THE GREAT PROCESSION OF JUNE 17.

IMAGE 1.1   Indian women in coronation suffrage procession, London,
30 June 1911
© The British Library Board, Lou.Lon 25 (1911)

willing to 'stand by English women in their fight for political freedom', but the 'dusky' hues were also evidently worth noting.[23]

Though more contemporary commentators have described these
women as 'Indian suffragettes', what were these women doing in the
procession? As a reporter in the *Dover Express* put it, they were included as 'emblematic representation of the Empire as a whole and of its
constituent parts'.[24] As we shall see later in this and the next chapter,
Roy and Bhola Nauth were to become involved in campaigns for votes

[23] E. G. W., 'The Suffrage Pageant', *Bath Chronicle*, 22 June 1911, 5. Annie
Besant was also a part of the pageant but she walked with the Co-Masons
group.
[24] 'Kent and the Woman's Suffrage Procession', *Dover Express*, 23 June
1911, 7.

for Indian women, but in the 1911 procession this did not seem to be on their agenda. They were involved in the empire pageant to show support for the British fight, and, more importantly, were used as symbols by British suffrage campaigners to represent the size of the empire and the breadth of interests British women could be called upon to influence through their votes in the imperial parliament. It is also noteworthy that the only non-'white' women in the procession were from India. There is no evidence of any women of African descent who lived in Britain, being involved publicly in the British suffrage movement before 1914.

There were other Indian women who had contact with the British suffrage movement at this time. In 1911, Anasuya Sarabhai went to England, with the help of her brother, and attended lectures at the London School of Economics. She attended lectures of the Fabian Society and came into contact with Sylvia Pankhurst and other British suffragettes. She returned to India in 1913, became a member of the Indian National Congress, and supported Indian female enfranchisement in public debates in 1918.[25] Meanwhile, Ramdulari Dubé became involved with the WFL and spoke at the International Suffrage Fair held at Chelsea Town Hall from 13 to 16 November 1912. She lived in London with her husband, a barrister.[26] Dubé addressed the audience on 16 November, having just arrived after taking part in the procession of suffragists that met the 'Brown women' on their arrival in London; they had marched together to Trafalgar Square. The 'Brown women' had walked 400 miles from Edinburgh to London, holding meetings and collecting signatures to a suffrage petition along the way. On the platform to open the fair that day, Dubé not only spoke about Indian women, particularly developments in their education, but also 'paid tribute to the devotion to their

---

[25] Aparna Basu, 'Sarabhai family (*per. c.* 1820–*c.* 2000)', *Oxford Dictionary of National Biography* (Oxford University Press, May 2007), available at http://www.oxforddnb.com/view/article/94947, accessed 7 August 2017; Aparna Basu, *Mridula Sarabhai: Rebel with a Cause* (New Delhi: Oxford University Press, 1996), 17–18, 22.

[26] 'International Suffrage Fair', *The Vote*, 16 November 1912, 41. She was secretary for the Indian Women's Congress and a member of the Lyceum Club in London, a private members' club for women.

homes of Western Suffragists', and declared that the 'political and social advancement of British women would be a help and encouragement to women in India'.[27] It also appears that there were other Indian female members of the WFL as early as 1910, according to a piece in *The Vote*. These Indian members may have been Bhola Nauth and Roy.[28]

However, it was Sophia Duleep Singh who was the most active and prominent non-'white' British suffragette. Singh, born in 1876 in Norfolk, was the daughter of the exiled maharaja of Punjab, Maharaja Duleep Singh, and the German-Abyssinian Bamba Muller. In 1896, Queen Victoria gave Sophia, her god-daughter, 'Faraday House' in Hampton Court as a 'grace and favour' home. Duleep Singh was a champion of women's rights, despite concern among royal circles that her activities were not appropriate for the former Queen's god-daughter. She joined the WSPU at the home of Una Dugdale in 1909. On 18 November 1910, the WSPU had organized a series of deputations of women to approach parliament to demand an audience with the prime minister. Duleep Singh was part of the first deputation, which was soon joined by many others to form a large crowd waiting for the prime minister's secretary. She joined Emmeline Pankhurst, Elizabeth Garrett Anderson, and nearly 300 other campaigners to urge Asquith's government to pass a limited suffrage bill, but the protest soon descended into police brutality and arrests.[29]

[27] 'The International Suffrage Fair: A Retrospect', *The Vote*, 23 November 1912, 60. Although there is little information about Dubé's activities in Britain beyond the Fair, she was present to garland Sarojini Naidu at a reception put on by the Oriental Circle of the Lyceum Club in November 1913 ('In Honour of Sarojini Naidu', *Indian Magazine and Review* [December 1913]: 324). Dubé was present at a reception for the viceroy, Lord Chelmsford, in London in March 1916 ('From the Editor's Study', *Indian Magazine and Review* (April 1916): 31) and part of a deputation to Montagu in August 1919 (see later in this chapter).

[28] Louisa Thomson-Price, 'Reviews', *The Vote*, 19 March 1910, 249.

[29] 'Outside the People's House', *The Vote*, 26 November 1910, 57. For more on Sophia Duleep Singh's suffrage activities, see Rozina Visram, *Asians in Britain: 400 Years of History* (London: Pluto Press, 2002), 164–8; Anita Anand, *Sophia: Princess, Suffragette, Revolutionary* (London: Bloomsbury, 2015);

Duleep Singh was not arrested on 'Black Friday' (as it became known), but became actively involved with the Women's Tax Resistance League (WTRL). The WTRL's main form of resistance was to refuse to pay any taxes, ranging from income tax or property tax to dog tax or carriage licences. They argued that as women did not have the vote they should not have to pay taxes. Bailiffs would impound objects from those who refused to pay taxes and then WTRL members would buy back the items at public auctions amid huge publicity. Duleep Singh's ability to refuse to pay taxes, a product of her aristocratic wealth, highlighted the arguments of the WTRL. In May 1911, Duleep Singh's refusal to pay licences for her five dogs, a carriage, and servant led to a fine of £3. In July 1911, when Duleep Singh refused to pay just 6 shillings in taxes, a warrant was produced to impound certain goods until she paid the arrears. The item chosen for bail was a seven-stone diamond ring, which was then bought back for her by her fellow suffragettes in a public auction.[30] In December 1913, she was fined £12 10s for refusing to pay for the licences for two dogs, a carriage, and a servant.[31]

Duleep Singh was also an active member of the Kingston and District branch of the WSPU, and later the Richmond, Surrey, branch. She was committed to raising funds and subscriptions and actively sold the WSPU's other weekly newspaper, *The Suffragette*, at a regular pitch outside Hampton Court Palace and at Saturday branch meetings. She was even pictured selling copies outside Hampton Court Palace for an issue of the paper.[32] In 1911, Duleep Singh also refused to sign the census, defacing the form with 'No Vote, No Census', so a registrar had to fill it in for her.[33] In the same year, she picketed

---

Sumita Mukherjee, 'Herabai Tata and Sophia Duleep Singh: Suffragette Resistances for India and Britain, 1910–1920', in *South Asian Resistances in Britain 1858–1947*, ed. Rehana Ahmed and Sumita Mukherjee (London: Continuum, 2012), 106–21.

[30] See Museum of London. Suffragette Fellowship Collection: Warrant on Sophia Duleep Singh, 15 July 1911.

[31] 'Princess Who Refused to Pay Taxes', *Evening Telegraph and Post*, 30 December 1913, 4; Visram, *Asians in Britain*, 167–8.

[32] *The Suffragette*, 29 November 1912, 105; 7 March 1913, 336; 18 April 1913, 447.

[33] The National Archives, RG 14/3561, 1911 Census Entry by Sophia Duleep Singh.

Downing Street to demand votes for women, as part of an organized effort by the WSPU to picket various Cabinet members' houses.[34]

In July 1915, Duleep Singh was involved in a procession of women in London to support a deputation led by Emmeline Pankhurst to the Ministry of Munitions. The deputation showed that women desired to serve their country in the war effort.[35] Involvement in the First World War led to a decline in activity for British suffrage campaigners but Duleep Singh had interests beyond the suffrage question. She was engaged, with other Indian women living in Britain, in raising funds and support for Indian soldiers who fought on the Western Front and the injured Indian soldiers who were sent to convalesce in special military hospitals in Britain. In 1914, Roy and Bhola Nauth became members of the 'Eastern League', which was set up by Indian and British women to raise money for the Indian Soldiers' Fund. They anticipated the needs of Indian soldiers in the war and raised appeals for items such as gloves, socks, jackets, hot water bottle covers, and food.[36] In November 1916, Duleep Singh organized a Ladies Day with Roy, Bhola Nauth, Mrinalini Sen, and others to raise money for Indian soldiers. They set up a pitch on Haymarket in London and sold 'India' flags emblazoned with elephants or stars, and also sold brooches.[37] However, women's equality remained a pressing issue. As the war effort continued and suffrage militancy decreased in Britain, the promise of political reforms offered for India encouraged Indian women to turn their attention to campaigns for Indian women's franchise. These campaigns, which focused on India's place within the empire, brought a new set of Indian women to London.

The 1917 Deputation

While British women were fighting for the vote with increasing militancy, in the 1910s women in India seemed, at first, to be untouched by those campaigns. The poet-turned-politician Sarojini Naidu

---

[34] 'Suffragists and the Government', *Manchester Guardian*, 7 February 1911, 6.

[35] 'The Procession', *The Observer*, 18 July 1915, 12.

[36] 'War-Work of Indians in Britain', *Modern Review* (July 1919): 56–7.

[37] 'India and the War: Our Day', *Indian Magazine and Review* (November 1916): 229–30.

stayed in Britain between 1913 and 1914, and was interviewed by a number of British journalists. In an interview with the *Daily News* in November 1913, Naidu explained that Indian women had been 'equal' in the past and there was need to regain the lost inheritance rather than embark on a novel struggle for women's rights.

> To us, you must understand, 'the vote' means nothing. Here, no doubt, it is a symbol standing for the idea of equality. There, it is an empty word suggesting a foreign ideal. What we are fighting for is not 'the vote', but a social and intellectual existence, equal to, while different from, that of men.[38]

Naidu did, however, appreciate that the suffrage movement had conferred solidarity among women of all classes in Britain, and that the increased solidarity of women was the finest outcome of the struggle, more so than any votes that might be achieved.[39]

Naidu was reluctant to describe herself as a feminist as she believed the term suggested sex antagonism. In an interview with the women's paper the *Queen* in February 1914, Naidu was keen to stress that Indian women did not face obstacles to public work from Indian men. 'Englishwomen are crying out for the vote; if ours wanted it (and the men could give it), they would get it.'[40] On 5 March 1914, Naidu gave an after-dinner speech at the Lyceum Club on Indian women. She told the attendees that India had enjoyed equal responsibility between the sexes 4,000 years ago and that the contemporary woman's movement was not solely confined to Europe: 'In this country you are asking for the vote, but the fundamental principle is the same: the demand of woman to fulfil her destiny.'[41] Although in 1914 Naidu did not think that the vote was an issue for Indian women, three years later she was to lead a deputation demanding female franchise. The issue of parliamentary representation was, by then, an issue that was exercising the minds of Indian men and women.

---

[38] 'Indian Poetess in England', *Daily News and Leader*, 13 November 1913, 6.

[39] 'Indian Poetess in England', *Daily News and Leader*, 13 November 1913.

[40] Basil Burton, 'Mrs Sarojini Naidu: A Chat with One of India's Eminent Women', *Queen: The Lady's Newspaper*, 28 February 1914, 412.

[41] A. A. Smith, 'The Indian Woman of Today', *Indian Magazine and Review* (April 1914): 89–93.

In 1917, Edwin Montagu, the secretary of state for India, visited India to join the viceroy in a survey with the view to implement a range of political reforms. Margaret Cousins, an Irish suffragette, had moved to India in 1915 with her husband, James. A Theosophist, she had immediately become involved in social reform activities in India. According to Cousins, her husband read the newspaper report about Montagu's visit and he asked her why she did not demand votes for Indian women. With her experience in Britain and Ireland, this seemed a natural fight to pursue in India too.[42] She arranged a delegation, which consisted of 14 women. They were, in addition to Cousins, Naidu, Annie Besant, Mrs Saralabai Naik, Dr I. Joshi, Mrs Srirangamma, Mrs Chandrasekhara Aiyar, Mrs K. Kibe, Herabai Tata, Mrs Lazarus, Dorothy Jinarajadasa, Nalinibai Daivi, Begum Hasrat Mohani, and Mrs Guruswami Chetty.[43] During the deputation, Naidu was delegated to read out a prepared address. Naidu, Naik, and Joshi were also given private interviews with the viceroy and secretary of state. Some of these women would continue to fight publicly for Indian suffrage but some were just well placed at the time. Begam Hasrat Mohani, for example, used the opportunity to appeal for the release of her incarcerated husband (the editor of *Urdu-e-Moalla*, jailed for sedition), to the displeasure of Naidu.[44]

Cousins had drafted the women's franchise address, which was published before the meeting in December. Rajwade (née Joshi) in 1957 recollected the following:

The official leader of the delegation was of course Mrs Sarojini Naidu but the unofficial ones were Mrs Annie Besant and Mrs Margaret

---

[42] BL, Mss Eur F341/31, M. Cousins, 'Votes for Indian Women: Introduction' in *Mrs Margaret Cousins and her Work in India*, ed. S. Muthulakshmi Reddi (Adyar: Women's Indian Association, 1956), 1; also James H. Cousins and Margaret E. Cousins, *We Two Together* (Madras: Ganesh & Co., 1950), 308–14.

[43] *New India*, 18 December 1917, 4; Joint Select Committee on the Government of India Bill, Appendix, 136; 'All-India Women's Deputation to the Secretary of State', *Stri Dharma* (February 1918): 16; Margaret Cousins, 'A Historical Deputation', *Indian Ladies Magazine* (November–December 1934): 228–9.

[44] Muhammad Siddiq, 'Hasrat Mohani', *Journal of the Pakistan Historical Society* 32, 1 (January 1984): 49.

Cousins. In fact, if I mistake not, the idea of such a deputation had really originated with Mrs Cousins, herself an ardent suffragist—and always a champion of women's cause anywhere in the world.[45]

The address presented the women as in 'touch with the new outlook of Indian women' and in support of self-government *within* the empire. They wanted women to be treated as 'people' as they were in other local governments across the British Empire. The address ended by reiterating that they wanted to bring their country 'politically, educationally and physically up to the level of other parts of the Empire' to which they were 'loyally devoted'.[46]

The deputation met Montagu and Chelmsford on 18 December 1917. They were supported by telegrams of sympathy from Mrs Mazhar ul-Haque, Hamabai Petit, Ramabai Ranade, Mrs O. Nehru, Saraladevi Chaudhuri, Mrs Sanjiva Rao, Mrs V. R. Nilakantha, Mrs Sharad Mehta, Miss K. Gokhale, and Miss Arundale.[47] Montagu wanted reassurances from the group that the main nationalist party, the Indian National Congress, supported women's suffrage before taking the matter further, and they were happy to assure him that Congress would pass a unanimous resolution on this issue.[48]

The meeting was reported upon with interest by various Indian newspapers. The English-language Punjabi paper *The Tribune*, printed in Lahore, noted that the demands for female enfranchisement in India had been inspired by the British movement and a 'universal awakening of women'. The reporter supported the demand for some concessions, arguing that 'Indian women are no less intelligent and deserving than British women'.[49] The comparisons with Britain continued; the paper remarked a month later that Indian women 'will

---

[45] Rani Lakshmi Bai Rajwade, 'A Tribute to Mrs M. E. Cousins', in Reddi, *Margaret Cousins*, 5.

[46] The Address is reprinted in 'The All India Women's Deputation', *Indian Journal of Gender Studies* (1998): 131–3.

[47] *New India*, 18 December 1917, 4.

[48] Edwin S. Montagu, *An Indian Diary* (London: William Heinemann, 1930), 115–16.

[49] JR, GB133 IWSA/3/105, 'All-India Women's Deputation', *The Tribune*, 11 November 1917.

not even wait until men have been enfranchised'.[50] Five months later, *The Tribune* continued to show interest in the issue of the franchise. A journalist remarked that the only way to get the support of the Labour party and British women for Indian self-government was to convince them that the nationalist movement in India considered the poor as well as women, and that they had to do this by demanding an extension of the franchise.[51]

News of the delegation reached Britain. A report in the WFL organ, *The Vote*, remarked: 'That Indian women are making themselves effectively heard in this connection will be welcomed as an important and historic fact in the world-wide progress of the woman's movement.'[52] Naidu recalled in 1935 how 'enterprising' they had felt to be part of this delegation and the attention they had given to what they were to wear. She remarked that women still liked to 'look picturesque though claiming equality in every form with men'. Though Naidu had earlier claimed that the vote was immaterial in the broader fight for equality, to get the vote was now seen as the symbol of emancipation.[53]

Despite the delegation, private interviews, and evidence of support, the Montagu–Chelmsford reforms failed to mention women at all. A new central legislative assembly as well as provincial assemblies were to be set up, but only men who would meet certain regional property qualifications were considered in the discussions of the electorate. As a result of the proposed reforms, Lord Southborough was appointed to chair a franchise committee, which toured India in 1918, to deal with the question of elections and franchise more closely.[54] There was now further opportunity for women to demand votes, if they wished to do so. In Bombay, the committee received a requisition signed by about 800 educated women for women to be included in the franchise. The 1917 deputation also re-sent its 'requisition', and there were

---

[50] JR, IWSA/3/105, 'Women and Constitutional Reforms', *The Tribune*, 22 December 1917.

[51] 'A Great Social Revolution', *The Tribune*, 14 May 1918, 2.

[52] 'Indian Women's Demand for Equality', *The Vote*, 10 May 1918, 245.

[53] Reddi, *Margaret Cousins*, 8.

[54] Francis John Stephens Hopwood, Baron of Southborough (1860–1947) was a trained barrister and civil servant.

similar demands presented from the Women Graduates Union in Bombay, the WIA, the Home Rule League, and other women's groups. Two women appeared as witnesses before the committee, representing Bengal and the Punjab.[55]

The WIA had been set up in 1917 in Adyar, the Theosophical Centre near Madras, inspired by the efforts of the British Theosophist Dorothy Jinarajadasa (who had set up a women's society in Madanapalle).[56] Women across India were encouraged to set up local branches dedicated to social reform activities, especially relating to health and education, and also franchise. However, Indian suffragettes were also looking to campaigners in Britain for their support on the franchise issue. Cousins, as secretary of the WIA, sent a letter to Millicent Fawcett about Indian women's demands. Fawcett, president of the NUWSS, was energized enough to write an article for *Common Cause*, the organ of the NUWSS, in July 1918. She also organized a letter sent to members of the Imperial Conference in 1918 by the NUWSS. Fawcett noted that British suffragists wondered what would happen to Indian women in the proposed Montagu–Chelmsford reforms, which had not been discussed by Montagu in parliament, and was concerned about the lack of public support from Indian male leaders. She was pleased though that Indian women were campaigning for suffrage with 'moderation'. Fawcett urged members of the Imperial Conference to ensure that the principle of allowing a share for women in national and political life be recognized. She argued that women were best fit for the responsibility for certain issues relating to education and the family. The letter concluded by forecasting that it would be a 'national disaster' if Indian women were totally excluded from the electorate.[57] Fawcett also wrote to Montagu, urging him to include women in the new electorates.[58]

[55] Reddi, *Margaret Cousins*, 14.

[56] Forbes, *Women in Modern India*, 72–3.

[57] Mrs Henry Fawcett (Millicent Fawcett), 'The Political Position of Indian Women', *Common Cause*, 5 July 1918, 144.

[58] JR, IWSA/3/144, 'Indian Women and Reforms', *The Tribune*, 30 November 1918.

The suffrage question in India was related to Irish suffrage too. On 6 February 1918, the Representation of the People Act was given the royal assent. The territorial extent of the Act included Ireland. Cousins arranged a victory meeting in Madras and passed a resolution sending congratulations to British and Irish suffrage societies. Another resolution was put forward by Miss Bell asking that British women resident in India be granted the same representation as their counterparts in the UK. Cousins and Besant both had strong Irish links; though they supported Irish Home Rule, Cousins regarded it as the duty of Irish women to bring the matter of Indian female suffrage 'strongly' before the House of Commons. The Irish Women's Franchise League sent a message of support to Indian suffragettes as a result.[59]

In the meantime, to counteract the suggestion that Indian men did not support female franchise, campaigners looked to prove that this was not the case. At the Indian National Congress meeting in Calcutta in December 1917, presided over by Besant (the first woman to do so), a woman suffrage resolution was on the agenda but was withdrawn without discussion.[60] It was decided that more public consultation was needed and the matter was referred to resolution at provincial meetings. The India Home Rule League (set up in 1915 by Besant) also asked branches to discuss the matter of female suffrage in schemes of Indian self-government. The Punjab Congress soon passed a resolution supporting the removal of sex disqualifications from the reforms. Naidu presided over the Madras Congress, and at Bombay in May 1918 she proposed a successful resolution to extend the franchise to women, which was supported by 100 women in Bombay.[61] A similar resolution was moved by Dorothy Jinarajadasa at the Malabar District conference and passed unanimously, and there was support in the Central Provinces, the United

---

[59] 'Correspondence', *Irish Citizen* (July 1918): 616; 'Correspondence', *Irish Citizen* (January 1919): 642–3; 'India and Suffrage', *Irish Citizen* (March 1919): 651–2.

[60] Joint Select Committee on the Government of India Bill 1919. Appendix, 136.

[61] 'Franchise for Women', *The Tribune*, 14 May 1918, 1; 'India's Women', *Fielding Star*, 19 December 1918, 2; 'Provincial Conference', *Times of India*, 8 May 1918, 8.

Provinces, and in Andhra.[62] In July 1918 *The Vote* noted the efforts of Sarojini Naidu, Herabai Tata, Dorothy Jinarajadasa, and Margaret Cousins in bringing publicity to suffrage matters. The paper also quoted E. I. M. Boyd in the *English Review*, who noted in response to these developments that 'India must no longer be looked upon as a field for beneficent charity or patronage', that British campaigners should work in cooperation with Indians, and noted the influence of literate Indian women.[63] As *The Tribune* observed, it was clear that Indians did not want a militant women's suffrage movement along the lines of the British example. Congress was aware of this and of the need to be conciliatory. It was also clear that the principle of allowing women to vote, along the same terms as men, would only enfranchise a very small number of women as so few possessed the required property qualifications of the time.[64]

On 1 September 1918, Naidu attended a special session of the Indian National Congress in Bombay and proposed a resolution that 'women, possessing the same qualifications as are laid down for men in any part of the scheme shall not be disqualified on account of sex'. She explained that though arguments relating to nationalism, politics, or economics could be used to support this resolution, her main justification was the pursuit of human rights. She also sought to reassure male delegates about the maintenance of separate spheres for Indian men and women.

> I do not think that there need be any apprehension that in granting franchise to Indian womanhood, Indian womanhood will wrench the power belonging to manhood. Never, never, for we realise that men and women have their separate goals, separate destinies and that just as a man can never fulfil the responsibility or the destiny of a woman, a woman cannot fulfil the responsibility of man.... We ask for franchise, we ask for vote, not that we might interfere with you in your official functions, your civic duties, your public place and power, but rather

[62] Joint Select Committee on the Government of India Bill 1919. Appendix, 137; BL, L/PJ/9/8, Cousins to Montagu, 4 June 1919.

[63] 'The Woman Suffrage Movement in India and South Africa', *The Vote*, 19 July 1918, 321.

[64] JR, IWSA/3/144, 'Women and Constitutional Reforms', *The Tribune*, 3 September 1918.

that we might lay the foundation of national character in the souls of the children that we hold upon our laps and instil into them the ideals of national life.[65]

Naidu's resolution was seconded by Anasuya Sarabhai (who spoke in Gujarati). Sarabhai had, as mentioned earlier, heard Sylvia Pankhurst and other British feminists speak when she had been a student in London. In her address, Sarabhai reassured delegates that Indian women would not imitate the struggle that Englishwomen had waged for the franchise, nor did she believe that India would commit the same 'blunders' as England had done on the franchise question. Another speaker, Rambai Morarji Kamdar, similarly reassured delegates that Indian women would not 'stand in antagonism' towards their men as their 'sisters in the West had done', but also congratulated Indian men for supporting the principle of sex equality in the franchise while men in Europe and America were only doing so grudgingly.[66] The resolution was carried. Cousins wrote to Montagu in October 1918 to inform him of the Congress resolution, demonstrating that Indian men supported female enfranchisement.[67] The Muslim League had passed the same resolutions in September 1918.[68]

In November 1918, Constance Villiers-Stuart, honorary organizing secretary of the Indian Women's Education Association (IWEA) based in Covent Garden, wrote to Sir James Dunlop Smith in the India Office. Her husband, Patrick, had been in the Royal Fusiliers and she had lived in India between 1910 and 1913 and then again from 1920 to 1922.[69] The IWEA raised money for scholarships to bring Indian

---

[65] Report of the Special Session of the Indian National Congress held at Bombay. On 29, 30, 31 August and 1 September 1918 (Bombay: D.D. Sathaye, 1918), 109–10.

[66] Report of the Special Session of the Indian National Congress held at Bombay, 111–12.

[67] BL, L/PJ/9/8, Cousins to Montagu, 28 October 1918.

[68] Joint Select Committee on the Government of India Bill 1919. Appendix, 137.

[69] British Library Collection Summary, available at http://www.bl.uk/catalogues/indiaofficeselect/OIOCShowDescs.asp?CollID=309236, accessed 7 August 2017.

women to Britain for teacher training courses. The first recipient of their scholarship had been Naidu's sister. On behalf of other members including Duleep Singh, Roy, Bhola Nauth, Mrinalini Sen, and Millicent Fawcett, Villiers-Stuart asked that evidence about the need for female franchise be brought before the newly appointed committee to deal with Indian franchise. She pointed out that Indian women were demanding the franchise and that they had Congress support, and so it would be invaluable to enfranchise some (not all) women in the upcoming reforms.[70] She enclosed an address which she hoped would be forwarded to the committee on behalf of the IWEA and NUWSS. It argued that it would be in the 'best interests of India, the Empire, and of the world at large' to include women in the new Indian electorate.[71]

In December 1918, Villiers-Stuart wrote to Sir James Dunlop Smith again, pleading for some Indian women to be included in the proposed electorates for British India. She suggested that women landowners and women graduates might be included, citing the support of the Aga Khan and Ameer Ali. Villiers-Stuart argued that enfranchising some women would also prevent them from being taken in by 'extremists'. Critical of the Theosophists, she pointed out that her plea had support from British people who understood conservative opinion in India, including the educationalists Sir Denison Ross and Sir Theodore Morison, as well as Lady Selbourne, Lord Haldane, Lady Lamington, and Khwaja Kamaluddin.[72] But, Dunlop Smith declined to support Villiers-Stuart's motion.[73] Indian suffrage supporters were beginning to see that the debates might have to be moved to Britain. The Salem (in Madras Presidency) branch of the WIA passed a resolution in December 1918 urging that a women's deputation headed by Besant and Naidu be sent to England to urge that women be treated on the same terms as men in the reformed councils.[74]

[70] L/PJ/9/8, Villiers-Stuart to Dunlop Smith, November 1918.

[71] L/PJ/9/8, Indian Women's Education Association to Indian Franchise Committee, November 1918.

[72] L/PJ/9/8, Villiers-Stuart to Dunlop Smith, 6 December 1918.

[73] L/PJ/9/8, Dunlop Smith to India Office, December 1918.

[74] Nehru Memorial Museum and Library (NMML), S. Muthulakshmi Papers, Subject File 3, Salem WIA to Southborough, 12 December 1918.

The issue continued to energize campaigners placed in Britain. Villiers-Stuart also wrote to the prime minister, Lloyd George, and Lord Southborough on behalf of the NUWSS and IWEA. She argued that women had a right to the vote, that they had a particular inputs to offer on education, marriage, and family, that purdah was not an issue, and that the franchise would be educative. She also pointed out that they were not demanding full adult suffrage.[75] Societies signing the franchise address (12 December 1918 to Southborough) included the Catholic Women's Suffrage Society, Church League for Women's Suffrage, Conservative Women's Reform Association, Men's League for Women's Suffrage, NUWSS, Actresses' Franchise League, WFL, and Women's International League. Individuals signing the address included various Indian men and women who lived in Britain, such as the Aga Khan, Sophia Duleep Singh, the former Conservative MP Mancherjee Bhownaggree, and Mrinalini Sen, as well as various British sympathisers and MPs.[76] The address and signatories were also reproduced in an issue of *India* (a British paper) in January 1919, the WIA journal, *Stri Dharma*, and in the *Indian Magazine and Review* (the journal of the National Indian Association).[77]

In January 1919, Villiers-Stuart wrote to Dorothy Jinarajadasa in India, explaining one of the additional reasons for her interest in female suffrage in India. She explained that her public appeals about the franchise were not merely about 'suffrage' as it was understood in Europe, but that 'our efforts for our sisters in India spring from a real consideration of past and present considerations there'—perhaps referring to imperial responsibilities though she was not specific about this. Villiers-Stuart explained that the franchise matter interested and affected Muslims throughout the British Empire, not just in India, and she was keen to inform Jinarajadasa

---

[75] L/PJ/9/8, Villiers-Stuart to Lloyd George, 11 January 1919; Villiers-Stuart to Southborough, 12 December 1918.

[76] Villiers-Stuart to Southborough, 12 December 1918; 'When East and West Meet', *Asiatic Review* (April 1919): 295.

[77] JR, IWSA/3/141. 'Female Suffrage in India', *India*, 24 January 1919; 'From England', *Stri Dharma* (April 1919): 76–8; 'Franchise for Indian Women', *Indian Magazine and Review* (March 1919): 42–3.

that she had received support and help from Muslim men in favour of enfranchising women.[78]

There was opposition too. Sultan Jahan Begam of Bhopal had told Villiers-Stuart and Southborough that she did not support the IWEA petition, suggesting that not all women should have a voice in political matters.[79] In January 1919, an English-language paper, the *West Coast Spectator*, printed in Calicut (Madras Presidency), criticized 'Indian suffragettes' for being under the thrall of Besant and the Theosophists, and argued that they did not represent Indian women.[80] In correspondence with the Irish suffragette Hanna Sheehy Skeffington, Cousins expressed some concern that Indian women were not showing any initiative (ignoring the work of Naidu and others) and described the 'white woman's burden' upon her, Besant, and Jinarajadasa.[81] In May 1919, an Indian woman, probably Oxford graduate Cornelia Sorabji, argued in the *Common Cause* that English women should not be advocating for Indian female suffrage because Indian women were yet to gain the status that English suffragettes had when they began their fight.[82] Her arguments that education and other social issues were more pressing than the vote and that Indian women should be understood in the 'vernacular' rather than as part of a universal womanhood demonstrate the discourse of opposition against suffrage that often brought in progressive arguments.

The Southborough Report from India, published in April 1919, ignored female franchise. No women were enfranchised at all. In fact, they were explicitly excluded on account of their sex. Thus, the division of franchise on the basis of sex was implanted from an

[78] 'From England', *Stri Dharma* (April 1919): 76; JR, IWSA/2/22, Harriet Newcomb to Miss Sheepshanks, 29 January 1919.

[79] Bodleian, Oxford, Southborough Papers, MSS Eng c.7355, Sultan Jahan of Bhopal to Southborough, 10 April 1919; Siobhan Lambert-Hurley, *Muslim Women, Reform and Princely Patronage: Nawab Sultan Jahan Begam of Bhopal* (London: Routledge, 2007), 168–9.

[80] L/R/5/126, Madras Native Newspaper Reports, Part I, 1919: *West Coast Spectator*, 4 January 1919.

[81] National Library of Ireland (NLI), Sheehy Skeffington Papers, MS 41,177/12, Cousins to Sheehy Skeffington, 13 July (no year).

[82] An Indian Correspondent, 'The Position of Women in India –I', *Common Cause*, 9 May 1919, 36–7.

early stage in India's democracy. Arguments about the obstacles to enfranchising women because of purdah, segregation, and their lack of literacy became enshrined in official opinion. However, a joint select committee was appointed to look further at the reforms from July 1919 in London and to take evidence from representative Indians. Besant and Naidu both went to London to give evidence. The female franchise question was not dead yet; the arena of debate had now shifted to the imperial metropolis.

The 1919 Southborough Committee in London

In July 1919, Margaret Cousins, on behalf of the 45 branches of the WIA, sent a letter to Edwin Montagu regarding the Joint Committee in London. She urged him to use his power and influence to remove the clause proposing to disqualify women from all rights of representation. Cousins explained that Indian women had 'in their quiet way' expressed their desire to be enfranchised through the 1917 delegation and subsequent memorials and petitions to the Southborough committee. Since then, there had also been protest meetings in 'important towns'. Cousins insisted that the right to vote was important as a principle and not all women would use the right, but that it would be a dishonour to 'stigmatise' Indian women as 'more backward than even the outcastes'. She also explained that it was a dishonour to have differential treatment 'compared with their sisters in other parts of the Empire'. As all the appeals regarding franchise had been directed to the British politician, it was clearly an imperial issue and for the British to address. Cousins went on: 'The Indian ladies tell me to say that they look to each Member of the Joint Committee as to a protector of their sex's honour and as an upholder of their modestly made but deeply desired claim for citizen rights with which to serve their country.'[83]

On 21 July 1919, Mrinalini Sen gave an address on 'The Future of Indian Women' to the East India Association (a politically minded organization for British and Indian people) at the 'Vogue' restaurant in Westminster. Besant, Naidu, and Bhola Nauth were also present. Mrinalini Sen was married to Nirmal Chandra Sen, the educational

---

[83] L/PJ/9/8, Cousins to Montagu, 22 July 1919.

advisor to Indian students appointed by the India Office (they had arrived in London in 1913 for this position).[84] Sen explained that educated Indian women had made an appeal for the vote but their attempts had been in vain so far. However, she noted that Indian women were not disheartened and appreciated the support of British women. 'Some of my greatest friends are British women', she remarked, and explained that there was no barrier between them. Furthermore, Sen noted that Indian women needed the support of not only Indian men, but also British men and women, because 'we all belong to the same empire'.[85] The chair, Lord Sinha, was sitting on the Joint Committee and was thus unable to comment directly but told the audience they could assume that they were 'preaching to the converted' in regard to enfranchising Indian women.[86] During the ensuing discussion with the audience, Besant articulated the hope (to cries of 'hear, hear') that the Joint Committee would reverse Southborough's decision regarding female franchise in India. She referred to the support evident in India through the 1917 deputation and various Congress resolutions, and was met with applause when she ended her remarks by hoping that the draft Government of India Bill would be amended to include women's franchise.[87]

In the interviews the Joint Select Committee held on 29 July 1919 with Annie Besant, who was there as representative of the National Home Rule League, she argued that the omission of women's suffrage would introduce a sex disability into Indian life which was alien to Indian spirit. She argued that objections to women's suffrage were weak and artificial. In the same month, Besant addressed the WFL on the topic of 'Indian Women as

[84] Nirmal Chandra Sen was the son of the famous Brahmo Samaj reformer Keshub Chunder Sen. An advisory bureau had been set up in 1908 following the 1907 Lee-Warner Report into Indian Students in the United Kingdom.

[85] Mrs N. C. Sen (Mrinalini Sen), 'The Future of Indian Women', *Asiatic Review* (October 1919): 552–67.

[86] S. Sinha was a barrister, former assistant of Montagu, and member of the King's Counsel, who was under secretary of state for India in 1919.

[87] 'Discussion of the Foregoing Paper', *Asiatic Review* (October 1919): 570–1; also reprinted in Mrinalini Sen, *Knocking at the Door (Lectures and Other Writings)* (Calcutta: Living Age Press, 1954), 22–57.

Citizens'. She proposed the resolution that Indian women possessing the same qualifications as men should be enfranchised and noted that Indian women 'need' the vote 'even more than English women'. The resolution was passed unanimously.[88]

Naidu positioned herself overtly as representative of the women of India and a 'symbol of Indian women' when she met the committee on 6 August. She explained that her 'comrades' were unable to come as many of them had young children but that she represented women of all religious communities including women of the Depressed Classes. She presented a memorandum entitled 'A Plea for the Franchise of Indian Women' in which she questioned why high profile women such as Pandita Ramabai, Kamala Satthianandhan, or Cornelia Sorabji (among others) were denied the vote. Naidu used the example of the Begum of Bhopal to show that Indian women could be political leaders and argued that purdah was not an issue if women supervisors were provided at polling booths.[89] In the committee hearing, Naidu declared that Indian women did not identify with religious communities but regarded themselves solely as 'women', and so enfranchising women would ensure cooperation between all sections of the Indian community. Tellingly, Naidu explained to the committee that the word 'franchise' was a new term introduced to Indians in 1917. Evidently, the Montagu–Chelmsford reforms had changed Indian perceptions of parliamentary democracy through the promise of reformed legislative councils and women were now aware of the possibilities open to them through these democratic structures. Naidu explained that women knew they wanted to be a part of the reforms, and she acknowledged the aid of Cousins, who, with her knowledge of the suffrage movement in Britain, had helped bring the 1917 deputation together.[90]

---

[88] 'Indian Women as Citizens', *Indian Magazine and Review* (August 1919): 126–7; L/PJ/9/8, Florence A. Underwood to Montagu, 11 July 1919. Naidu was also present at the meeting, having seconded the resolution, and Anglo-Irish suffragist Charlotte Despard was in the chair.

[89] E. K., 'Votes for Indian Women', *The Vote*, 15 August 1919, 293.

[90] Joint Select Committee on the Government of India Bill, vol. 1 (1919), 215–17.

Naidu's appeal to 'English chivalry' was noted with interest in the London *Times*. Naidu was clear that the desire for female enfranchisement was unanimous in India. She did not want to overplay this demand, but asked for this 'gift' from British statesmen. Indian women did not seek office or power, according to Naidu, and the Indian home was unlikely to be affected. She explained that there was some need for Indian women's views to be expressed, which would be best served through an electoral voice, and that it was their right by historic tradition. *The Times* also reported that a large number of Indian men and women attended the hearings, and one must suspect that apart from other delegates the Indian community living in London—people such as Roy, Bhola Nauth, and Sen—would have been part of those interested audiences.[91]

As reported in the *International Woman Suffrage News*, it was the British witnesses to the committee, such as Sir James Meston and Sir Frank Sly, who opposed female suffrage in India. Not only did Naidu and Besant present arguments in favour of female enfranchisement, so did Surendranath Banerjea (ICS) and Srinivas Sastri.[92] The Aga Khan wrote a letter into *The Times* endorsing the support for female suffrage in India.[93] As the report in the *International Woman Suffrage News* remarked, just a year after British women had been enfranchised, the question of Indian women's suffrage was in the hands of parliament. It was clearly a decision for British politicians (rather than Indians) at this time and an issue of imperial policy. The writer pleaded with MPs who had once defied the government line in favour of enfranchising British women to do the same in this instance.[94] At the same time, various Indian men visited London to petition the committee about other political concerns relating to the Montagu–Chelmsford reforms. Indeed Indian men had been travelling to Britain since the nineteenth century to petition parliament,

---

[91] 'Indian Women's Claims', *The Times*, 7 August 1919, 4.

[92] 'Women Suffrage and the Government of India Bill', *International Woman Suffrage News* (September 1919): 172–3.

[93] Aga Khan, 'Indian Women and the Vote', *The Times*, 11 August 1919, 6.

[94] 'Women Suffrage and the Government of India Bill', 172–3; see also BL, IOR L/R/5/176 Bombay Native Newspaper Report Part II 1919, 15–16: *Indian Social Reformer*, 17 August 1919.

as was their right as British subjects. The British parliament had housed MPs of Indian heritage, such as David Octherlony Dyce Sombre, of mixed Indian descent, who was elected MP for Sudbury in 1841; Dadabhai Naoroji, elected Liberal MP for Central Finsbury in 1892; and Conservative Mancherjee Merwanjee Bhownaggree for North East Bethnal Green in 1895 and again in 1900.[95] Indian politicians were adept at situating themselves within British metropolitan political circles. Indian suffragettes were equally adept.

The day after her meeting to give evidence, Naidu headed another deputation to Montagu to protest against the Southborough recommendations regarding female franchise. The London paper the *Pall Mall Gazette* was particularly complimentary of Naidu's ability: 'It would be difficult to find a better advocate for the Indian women's cause.' Naidu asserted that there was unanimity between Indian men and women on the issue and pressed for female inclusion in the new electorates.[96] Mrinalini Sen also spoke, reiterating that purdah was not an obstacle to the franchise in India.[97] As St Nihal Singh, a journalist of Indian origin, wrote for the *The Observer*, the deputation reflected the 'progressive character of India'.[98] Indian delegates included Naidu, Sen, Duleep Singh, Besant, Lolita Roy, Bhola Nauth, Dubé, and Mrs Kotwal (as well as male supporters such as A. Yusuf Ali, Ramaswami Aiyar, and P. C. Roy).[99] An evocative description was written by the London correspondent for the *Glasgow Herald* (reproduced in the *Dundee Evening Telegraph*), which described it as a 'picturesque scene' bringing

---

[95] Michael H. Fisher, *The Inordinately Strange Life of Dyce Sombre: Victorian Anglo-Indian MP and Chancery 'Lunatic'* (London: Hurst, 2010); Sumita Mukherjee, '"Narrow-majority" and "Bow-and-agree": Public Attitudes towards the Elections of the First Asian MPs in Britain, Dadabhai Naoroji and Mancherjee Merwanjee Bhownaggree, 1885–1906', *Journal of the Oxford University History Society* 1 (2004): 1–20.

[96] *Pall Mall Gazette* article quoted in 'India and Woman Franchise', *Lancashire Evening Post*, 24 July 1919, 2.

[97] 'Woman Suffrage for India', *The Times*, 8 August 1919, 13.

[98] St. Nihal Singh, 'Indian Women and the Franchise', *The Observer*, 10 August 1919, 4.

[99] St. Nihal Singh, 'Indian Women and the Franchise'; 'Woman Suffrage for India', *Indian Magazine and Review* (September 1919), 134–5.

a 'touch' of the 'colour of the East' to the India Office through the bright 'oriental costumes' of the Indian women. The only woman wearing 'British' clothes was Duleep Singh.[100]

The Tatas and the Government of India Bill

It was clear that the efforts of Naidu were unlikely to change the official opinion set out in the Southborough Report, but Indian women were still anxious that more pressure should be brought upon the government in London. Two other Indian women were to take up the cause in the last quarter of 1919 with more vigour: mother and daughter Herabai and Mithan (also known as Mithibai) Tata from the Tata family of industrialists. A Theosophist, Herabai's interest in a public role to advance the right of women was aroused by a meeting with Duleep Singh in 1911. Her daughter, Mithan, who was thirteen at the time, remembers the holiday they took in Srinagar, Kashmir, where they met Duleep Singh.

> She always wore a small green, white and yellow badge with 'votes for women' inscribed on it. Naturally, my mother's attention was drawn to it, and as we got friendly, she informed us that she was a member of the 'Women's League for Peace and Freedom' in Britain.... Thereafter, she became a firm believer and worker for the cause of women's suffrage.[101]

In an article for *Stri Dharma* (the WIA journal), published in May 1918, Mithan drew comparisons between the Indian and British female suffrage movements. She argued that Indian men and women should receive the same democratic rights together.

> We have seen that it has taken English women more than 80 years of bitter agitation to get their rights. Surely, if we call ourselves human and rational beings, we ought to beware, and not make the same mistake as the English people.... All the vague fears which were conjured up about woman's suffrage in England have proved to be illusions. So also will

---

[100] 'Indian Women Seek the Franchise', *Dundee Evening Telegraph*, 8 August 1919, 11.

[101] BL, Mss Eur F341/147, Mithan Lam, 'Autumn Leaves: Some Memories of Yesteryear'.

our Indian reactionaries see that their fears about granting women the vote are made of soap-bubble material.[102]

Mithan also drew upon differences between the status of Indian and British women in the past. She drew upon (Hindu) nationalist arguments about the glory of ancient India, arguing that in 'olden days' Indian women were rulers, philosophers, and took part in village councils.

In June 1919, Herabai Tata's rationale for enfranchising the women of Bombay was published in the *Times of India*. She explained that the principle of female voting was already in place in Bombay in municipal elections and appealed to the Bombay government to put pressure on the Southborough Committee.[103] A public meeting of Bombay women was then held in July to protest against the non-enfranchisement of women in the Southborough reforms; Herabai spoke at this event.[104] This was followed by another meeting on 1 August 1919 where it was resolved that Herabai and Mithan would be sent to London, with Sir Shankaran Nair who was travelling to give evidence to the Select Committee. It was on short notice (five days) but the Tatas evidently had the means, time, and desire to continue their campaigns in Britain.[105]

Herabai and Mithan arrived in London in September 1919. Upon arrival in Tavistock Square, they sent a letter to the secretary of state, asking to give evidence before the Joint Select Committee. They included a resolution from the Bombay meeting on 1 August, which they had also cabled before leaving India. The resolution noted that the meeting protested against the recommendations of the Southborough Committee to disqualify women from the franchise, drawing attention to the fact that women in Bombay, and other parts of the country, voted in municipal and other elections. It asked

---

[102] Mithan A. Tata, 'Why Indian Women should have the votes', *Stri Dharma* (May 1918): 37.

[103] Herabai A. Tata, 'Votes for Women', *Times of India*, 13 June 1919, 10.

[104] 'Votes for Women', *Times of India*, 14 July 1919, 12; G. R. Josyer, 'Indian Women's Demand for Suffrage', *The International Woman Suffrage News* (September 1919): 173.

[105] 'Women and Franchise', *Times of India*, 2 August 1919, 13.

parliament to reconsider the question.[106] Their statement 'Why Should Women Have Votes?', sent to the India Office on 25 September 1919, laid out a number of reasons for Indian women to have the vote:

> It has been recognised now in all countries that the sex barrier has been a grave mistake, is out of date, unworthy of the times, a relic of past days when might was above right.... Why should India lag behind others in this respect and create a sex barrier where one does not exist, and thus brand Indian women as inferior to their sisters in other countries.[107]

The same Joint Statement by the Tatas was received by the Joint Select Committee on 13 October. The Tatas described themselves as representatives of 'Bombay Women' and the WIA. They argued that Indian women had been treated equally over 5,000 years ago, and in the past few decades, with the rise of female education, their stock was rising again. They noted the continued existence of purdah in some communities but did not see this as a hindrance to female suffrage. They vehemently criticized the Southborough Committee for their total rejection of women from the electorates and for listening to base prejudices about women's inferiority. In their argument for the vote, the Tatas referred back to British history:

> The Government ought not to commit the same mistake as was made in England at the time of the Reform Bill of 1832 and the later Bills, of excluding women from political life, a course which led to very great bitterness, and created great disparity between the political education of men and women. We in India are now in the happy position of being able to start our political education on terms of equality.[108]

The Tatas pointed out that many Indian women were demonstrating a keen interest in political affairs, and that conceding the vote to

[106] L/PJ/9/8, Herabai and Mithibai Tata to Private Secretary to Secretary of State for India, 24 September 1919.

[107] L/PJ/9/8, Herabai and Mithibai Tata, 'Why Should Women Have Votes?' Statement, Bombay 1919.

[108] BL, Mss Eur F136/54, *Joint Select Committee on the Government of India Bill. Vol. III. Appendices* (1919), 134. See also L/PJ/9/8. Herabai and Mithibai Tata, 'Why Should Women Have the Votes?' Statement, Bombay 1919.

women would be a spur for female empowerment. They also pointed out that granting suffrage did not mean that all people would exercise their right to vote. This was an attempt to reassure the government that it would be mainly educated, upper-class women exercising their rights: 'Even in enlightened England all women do not exercise the vote.' They further remarked that even in Britain there had been Conservative opposition to the extension of the franchise to women up until 1917. As Herabai Tata explained in 1920:

> We did not ask the votes for all women, as for some time to come universal suffrage may not be practicable in India, but we do claim that women who possess the same qualifications as are laid down for men, should not be debarred from the enjoyment of the right to vote on account of their sex.[109]

Herabai and her daughter Mithan toured Britain meeting with various women's groups looking for support and advice. In their support, as might be expected, the main women and suffrage organizations in Britain, the WFL, the National Union of Societies for Equal Citizenship (NUSEC), and the National Council of Women of Great Britain and Ireland, sent letters and resolutions to the India Office. The India Office soon became inundated with letters of support from individuals and local associations across the breadth of Britain. They included resolutions urging that Indian women be enfranchised on the same terms as men and that the Government of India Bill remove any allusion to sex disability. These resolutions were sent between September and December 1919 from the Glasgow Study Circle, a group of Glasgow citizens, the Glasgow Society for Women's Suffrage, a public meeting of Newcastle citizens, the Huddersfield, Bristol, and Manchester branches of the Women's International League, the Liverpool Council of Women Citizens, the Cardiff branch of the Britain and India Association, the Letchworth and Swansea branches of the WFL, and the New Cross branch of the National Co-operative Men's Guild, among many others. British individuals also sent in letters of support for Indian women to the

---

[109] Herabai Tata, *A Short Sketch of Indian Women's Franchise Work* (London: The Pelican Press, 1920), 7.

India Office.[110] The Women's International League (the British branch of the Women's International League for Peace and Freedom [WILPF]) passed a resolution through its council in October 1919, urging the government to grant equal political status to Indian women and thus recognize the principle of equal human rights in 'our Eastern Empire'.[111]

Herabai Tata's letters to Jaiji Petit, chair of the Bombay Women's Committee for Women's Suffrage, on her activities in Britain in the last quarter of 1919 reveal the amount of support Tata received. Her letters recount the large number of organizations Herabai spoke to, with Mithan, across London and other British centres. The mother and daughter duo visited various towns and cities, including Birkenhead, Bolton, Edinburgh, Glasgow, Harrowgate, Liverpool, Manchester, and Newcastle, to spread the message of Indian women. Annie Besant had been helpful in arranging some of the public meetings that they spoke at, and had introduced them to various suffrage societies.[112] The organizations they visited in October and November included the National Council of Women of Great Britain and Ireland; Social and Political Union of Bedford College; Council of the Women's International League; Quakers' Friends' Mission; Westfield Ladies' College; Unity Hall, Wood Green; Adult School, Wesleyan Mission; Holloway Women's Co-operative Guild; New Cross Men's Cooperative Guild; British Dominions Women Citizen's Union (BDWCU).[113] The Tatas were becoming notorious among campaigning groups and were making their presence felt well beyond the metropolitan centre, engaging well with a range of British people and asserting their right to debate with these people as British subjects and imperial citizens.

[110] L/PJ/9/8. Representations etc relating to Franchise for Women in India under the Reforms Scheme (1918–1919)

[111] LSE Archives, Women's International League for Peace and Freedom Papers, WILPF/4/2, Resolutions Folder.

[112] Herabai Tata, 'Mrs Besant & Women's Franchise Work', *United India*, 25 February 1920, 345–6.

[113] NMML, Misc. Items Acc. no. 612 [Tata Collection—hereafter TC], 'Activities in Great Britain', *United India*, 19 November 1919, 126; 'Activities in Great Britain', *United India*, 26 November 1919, 143.

The Tatas' activities were reported frequently upon in *United India*, a paper edited by Besant and others in London for the Home Rule for India League. In November 1919 Herabai's response to the report of the Joint Select Committee was published, in which she wondered whether women had not shown enough initiative and statesmanship in getting their voice heard. She pointed out that the government had listened to 'outcastes and depressed classes, non-Brahmanas, urban and rural wage-earning classes' and yet ignored female representations.[114] It is evident in looking at government responses that the government did not yet see women as a political caucus in the way they dealt with other 'political communities'. She expressed concern that Indian provincial councils might not enfranchise Indian women and stressed the imperative need for the question to be decided by parliament rather than Indian men. Herabai was not alone in urging the British government, in London, to act upon the Indian female vote. This was not merely a domestic concern or something that Indians could be trusted to decide. Campaigners actively wanted imperial intervention on this issue and expected parliament to exercise its imperial responsibility. Indian women were willing to be positioned as imperial subjects in this matter.

Mithan was as active as her mother. Her article on the Indian women's struggle was featured in *Jus Suffragii*, the monthly journal of the IWSA, in November 1919.[115] Furthermore, Mithan's address to the WFL at the Minerva Café in London was promoted heavily in *The Vote*, the WFL's journal, which included a summary of her talk in the 12 December edition. She argued that enfranchising women on the same terms as men would only enfranchise about one million women. She also offered some statistics on the number of educated women in India, though she observed that the qualification to vote was based on property rather than literacy. Mithan further remarked that the government had allowed the principle of 'outcasts' in India to vote and yet hesitated when it came to women.[116]

---

[114] H. M. Tata, 'The Indian Woman', *United India*, 26 November 1919, 134.

[115] M. Tata, 'Indian Women and the Vote', *International Woman Suffrage News* (November 1919): 18–19.

[116] 'Forthcoming Events', *The Vote*, 21 November 1919, 407; 'Our Wednesdays', *The Vote*, 12 December 1919, 430.

As Mithan was to recall decades later in an unpublished memoir, the Tatas had earned the support of well-known leaders of the British women's suffrage movement including Charlotte Despard, Millicent Fawcett, Maria Ogilvie Gordon, and Margery Corbett Ashby. These women were instrumental in helping arrange meetings across England and Scotland, providing assistance with accommodation when the Tatas travelled outside of London, passing resolutions, and forwarding these resolutions to members of parliament.[117] Although the Tatas evidently had money, they were reliant on further help from these hosts. As Herabai told Jaiji Petit on 7 December, utter strangers in Britain had been of more help than Indians in India.[118] The inspiration of British suffragettes was felt beyond the direct aid they gave to the Tatas. Mrinalini Sen also recalled, decades later, the inspiration of Lady Constance Lytton on Indian campaigners for the female vote.[119]

Despard later noted that Besant had usefully explained to British audiences that 'women in Indian society are not the subject, inapt human beings that many Europeans imagine them to be' and that the political distinction of Indian men and women would actually be a new departure in the history of India.[120] At the end of 1919, Despard wrote an address to Indian women for the new magazine *Britain and India*, edited by the Theosophist Josephine Ransom in London. She explained that Besant and Indian women in Britain had carried out effective propaganda and made it clearer to her, at least, that 'womanhood everywhere is one'. Despard expressed her sympathy towards Indian women who had to ask for the elementary right of franchise, which Indian men appeared to be willing to grant, from 'men of a different race'. However, she assured them that 'women of Great Britain are with you'.[121]

Following the Joint Committee meetings in the summer of 1919, it was clear that pressure now had to be borne in upon MPs involved in readings of the Government of India Bill through parliament.

[117] Lam, 'Autumn Leaves', chapter VII.

[118] TC, Herabai Tata to Petit, 7 December 1919.

[119] Sen, *Knocking at the Door*, 143.

[120] Charlotte Despard, 'Mrs Besant and Indian Women's Franchise', *United India*, 10 March 1920, 376.

[121] 'To the Women of India', *Britain and India* (January 1920): 12–13.

The committee had decided to leave the decision of female enfranchisement up to the provinces in India, but the Tatas and their supporters were keen that the principle should be enshrined in law in the new Reform Bill. As E. Knight put it for *The Vote*, the 'Mother of Parliaments' was shifting its responsibility on this issue to newly created provincial legislatures, which was a 'ludicrous position' when so little else of imperial management had been devolved to India. Knight quoted from Herabai Tata who lamented that 'India has already spoken, and yet she is to be made to wait'. The WFL had taken this issue to heart since Indian men and women had asked for their help in the spring of 1919. The imperial responsibility (and burden) was felt. Knight urged every member of the WFL to write to their MP to vote for the amendments to the bill to prevent 'shame from being done by your Country in your name' and to 'share in giving Right and Justice to this great and ancient Empire'.[122]

The Women's International League had a public meeting at Queen's Hall in November 1919 to protest against the Government of India Bill when it was clear that women were being excluded from the franchise.[123] In a circular invitation to the event, Emmeline Pethick-Lawrence, treasurer of the Women's International League, explained that the meeting was organized so that British women could demonstrate their support towards their 'Indian sisters' in protest of the exclusion of women from political rights and for being 'classed amongst lunatics, criminals and children'.[124] The meeting was presided over by Ramsay MacDonald (the Labour politician who had lost his seat in the 1918 election), and Naidu, Mithan, and Besant all spoke. Mithan recalled later how MacDonald 'made an impassioned speech for the passage of the India Bill, so that Indians could have greater rights in the affairs of their own country'.[125] Naidu put forward the resolution of protest and said that she spoke to the 'spirit and ideals of the English nation'. As in previous addresses, Naidu explained that Indian women had historically enjoyed similar rights

[122] E. Knight, 'Government of India Bill', *The Vote*, 28 November 1919, 412.
[123] LSE Archives, WILPF/4/2, Resolutions Folder.
[124] JR, IWSA/2/33, Women's International League circular, 20 October 1919.
[125] Lam, 'Autumn Leaves', chapter VII.

and pointed to examples of female rulers such as the Maharani of Gwalior and Begum of Bhopal. Mithan argued that women were as just a part of the country as men, and that they should be given the franchise at the same time to learn how to exercise it together. Besant emphasized the Indian male support for female franchise, and the meeting also included supportive comments from Indian men.[126]

Apart from encouraging public and private associations to petition the India Office, Herabai was keen to persuade MPs in the House of Commons to pass an amendment to the Government of India Bill to remove any sex disabilities. Lord Lytton was an early ally in this mission, an advocate of female franchise owing to his sister, Lady Constance Lytton, who had been involved in hunger strikes in prison. The Tatas also had the support of another Lytton sister, the Theosophist Emily Lutyens, who wrote to the suffragist Tories Lord Hugh Cecil and Lord Henry Cavendish Bentinck.[127] Lytton went on to talk to Lord Robert Cecil (brother of Hugh) who introduced Herabai to Major Hills, who, in turn, was able to arrange to book a committee room in the House for a meeting.[128] The Tatas held two meetings for MPs. One was on 25 November, which Naidu also attended, but only 15 members attended as a vote was going on at the same time.[129] In the meantime the Tatas wrote letters to MPs who they knew had been in favour of enfranchising British women.[130] They then had another meeting on 1 December, again without a favourable turnout because it coincided with Lady Nancy Astor taking her seat, a momentous occasion which Herabai was very aware of. It was this occasion of a female MP taking up a seat in the House of Commons which encouraged Herabai to realize that the focus needed to be not only on the vote, but also in getting women appointed as members of legislative

---

[126] They included Jamnadas Dwarkanath and a Mr Patel ('Votes for Indian Women', *United India*, 19 November 1919, 123–4).

[127] TC, Herabai to Petit, 1 November 1919.

[128] TC, Lytton to Herabai, 5 November 1919. John Waller Hills had served in the British Army during the First World War and was Liberal Unionist MP for Durham City.

[129] TC, Herabai to Petit, 26 November 1919.

[130] TC, Herabai to Petit, 25 November 1919.

councils.[131] Naidu, the Tatas, and Lolita Roy were all present at the meeting. They were particularly keen to disabuse members of the preconception that Indian men did not support female enfranchisement.[132] As the honorary secretary of the BDWCU put it, these Indian women created a deep impression by their 'calm and convincing logic', as well as their 'striking eloquence'. Representatives of most of the major British women's societies were reported to have been present too.[133]

As Major Hills put it in that meeting, the 'safest as well as the justest' plan would be to enfranchise eligible women. It was also reported that when Montagu explained that the question was one for Indians to decide, Astor retorted that it was to be decided by Indian men. When Montagu responded that the question of women's franchise had been decided by men in Britain, Astor reminded him that this was 'only after enormous pressure from the ladies'.[134] As Lutyens put it in an article for *United India*, supporting Astor's remarks, the Government of India Bill continued to maintain their belief in the inferiority of women. 'It therefore now remains for Indian men to prove that the East can still teach a lesson in justice and wisdom to the West,' she remarked. 'The women of the West look to the Motherland of the Aryan race to accomplish an act of justice towards its women, denied to them by the blind prejudice of English men.'[135]

The enfranchisement of Indian women was a matter of pride and responsibility for many British campaigners. Emmeline Pethick-Lawrence wrote to the India Office in November 1919 to explain that the 'women of Great Britain' were 'exceedingly anxious that the stigma of sex prejudice and injustice shall not fall upon the British people'. Believing that the 1918 enfranchisement of British women (though not all women were enfranchised) was a victory for the principles of British democracy, Pethick-Lawrence argued that imposing sex

[131] TC, Herabai to Petit, 7 December 1919.
[132] 'Enfranchisement of Indian Women', *Britain and India* (January 1920): 26.
[133] 'Deputation of Indian Women', *Daily News (Perth)*, 17 February 1920, 5.
[134] 'The Way of the World', *United India*, 10 December 1919, 162.
[135] Emily Lutyens, 'Votes for Indian Women', *United India*, 31 December 1919, 212.

discrimination on Indians would be a violation of British principles and would bring contempt upon British people.[136] As has been evident through the efforts and support afforded to the Tatas, the campaign to enfranchise Indian women was seen as an imperial policy issue, though the government was shifting that responsibility to India. This created resentment because there was an obvious sex disparity in the reforms. Elizabeth Abbott found it 'atrocious' that the government gave an opinion on 'almost every other subject' except that relating to Indian women.[137] As Maude Royden explained:

> If India is allowed to settle her own franchise, that is good; but for Great Britain to settle the franchise for men, and then tell them to settle that for women, is not democratic—it is not leaving India to settle her own affairs: it is leaving it to the men to settle the affairs of the women.[138]

Following the 1 December meeting, the Tatas were tasked by Hills to produce more statistics and arguments in favour of enfranchising women. An unnamed Labour MP intended to ask for the inclusion of Indian women as political candidates too, but the Tatas and Naidu were concerned that Conservative MPs would not approve of this amendment so they focused solely on a resolution regarding the vote.[139] On 5 December 1919 Naidu and the Tatas attended a reading of the Government of India Bill in the Strangers' Gallery.[140] Mithan recalled later how packed the gallery was. The majority of MPs felt they did not know enough about India and wanted to leave the decision of enfranchising women up to Indian men in the legislatures. It is interesting to note that in this sphere alone British politicians felt that this argument was defensible, which could be an acknowledgement of the frailties of imperial rule. It actually proved that the female sphere was not deemed important enough for the imperial parliament. In Mithan's memoirs, she suggested that she was 'happy'

[136] L/PJ/9/8, Pethick-Lawrence to India Office, 25 November 1919

[137] JR, IWSA/2/25, Elizabeth Abbott to Pinja Powallah, 25 November 1919.

[138] 'To the Women of India', *Britain and India* (January 1920): 14.

[139] TC, Herabai to Petit, 4 December 1919.

[140] J. D. W., 'From the Ladies' Gallery, 5th December 1919', *Indian Magazine and Review* (January 1920), 6.

with the decision of the Government of India Bill readings because the door was not fully closed.[141]

Therefore, the 1919 Government of India Act enlarged the democratic parliamentary principle in India. Provincial governors and the viceroy still had reserved powers to certify legislation, and the Government of India was still responsible for foreign policy, the military, income tax, currency, and criminal law. However, public health, education, land revenue administration, and 'law and order' were devolved to the provincial governments and hence the Indian electorate now had some influence on these matters. Elected Indians now had more responsibility on social reform issues through this new system known as 'dyarchy'. All provincial legislatures, though, had some seats that were reserved through nomination rather than election. They also had seats reserved, either through special constituencies or through general constituencies, for certain 'communities' and 'interests'. These varied by province but included Muslims, Sikhs, Anglo-Indians, Christians, Europeans, Landowners, Depressed Classes, Labour, and university seats. With such fundamental reforms taking place in Britain's imperial possession, the debates about the bill exercised MPs for a number of different reasons. They had already had two readings of the bill by June 1919 before Indian suffragettes had become more vocal in the metropolitan centre about women's rights. It was clear that enfranchising women was not a priority for the MPs, which is why the concession to ensure that women were not permanently excluded was seen as a small victory for Mithan and other campaigners.

While the Tatas had been touring, Mrinalini Sen had also been publicizing the Indian fight, giving a lecture on 'Indian women' in Liverpool in October 1919.[142] Following the passing of the bill, Sen had a piece published in the *Africa and Orient Review*. Though she was happy for the reforms in general for Indian men, she expressed disappointment with the lack of public support from Indian men (apart from the Aga Khan) for the demands made by women. Sen also complained that Indian women were not treated as if they 'belonged to the British Empire'. As she explained, Indian women

---

[141] Lam, 'Autumn Leaves', chapter VII.

[142] 'Activities in Great Britain', *United India*, 29 October 1919, 76.

were subject to the laws of the British government and had to pay taxes if they had incomes, and yet on the issue of franchise they had been ignored and the issue was left in the hands of Indian men. She concluded with the observation: 'I dare say we shall get our rights in time, but it is likely to cost us some agitation, some stirring up, some wasting of time before we achieve it.'[143]

The Regionalism of the Indian Suffrage Movement

Disappointed that the amendment to enfranchise women through the Government of India Bill had not been accepted, and that the responsibility had been left to the legislative assemblies in India, Herabai Tata began to focus her attention back on Bombay and her own regional legislative assembly. The 1919 bill had devolved franchise to the regions, and Herabai took regional loyalty seriously. She had always positioned herself as a representative of Bombay rather than 'Indian' women.[144] The Tatas remained in London until 1923 as Mithan pursued a postgraduate degree at the LSE and trained as a barrister at Lincoln's Inn (one of the first ten women to be called to the Bar in the UK). They continued to maintain links with British feminists such as Despard and Fawcett; and in February 1920 the Tatas and Lolita Roy addressed the Cambridge Majlis (an Indian student society) on the need to enfranchise Indian women.[145] Meanwhile, Herabai urged Petit to start calling meetings and organize petitions to the male members of the Bombay Legislative Council and Imperial Council to urge them to remove the sex disability in Bombay.[146] Herabai used her connections with British women's organizations to ask them to start sending letters to Bombay, too, and the Women's International League did so in February 1920.[147] She continued to campaign on the

---

[143] Mrinalini Sen, 'The Indian Reform Bill and the Women of India', *Africa and Orient Review*, 1, II (February 1920), reprinted in Sen, *Knocking at the Door*, 67–70.

[144] See L/PJ/9/8 files, Representations etc. relating to Franchise for Women in India under the Reforms Scheme (1918–1919).

[145] 'In Britain and India', *Britain and India* (April 1920): 137–8.

[146] TC, Herabai to Petit, 8 February 1920; 29 September 1920.

[147] TC, K. E. Royds to Herabai, 24 February 1920.

issue of women's franchise, writing to Montagu and putting pressure on the Imperial Council through resolutions sent on by the Women's International League, the BDWCU, and NUSEC. Herabai also urged Petit to send on copies of these resolutions regarding Bombay to the local press such as the *Bombay Chronicle* and *New India*.[148] As Herabai explained to Petit, it was important to record that English women supported the extension of the franchise to Indian women.[149] The secretary of the National Council of Women of Great Britain and Ireland, though, declined to continue involvement in direct action as the council believed it was beyond their scope to comment on legislative measures in India. With the shifting of the political debates to the geographical space of India, the matter became less immediate to British suffragists.[150]

As directed by the Government of India Act, it was up to members of provincial legislative councils to propose a resolution to enfranchise women, and then for the resolution to be passed by a majority. Herabai became particularly competitive with Madras and the work that Cousins was doing there to enfranchise women, repeatedly telling Petit that she wanted Bombay to be the first province to allow women to become voters. She was keen to point out, as before, that Bombay women had the municipal vote and were well placed to exercise a parliamentary vote.[151] The Bombay campaign certainly appeared to be the most 'vigorous', as Jana Matson Everett put it, with 19 women's associations in participation.[152] In July 1921, Bombay enfranchised women on the same terms as men.[153] Following the resolution, a Karachi paper the *Sind Observer* remarked that enfranchising women would be in the interests of the British government as it would prevent women from turning extremist. The paper also pointed out that the systems of education, industry, and government had all been

---

[148] TC, Herabai to Petit, 10 March 1920.

[149] TC, Herabai to Petit, 29 September 1920.

[150] TC, Norah E. Green to Herabai, 19 February 1920.

[151] TC, Herabai to Petit, 28 March 1920; 24 September 1920.

[152] Jana Matson Everett, *Women and Social Change in India* (New Delhi: Heritage, 1981), 107.

[153] Gail Pearson, 'Reserved Seats—Women and the Vote in Bombay', *Indian Economic and Social History Review* 20, 47 (1983): 51.

imposed by the colonial government and thus British concerns about 'tradition' were not appropriate when thinking about the new society and norms that India lived under.[154]

As Herabai focused on her locality, Cousins too focused on her immediate sphere of influence: Madras. As she was to put it later to Elizabeth Abbott of the British section of the IWSA, the vote for women in Madras was won almost entirely due to the work of the WIA.[155] The WIA approached every candidate for the new council in November 1920, asking them to pledge to support the vote for women.[156] It is worth noting that a group of women in Mangalore, where Jinarajadasa was based, held a protest meeting about the sex disqualification in the Madras Presidency in April 1920. They argued that they were only asking for the vote for qualified women and that 'Western women, who would have [had] the vote had they been in any other part of the Empire, were denied it in India, because they had to be pulled down to the status of Indian women'.[157] Clearly, suffrage debates were not always inclusive and often used socially charged language. However, the *Swadesamitram*, a Madras paper, was keen to point out that the privilege of voting should not be denied to women in India while women in various other countries including 'conservative England' were sitting as members of parliament.[158] Britain remained the obvious focal point for comparison in these debates.

Unfortunately for Herabai, Madras women were enfranchised (on the same terms as men) before Bombay—in April 1921. Jinarajadasa,

[154] L/R/5/179, Bombay Native Newspaper Reports 1921, *Sind Observer*, 3 August 1921.

[155] Cousins to E. Abbott, 19 May 1921 in S. Muthulakshmi Reddi, *Mrs Margaret Cousins and Her Work in India: With a Brief Life Sketch of Her Colleagues and Comrades* (Adyar, Madras: Women's Indian Association, 1956), 29.

[156] All-India Women's Conference Library, Delhi, File no. 1-II (1920–27), WIA Circular, November 1920.

[157] 'Indian Women Claim the Rights of Citizenship', *United India*, 19 May 1920, 99.

[158] L/R/5/129, Madras Native Newspaper Reports 1921, *Swadesamitram*, 2 April 1921.

Cousins, and 58 other women sat in the gallery to hear the debate.[159] Cousins hailed the victory for taking place in the city where the women's deputation had met Montagu in December 1917, and for only taking three years unlike the forty-five in Britain.[160] In analysing the success, Jinarajadasa was amazed at the contrast between her experiences as a suffragette in Britain where she had witnessed police brutality and comrades being imprisoned. She noted that British women did not yet enjoy franchise equality with men but that Madras women did (disregarding the minimal number of women who would be able to vote in Madras).[161] The efforts in Bombay and Madras had evidently been spearheaded by keen activists, but also through the financial backing of their supporters. It is not my intention to interrogate the local debates about women's franchise further, as my focus is on the transnational networks of Indian suffragettes, but it should be noted that all the Muslim members of the council voted against the resolution.[162]

Following the success in Madras, Cousins directed her attention to Bengal. She believed that personal appeal was the best method to influence public opinion.[163] She was keen to ensure that all provinces enfranchise women and started linking this to nationalist arguments—that enfranchising women would place India in a position of equality with other countries in the empire and demonstrate India's fitness for self-government.[164] Cousins attended a debate in the Bengal Legislative Council alongside Indian suffragists including Mrinalini Sen who had actively lobbied members even though they had only

[159] AIWC Library, File no.1-II (1920–1927), L. W. Swamikanna to D. Jinarajadasa, 24 March 1921.

[160] Cousins, 'Votes for Women: What Madras Has Done', *Times of India*, 21 April 1921, 10; NLI, Sheehy Skeffington Papers, MS 41,177/12, Cousins to Sheehy Skeffington, 29 April 1921.

[161] Dorothy Jinarajadasa, 'Women's Franchise in India and England' (1921) in Reddi, *Margaret Cousins*. See also Smith College, Sophia Smith Collection [hereafter SSC], India, Box 20, Folder 2, Dorothy Jinarajadasa, 'How We Won Equal Suffrage in South India', *Life and Labor* (June 1921).

[162] 'Votes for Indian Women', *The Times*, 29 April 1921, 9.

[163] Cousins and Cousins, *We Two Together*, 408.

[164] Cousins, 'When Will Bengal Give Woman Suffrage?' *Modern Review*, 30, 3 (September 1921), 328–30.

learnt of the tabling of the resolution 17 days beforehand.[165] Sen was the figurehead of the women's movement in Bengal, largely through the efforts of the women's group the Bangiya Nari Samaj. However, as Sen pointed out a decade later, British interest and knowledge of female suffrage activities outside of Madras and Bombay were minimal because the connections that Cousins, Tatas, and others had built were primarily between Madras and Bombay women's groups and international women's groups.[166] A women's suffrage resolution in Bengal was defeated in 1921; it was only in 1923 that women were allowed to vote in municipal elections in Bengal. An amendment allowing women to vote in legislative elections was finally passed in August 1925 (and again opposition mainly came from British and Muslim members).[167]

Despite the rhetoric put forward by Cousins, Naidu, and others that Indian women faced little opposition to suffrage from Indian men, the campaigns to enfranchise women on provincial levels were not straightforward. Suffrage campaigners were not yet organized regionally or nationally, and they faced hostile opposition and apathy from Indian men and women. Dhanvanthi Rama Rau, for example, recounts a suffrage meeting for women in Quetta, near the Afghan border, in the 1920s where the audience appeared to have neither enthusiasm for the advances in Madras nor interest in gaining those same voting rights.[168] As Bharati Ray has argued in relation to the Bengali suffrage movement, campaigners were generally from elite backgrounds—middle-class women who were unable to involve the vast majority of women in rural areas as

---

[165] Cousins, 'Backward Bengal: Woman Suffrage Defeat' (no date) in Reddi, *Margaret Cousins*.

[166] Sen, *Knocking at the Door*, 83, 146.

[167] For more on the Bengal suffrage campaigns, see Southard, 'Colonial Politics and Women's Rights'; Barbara Southard, *The Women's Movement and Colonial Politics in Bengal: The Quest for Political Rights, Education and Social Reform Legislation, 1921–1936* (Delhi: Manohar, 1995).

[168] Bharati Ray, 'The Freedom Movement and Feminist Consciousness in Bengal, 1905–1929', in *From the Seams of History: Essays on Indian Women* (New Delhi: Oxford University Press, 1995), 191, 210. Dhanvanthi Rama Rau to Cousins (no date) in Reddi, *Margaret Cousins*, 53.

their aspirations were based on urban ideals and finding room in established power structures.[169] Nevertheless, resolutions were put forward in provincial assemblies by male members. Women were enfranchised in Punjab and Assam in 1926, Central Provinces and Berar in 1927, and Bihar and Orissa in 1929 (having been defeated twice before).[170] The question was simultaneously raised about the qualification for women to sit as members of legislative councils, which required further resolutions. These were passed in the Central Assembly, Bombay, Madras, Punjab, Central Provinces, United Provinces, and Assam by 1927.[171] Indian States that were not under the jurisdiction of British India and the 1919 Bill were also inspired to enfranchise women: Travancore in 1920, Jhalwar in 1921, Mysore in 1922, Rajkot in 1923, and Cochin in 1924, which also allowed women to become members of the state legislature. Mary Poonen Lukose was the first female legislator in Travancore and became minister of state to the Travancore government in 1925.[172] By 1930, the ratio of male to female voters was about 25:1 and the percentage of women voters compared to the adult female population was under 1 per cent in most provinces.[173]

The ongoing developments in Indian franchise and female electoral activity continued to be viewed with interest in the British feminist periodical press. Herabai wrote a piece for *The Vote* in April 1922 discussing developments beyond Bombay and Madras.[174] Cousins contributed an article in November 1923 discussing the elections

---

[169] Bharati Ray, 'The Freedom Movement and Feminist Consciousness in Bengal, 1905–1929', in *From the Seams of History: Essays on Indian Women*, ed. Bharati Ray (New Delhi: Oxford University Press, 1995), 191, 210.

[170] IOR, L/PJ/6/1878, Women Suffrage and Eligibility of Women for Membership of Legislative Bodies.

[171] Everett, *Women and Social Change in India*, 108–9.

[172] R. M. Gray, 'Women in Indian Politics', in *Political India 1832–1932: A Co-operative Survey of a Century*, ed. John Cumming (London: Oxford University Press, 1932), 159.

[173] IOR, L/I/1/171, Indian States: Enfranchisement of Women, *Times Educational Supplement*, 8 November 1930.

[174] Herabai Tata, 'Indian Women's Enfranchisement', *The Vote*, 28 April 1922, 130.

where women in India were able to exercise their right to vote for the first time.[175] However, women could not yet stand for election at this time.[176] In April 1925, the Women's International League had a meeting and passed a resolution, sent on to the India Office, calling for the British government to support Indian women to be allowed to be nominated or elected to all Indian legislatures.[177] The first women to contest legislative council seats did so in 1926. In these elections only 4.62 per cent of the total number of votes was cast by women.[178] Although Kamaladevi Chattopadhyay (sister-in-law of Naidu) contested a seat in the 1926 elections for the Madras Legislative Council, she was defeated by a few hundred votes. Cousins had been involved in Kamaladevi's campaign and had hosted the British suffragette Emmeline Pethick-Lawrence in Adyar at the same time. As Cousins told Irish suffragette Hanna Sheehy Skeffington, Pethick-Lawrence was 'entirely surprised to find Indian women in advance of the British women both in their political accomplishment [and] their present enthusiasm'.[179] Hannah Angelo contested the reserved seat for Anglo-Indians but was also unsuccessful. Instead, following the elections, the Madras Legislative Council nominated Dr Muthulakshmi Ammal (Reddi) to the council. She was the first woman to hold a seat and became deputy president of the council.[180]

In an article in Gandhi's *Young India* in 1920, Herabai Tata was criticized for enlisting the help of Carrie Chapman Catt, president of the IWSA, and for modelling the Indian fight for suffrage on that in Britain.[181] *Young India* argued that the priority in India was to fight the

[175] Cousins, 'Indian Womanhood at the Polls', *The Vote*, 30 November 1923, 379. See also 'Women of India Call for Equality', *The Vote*, 12 September 1924, 293.

[176] Cousins, 'Our Special Article: Women at Home and Abroad', *New India*, 27 October 1923, 4; Cousins, 'Our Special Article: Women at Home and Abroad', *New India*, 10 November 1923, 4.

[177] L/PJ/6/1878, Dorothy Evans to Earl of Birkenhead, 9 April 1925.

[178] L/PJ/6/1848, Joint Secretary to Government of India, 28 March 1929.

[179] NLI, Sheehy Skeffington Papers, MS14,177/12, Cousins to Hanna Sheehy Skeffington, 29 October 1926.

[180] Reddi, *Margaret Cousins*, 58, 63, 66.

[181] 'Women and Vote', *Young India* (24 November 1920), 4.

British first rather than cooperate with them by demanding representation within an imperial parliament. In the 1910s and 1920s, British and Indian women had fought to have a voice within a structure that was patriarchal, imperial, and conservative. They did not put forward a coherent plan to dismantle the very institutions that had been suffocating them for so long, though some may have described themselves as 'nationalist'. In fact, they depended upon their rights as British subjects and the imperial networks in place to use the help of British campaigners in their initial fight for female suffrage. Although the concessions were small, it was with insistent campaigning and British support that Indian suffragettes were at least able to convince the government to allow the provinces the right to enfranchise women if they saw fit. In addition, there were some provinces that benefitted more directly from transnational (and imperial) links. Therefore, despite a fight based on the right to citizenship and participation in a democratic state, Indian campaigners had to assert these rights within an imperial context.

The relationship between Indian and British suffragettes was not equal. British women asserted their own ideas about imperial responsibility and only engaged with a select few elite Indian women in Britain. In turn, these well-connected women dominated the movement in India. Indian campaigners such as Naidu and Tatas had also felt compelled to air their demands in Britain and engage with British bodies and individuals rather than on a national Indian stage. The Indian suffragettes, at the beginning of their campaign, were projecting themselves within a binary imperial relationship. They were demanding their rights as subjects of the British Crown, as imperial subjects. The Indian suffrage movement also became unequally focused on winning votes on a province-by-province basis, rather than becoming a struggle that was united nationally at this stage. The suffragettes were not asserting their national identities in this fight yet.

As many Indian suffragettes reflected, the fight to gain franchise on the same terms as Indian men was not particularly drawn out, especially not when compared to the violent roller-coaster struggle for British women. Cousins was keen to gloat in 1927 that Indian women had been granted equality of status on equal terms as men in the political sphere while 'Britain is still treating a boy of 21 as the superior in citizenship of any women under 30!'[182] However, the inherent inequalities within Indian society were clearly exemplified by the minuscule proportion of women who were enfranchised by 1930. The fight for suffrage equality was not over. The government in Britain had abrogated themselves of their responsibility with the 1919 Government of India Act. Although this encouraged Indian suffragettes to turn their attentions to campaigns on Indian soil, in fact, their experience of engaging and campaigning with British activists encouraged them to continue to think of their suffrage rights as part of a broader movement, beyond the 'nation'. Indian suffragettes could now draw from larger, broader, networks of feminists in the next stage of ensuring that more Indian women could have equal political rights and a voice in Indian and imperial affairs.

[182] Margaret E. Cousins, 'Miss Mayo's Cruelty to Mother India' (Women's Indian Association pamphlet, no date), 2.

2

Indian Suffragettes and Commonwealth Networks

I ndian suffragettes had an obvious, politically determined link to Britain and British suffrage campaigners. Naidu and the Tatas had exploited this to good effect in the immediate post-war period. Their engagement with the British government and MPs in London had been necessary as a practical measure because the Government of India Bill readings were in the House of Commons, and the Southborough Committee had met in Westminster too. In what ways, though, were Indian suffragettes thinking of themselves as British subjects and citizens of empire? Engaging with the issue of franchise meant that campaigners had to reflect upon their political participation and representation, and what it meant to be not only a 'citizen' of 'India', but also a subject of the British Crown. Many Indians lived overseas in other parts of the empire; India was part of a larger empire and 'Commonwealth', whose relationships were constantly being reimagined and reinforced over the twentieth century. As discussed in the introduction, the empire consisted of multiple, layered webs of connections that did not just emanate from Britain to colony.

Indian suffragettes used nationalist reasoning (as we shall see in Chapter 5) to demand citizenship rights and the vote in the interwar period. They focused on imperial reasons, too, to explain why the British government should award them the right to vote (as we have seen in the previous chapter). They also looked beyond India and Britain, to the wider expanse of empire, for inspiration in their campaigns for female suffrage. They did this in two ways. First, they drew inspiration from the earlier enfranchisement of women in Australia and New Zealand, and subsequent enfranchisement of women in the other white dominions, arguing that Indian women should be on a par with their 'sisters' in other parts of the empire. Second, they were also drawn in (to some extent) by the female suffrage fights that Indian women who lived in other parts of the empire were engaged with, especially Kenya and South Africa. Thus, they drew upon and cemented new transnational ties of feminist campaigning, ties that have generally been overlooked by historians—that of Indian feminist positioning within 'colonial' feminist webs. Though Woollacott has used the term 'Commonwealth feminism' to discuss some of these networks, the Commonwealth is largely used to discuss the white dominions before the Second World War and white settlers. 'Imperial Feminism' is a term used by Burton and others that denotes the imperialist thinking of British feminists. I use the term 'colonial feminism' here, appropriately to discuss these webs of feminism between women of empire, beyond the metropole.

The earliest global victories for women's suffrage were in the British dominions: in New Zealand and Australia. Their example had been important for British suffragists, as they would also prove to be for Indian women. Indian women met women from the dominions in Britain, but considered their relationship to be different to that with British women. 'Colonial feminism' was a more benign sisterhood than that of British imperial feminist relations. In this chapter, I will explore these colonial relationships, with particular reference to Indian suffrage connections in the British Dominions Women's Suffrage Union (BDWSU) and the BCL. As Indian suffragettes were thinking globally and exploiting transnational networks for their campaigns, the position of Indians in other parts of the empire and their political rights were naturally raised. The practice of indenture had forced Indian men and women to migrate to Fiji, Guyana, Malaya, and South Africa, and imperial routes had also encouraged Indians to migrate to all parts of the world including Australia, Canada, Kenya, and South Africa. In this chapter, I will discuss the development of female franchise rights for Indians in selected colonies outside of India to explore the ways in which citizenship was being considered in these different spaces.

On 17 June 1911, Indian women carried a flag of India and marched alongside other women from the British Empire in a coronation procession in London organized by British suffragettes to demand votes for women. As we have seen, Mrs P. L. Roy, Bhola Nauth, and Leila Mukerjea were living in Britain at the time and were part of this contingent.[1] They were included in the Empire Pageant with British and Irish women, alongside Australia, New Zealand, Canada, and South Africa, as a symbol of the so-called sisterhood of suffrage campaigners across empire. No other colonial women were represented, only women from the 'white' dominions, and India. Following this, in the 1920s and 1930s, Indian women were involved in the BDWSU and BCL alongside women from the white dominions, though other women 'of colour' were not.

The issue of race within suffrage networks and imperial racial hierarchies need to be discussed here. Though Indian women were campaigning for political rights, they often remained silent on issues of racial, class, and caste prejudice within India and empire more broadly. This is particular evident in the positioning of Indians in colonies such as Kenya and South Africa, where solidarity with 'black' Africans was not always forthcoming. While British women and women from other dominions welcomed Indian suffragettes, who were educated, well-dressed Anglophiles, the suffrage rights of other women of colour within empire were summarily ignored. Indian women did little to address these issues. While there has been a great addition in recent years to the scholarship on female suffrage in empire, and the intersections of race, class and gender, I wish to explore the relationship between Indian women and other colonized women further, including those in the 'white' dominions.

---

[1] 'The Women's Procession', *The Vote*, 17 June 1911, 95; 'Women's Coronation Procession', *Votes for Women*, 16 June 1911, 615; 'Echoes of the Procession', *Votes for Women*, 30 June 1911, 640.

Indian women were beginning to reject British feminist intervention by the late 1920s, but they wanted to engage in transnational networks, and certainly did not want to be isolated in their feminist campaigning. In 1925, *Stri Dharma*, the journal of the WIA, suggested, in relation to the BCL, that there had been a shift in feminist connections for Indian women: 'The British Commonwealth League is becoming an important power in the British Commonwealth, and it is not Imperialistic, but stands on the ground of our common feminism.'[2] Despite interactions with white colonial women who asserted similar conceptions about race and empire as British women, Indian women appeared to view organizations such as the BCL as substantially different from other female organizations. In this chapter, I explore the ways in which Indian women built up networks with women across the empire, the ways in which 'imperial citizenship' was considered, and the place of racial hierarchies in these conversations. I discuss the tour that Dorothy Jinarajadasa took of Australia in the 1920s, the interactions of Indian women with the BDWSU and the BCL, both based in London, and the campaigns Indian women were involved in for greater franchise in other parts of the empire. I argue here that Indian women looked across the empire—to colonial feminism—for a new web of solidarity, and discuss the ways in which they used these networks to engage with issues of race and female citizenship in empire—in both metropole and various peripheries.

Early Colonial Connections and Dorothy Jinarajadasa

The fight for female franchise in Australia and other white dominions always had an international, and imperial, dimension. It was not only British suffragettes who were compelled to justify their fitness to vote on matters relating to empire. For example, Lord Milner, at the Women's Canadian Club in Montreal in 1908, argued that the common citizenship and networks of empire benefitted feminism: '"The women's movement" can only gain, and may gain

---

[2] Quoted in Mrinalini Sinha, 'Suffragism and Internationalism: The Enfranchisement of British and Indian Women under an Imperial State', *Indian Economic and Social History Review* 36, 4 (1999): 477.

immensely, from an exchange of experiences, from the women of one part of the Empire following the efforts, and learning from ... women in other parts.'[3] Ian Tyrrell has described the cooperation between the Women's Christian Temperance Union (WCTU), founded in America, and suffrage groups in Australia, Canada, New Zealand, and South Africa in the late nineteenth and early twentieth centuries.[4] Despite the prominence the WCTU gave to female suffrage and the fact that they had branches in India from 1887, the organization was not visibly involved in raising issues about the votes for Indian women either in the nineteenth or the twentieth century.

Early connections between Australian and Indian feminists were between 'white' women in both countries. In June 1910, a meeting on women's suffrage in Britain took place in the Indian hill town of Simla. During the meeting, the examples of Australia and New Zealand were raised as positive cases where female suffrage had been awarded, and 'all women of the British Empire' were called upon to help the British cause. Nevertheless, the meeting voted against the motion on British female suffrage—with 74 in favour, and 82 against.[5] British women in India also began to consider their suffrage rights within India. The Mussoorie Suffrage Society had been set up by white women, including the British suffragist Frances Hallowes, by 1912, not only to support suffrage campaigns in Britain but also to discuss the ways British women living in India could have a say in the political process. In 1913, 400 people attended a suffrage debate and they sought affiliation with the National Union for Women's Suffrage.[6] However, they faced opposition from the all-India branch of the National League for Opposing Woman Suffrage, founded in 1913 and presided over by Lord Curzon. The former viceroy opposed British female suffrage

---

[3] Quoted in Anna Snaith, *Modernist Voyages: Colonial Women Writers in London, 1890–1945* (Cambridge: Cambridge University Press, 2014), 29.

[4] Ian Tyrrell, *Woman's World Woman's Empire: The Woman's Christian Temperance Union in International Perspective, 1880–1930* (Chapel Hill: The University of North Carolina Press, 1991), chap. 10.

[5] 'Women's Suffrage', *Times of India*, 30 June 1910, 7.

[6] 'Indian News in Brief', *Times of India*, 30 July 1913, 7; *The Brisbane Courier*, 22 October 1913, 21.

and argued that Indian men would be too alarmed by the enfranchisement of British women, which would have disastrous effects on British rule in India.[7] In response, the Mussoorie Society produced a pamphlet citing the successful examples of Australia and New Zealand and argued that enfranchised British women would have the power to improve educational and medical services for Indian women.[8]

The Mussoorie Suffrage Society continued to discuss female enfranchisement while the battle raged on in Britain. Their activities were infrequently reported upon in British suffrage periodicals.[9] The British campaigner Emily Hobhouse, who spent much of her career focusing on reform in South Africa, wrote to Hallowes in October 1915 upon hearing of the successful suffrage meeting of the society through *Jus Suffragii* (the IWSA newspaper).[10] Following notice of the partial enfranchisement of British women in 1917, Hallowes presided over a celebration to express 'India's congratulations to the Empire's enfranchised daughters'.[11] There is little evidence of the work of the society after (some) British women were enfranchised in 1918. Hallowes left India towards the end of 1919, following the death of her husband.[12] Little was done to enfranchise Indian women in India.

The work of the Mussoorie Suffrage Society was, in many ways, superseded by the WIA founded in 1917. A social reform organization primarily concerned with Indian women's rights rather than British women in India, it was, however, set up by non-ethnically Indian

---

7 'Opposing Woman Suffrage, *Times of India*, 4 August 1913, 7.

8 'India and Women's Suffrage', *Times of India*, 5 August 1913, 7.

9 See also JR, GB133 IWSA/3/105, 'Votes not Vanities', *Evening Standard and St James's Gazette*, 25 September 1916.

10 Swarthmore College Peace Collection (SCPC), Women's International League for Peace and Freedom, India Section, Reel 133.76, Hobhouse to Hallowes, 31 October 1915.

11 JR, GB133 IWSA/3/105, 'Mussoorie Women's Suffrage Society', *Mussoorie Times*, 21 September 1917; 'India: Mussoorie Women's Suffrage Society', *International Woman Suffrage News* (1 December 1917): 39.

12 SCPC, WILPF India Section, Reel 133.76, letter to Hallowes, 3 October 1919; 'The Woman Suffrage Movement in India', *The Vote*, 28 June 1918, 301.

women, Annie Besant, Margaret Cousins, and Dorothy Jinarajadasa (alongside Indian founding members). Though the work of Besant and Cousins in relation to Indian social reform is better known, that of Jinarajadasa has often been overlooked. As noted in the previous chapter, Jinarajadasa was one of the members of the 1917 suffrage deputation to the viceroy. Avabai Wadia described Jinarajadasa as a 'beautiful Scotswoman' who greatly helped the Indian women's movement.[13] Born Dorothy M. Graham, she was married to the Sri Lankan Theosophist Curuppumullage Jinarajadasa, who was the president of the Theosophical Society from 1945 to 1953. In contemporary literature, Jinarajadasa was invariably described as English and her husband Indian, though she was often 'mistaken' for an Indian woman because of her surname.[14] Jinarajadasa had been involved in the British suffrage movement before her arrival in India; she was arrested, but never imprisoned for her involvement in protests. She did not suggest using militant measures of protest during her career in India.[15] Despite her ethnicity, I would like to include Jinarajadasa within my definition of Indian suffragettes. She lived and worked in India and identified closely with the Indian women's movement. As she put it herself, 'I am English by birth, but legally and by marriage I am an Indian woman.' Further, though Jinarajadasa asked for the support of women around the world, she noted 'the *women of India* must do this work'.[16] In 1919 and 1920, Jinarajadasa conducted a speaking tour of Australia and New Zealand to discuss Indian women's rights and the franchise issue. It is in this example that we can see some ways in which Indians were exploiting colonial networks for their own suffrage campaigns.

The Theosophists had strong connections with Australia. The Australian section had been founded in 1895 and leading member Charles Leadbeater had moved there in 1915. The Jinarajadasas were

---

[13] Avabai B. Wadia, *The Light Is Ours: Memoirs and Movements* (London: International Planned Parenthood Federation, 2001), 27.

[14] Geraldine Forbes also mistakenly describes Jinarajadasa as Irish in Forbes, *Women in Modern India*, 72.

[15] 'Suffragette from Madras', *Daily Herald (Adelaide)*, 6 November 1919, 2.

[16] Dorothy Jinarajadasa, 'The Women's Suffrage Resolution', *Stri Dharma* (October 1918): 53. Emphasis in original.

able to take advantage of these links when they visited the Antipodes, but Jinaradasa also exploited interest in feminist issues. In her tour, Jinarajadasa spoke at a number of places on the status of Indian women, discussing matters such as education and the franchise. The tour was an attempt to educate Australian and New Zealand women about the situation in India and the work that she and other reformers were doing there. Examples of where Jinarajadasa spoke include the National Council of Women in Brisbane in September 1919; the National Council of Women in Australia in Melbourne in October 1919; the Australian Women's National League in October 1919; Burns Hall, Otago, under the aegis of the Women's Citizens' Association on 29 January 1920; the Literary Institute Perth in June 1920; and a reception (with her husband) at the Mohammedan Mosque in Perth from Indian and Afghan residents in June 1920.[17] She also addressed the first meeting of the Theosophical Women's Union of Service in Melbourne, which she presided over, and ensured that a resolution of sympathy with the efforts of Indian women to obtain the franchise was passed.[18]

Local newspapers reported upon the activities of Jinarajadasa with interest. The Brisbane (Queensland) paper *Daily Mail* interviewed Jinarajadasa about her work with the WIA and Indian women in November 1919. It reported how there was no opposition from Indian men on extending the franchise to women, as evidenced by the motion carried at the Indian National Congress meeting on this issue. The interviewer noted with interest that the National Council of Women of Great Britain strongly supported Indian women in their fight for suffrage, but remarked: 'Of course, India is not asking for suffrage on the principle of "one woman, one vote", but is desirous of giving voting power to women in professions and women landowners.'[19] The correspondent for the Sydney *Evening News*, in discussing

---

[17] 'Women's Department', *The Queenslander*, 27 September 1919, 5; 'Women's National Council', *The Argus*, 31 October 1919, 9; 'Suffragette from Madras', *Daily Herald*, 6 November 1919, 2; 'The Women's Movement', *Otago Daily Times*, 30 January 1920, 6; 'Indian Womanhood', *West Australian*, 14 June 1920, 7; 'Mr Jinarajadasa', *West Australian*, 21 June 1920, 6.

[18] 'Editorial Notes', *Stri Dharma* (July 1920): 151.

[19] Quoted in 'World Sympathy with India', *United India*, 5 November 1919, 91.

Jinarajadasa's trip, highlighted the ways in which Indian women were agitating for the right to vote by approaching political conferences and writing to the heads of government.[20] According to Jinarajadasa, in an interview reported in *The Dominion* in January 1920, the 'great objective' of Indian women at that present time was suffrage and they were throwing their 'whole energies' into the movement. Noting that there was no opposition from Indians, the article explained that the only obstacle came from the British government. Explaining that the female franchise issue was left to the provinces, Jinarajadasa said that this was a 'good thing' as it gave women something to 'strive for': 'If the franchise came too easily they might grow apathetic.'[21] Jinarajadasa not only stressed the lack of Indian male objection to the female franchise, she also drew attention to the nationalist narrative that Indian women in ancient times had previously enjoyed high status.

On 10 February 1920, Jinarajadasa gave an evening lecture at the Concert Chamber in Wellington in New Zealand in which she considered colonial networks, the inspiration of women in the dominions, and Indians overseas. At the outset, she noted that New Zealand was always of interest to women internationally because women in New Zealand had enjoyed equal suffrage for many years, but she expressed surprise at the lack of women sitting in the New Zealand parliament. After tracing developments in 'England', she reminded the audience that Indian women were 'sisters in the British Empire'. She explained that it was probably largely due to the evidence given by Indian men and women to the Southborough Committee in London that the principle of female suffrage was at least delegated to the provinces. Jinarajadasa also noted the interest that Indian women had taken in their fellow countrymen in Fiji and South Africa. The meeting passed the following resolution: 'That this meeting of Wellington citizens desires Mrs Jinarajadasa to convey our fraternal greetings to the women of India, and to express the hope that the Indian Legislative Council will grant the franchise on the same terms as men, giving the same political status as in all parts of the British Empire.'[22]

---

[20] See 'Women of India', *United India*, 26 November 1919, 134.

[21] 'The Women of India', *The Dominion*, 21 January 1920, 4.

[22] 'Women's Movement', *Evening Post*, 12 February 1920, 10; 'The Women's Movement', *The Dominion*, 11 February 1920, 4.

Emphasizing the colonial comparison might prove to be a useful argument for Indian suffragettes.

Jinarajadasa forwarded the resolution to Annie Besant and the editorial team of *United India*, the weekly London paper that distributed news about Indian affairs and policy to interested British politicians and readers. She remarked how her tour of Australia and New Zealand had been successful and she had found that the people there had great interest in the 'development of Indian women'. She explained that she had held meetings in every large town she had visited to dispel some of the ignorance about Indian women, remarking on the surprise and interest expressed by the audiences about the work Indian women were doing in connection with their enfranchisement. With a similar sentiment to the resolution passed in Wellington, Jinarajadasa explained:

> The people in Australia and New Zealand feel that, if India is to be acknowledged as an equal by all the other parts of the Empire, the women of India must necessarily occupy the same position and status as the women in the other parts of the Empire, and, therefore, they feel that it is a matter of the first importance that a measure of women's suffrage should be passed by the Indian Legislative Councils at the first possible opportunity.[23]

This colonial sisterhood differed from that with British suffragettes, who were still fighting for their own franchise rights. It was, however, not acknowledged in these resolutions and meetings that indigenous women in Australia were not afforded the same position and status as women in other parts of the empire. This comparison was simply not considered, as I will discuss in the next section.

Following her return to India, Jinarajadasa published an eight-page pamphlet, *Why Women Want the Vote*, from the WIA press in Adyar in March 1921. In it she discussed Commonwealth networks, arguing that Indian women should be enfranchised as their 'sisters' in other parts of the empire.

---

[23] Jinarajadasa to editor of *United India*, 16 February 1920, in 'New Zealand's Sympathy with the Political Aspirations of India's Women', *United India*, II, 2 (14 April 1920), 20.

India is part of a great federation of Nations that makes up the British Commonwealth, and in all the countries of this Commonwealth, women have equal voting rights with men, except South Africa, (and there the vote will be conceded almost at once,) and it is impossible that a slight should be put upon the women of India, in making them of inferior status and position to their sisters in all other parts of this Commonwealth. And not only that: in almost every civilised country of the world women have the vote, and Indian women have the right to ask that they shall not be left unenfranchised with the criminal, the infant, and the lunatic of other countries.[24]

Jinarajadasa claimed that Australia had huge success and was better off for having enfranchised women 16 years earlier. She also raised the examples of Tasmania and New Zealand, explaining how the female vote had helped 'purify' politics.[25] It must, however, be reiterated that it was not only the criminal, 'lunatic', or infant who were disenfranchised in other parts of the empire, it was also Aborigine women in Australia. Not only was it likely that Jinarajadasa was ignorant of the legal restrictions to Aborigine franchise, it is also clear that she did not, like many of her counterparts, consider the rights of Aborigines as noteworthy or comparable to the fight by Indian women.

On Jinarajadasa's return to Adyar after her Australian tour, Margaret Cousins encouraged WIA branches to send addresses. The Tirumeyachar branch sent a letter to Jinarajadasa in December 1920 looking forward to her return. The branch suggested: 'Your tour abroad, your movement with the various races and people of the world at the present time has, we hope, increased your energy and enthusiasm which would be very useful in the coming months for work on our behalf.'[26] Jinarajadasa continued to work with the WIA on issues of social reform, but there is little evidence that her tour of Australia and New Zealand changed the focus of debates within Indian suffragette circles. What they did do was raise consciousness in the Antipodes about Indian suffrage campaigns, which would

---

[24] Dorothy Jinarajadasa, *Why Women Want the Vote* (Adyar: Women's Indian Association, 1921), 2.

[25] Jinarajadasa, *Why Women Want the Vote*, 6–7.

[26] NMML, S. Muthulakshmi Reddi Papers, Subject File 2, Tirumeyachar WIA to Dorothy Jinarajadasa, 17 December 1920.

prove useful in the next stage of these networks when Indian women engaged with Australian-led women's organizations in London.[27]

'Indians Overseas' in the Commonwealth

Indians were subjects of the British Empire. This allowed them free movement within the empire and access to the British government. The 1914 British Nationality Act confirmed that issued passports conveyed a common citizenship for all subjects within the British Empire.[28] Sukanya Banerjee has explored this notion of 'imperial citizenship' for prominent Indians in the late Victorian era such as Mohandas Gandhi, Dadabhai Naoroji, Surendranath Banerjea, and Cornelia Sorabji. Though this was a changing concept in the period, and Banerjee notes the difference between British concepts of citizenship and those for Indians who were British *subjects*, many Indians used this notion to argue that they should have the same rights as others within the empire. As nineteenth-century discussion about citizenship was often related to the right to vote, Banerjee argues that the award of (male and female) franchise in the colonies *before* Britain raised debates that led to an expanded trans-imperial framework of citizenship. This is evident in the way British suffragettes, influenced by the incongruous position where colonial women had the vote before them, highlighted the position of Indian women who had fewer rights than them and used this to argue for the need for the British female vote.[29]

There has been more attention to imperial citizenship in British political thought. In addition, Daniel Gorman has argued that 'imperial citizenship' is a notion that was not shared by the dominions in the early twentieth century. Gorman argues that the dominions

---

[27] Dorothy Jinarajadasa received a note of congratulations for the women of Madras when they won suffrage in 1921, from the Women's Service Guild of Australia, reprinted in BL, Mss Eur F341/31, *Mrs Margaret Cousins and Her Work in India* (Adyar: Women's Indian Association, 1956).

[28] Hugh Tinker, *Separate and Unequal: India and the Indians in the British Commonwealth 1920–1950* (London: C. Hurst & Co., 1976), 37.

[29] Sukanya Banerjee, *Becoming Imperial Citizens: Indians in the Late-Victorian Empire* (Durham: Duke University Press, 2010), 18–21.

were disabused of this ideology, particularly influenced by concerns relating to intra-imperial migration in this period.[30] So while migrant Indians may have been more eager to justify their campaigns for political rights based on the notions of British subjecthood, dominion governments were increasingly wishing to assert their independence in such matters faced by threats to their fragile national identities based on racial exclusiveness.

Although Indian suffragettes were mainly concerned about their vote in India, it is useful to consider here the plight of Indians living in other parts of the empire, and their campaigns for citizenship rights, in relation to these notions of imperial citizenship. Indian women were involved in some of these campaigns, though the issue of franchise was often occluded by other concerns. The numbers of Indians recorded in the white dominions at the turn of the century was low. The Australian colonies had 9,184 recorded in 1901 (less than 0.2 per cent of the total population); British South Africa had 118,799 in 1904 (about 10.6 per cent), and New Zealand only had 24 recorded in 1901.[31] However, for those Indians invested in the concepts of British subjecthood and citizenship within empire, the political position of Indians in these and other parts of empire had important ramifications for the nationalist position in India as well. In the following section, I discuss the ways in which the franchise for Indians was discussed in Australia, Kenya, and South Africa. The issue was negligible for Indians in Canada and New Zealand. Although many Indians lived in the Caribbean, and other countries, and engaged with citizenship issues, they did not engage directly with the female franchise question which is the focus of this book.

When women over 21 were enfranchised in South Australia in December 1894 there was no race bar. It was only in Queensland and Western Australia that Aborigines were specifically barred from voting. However, in 1902, when women in all states were enfranchised

---

[30] Daniel Gorman, 'Wider and Wider Still? Racial Politics, Intra-Imperial Immigration and the Absence of an Imperial Citizenship in the British Empire', *Journal of Colonialism and Colonial History* 3, 3 (2002), available at https://muse.jhu.edu/article/38080, accessed 7 August 2017.

[31] Figures from P. E. Lewin, 'Appendix', *Journal of Royal Society of Arts* (24 April 1908), quoted in Gorman, 'Wider and Wider Still?'.

in Australia, under the 1902 Franchise Bill, it was explicitly stated that Aborigines (male or female) were not entitled to vote, unless they already had the right (for instance, in South Australia). 'Natives' of Asia, Africa, and the Pacific Islands were also explicitly excluded from the Commonwealth franchise in 1902; Indians were neither allowed to become naturalized nor vote in Australia.[32] However, in 1904, South Australia amended its Electoral Act to allow Indians to vote.[33] Alongside this, the 1901 Immigration Restriction Act (known as the White Australia policy) deemed Indians as 'prohibited immigrants' despite the fact that they were British subjects. It was only after 1919 that Indian men in Australia were allowed to apply to bring wives and children to Australia too.[34]

The issue of imperial citizenship in the dominions, particularly for Indians, gained political traction after the First World War.[35] Resolutions from the 1917 and 1918 Imperial War Conferences put pressure upon the Australian government to reform their constitution and allow British Indians the right to vote (and receive a pension). Although a cabinet subcommittee was willing to allow Indians to receive pensions, they were not willing to enfranchise them. However, further pressure was brought to bear on the government, following the 1921 Imperial Conference. This meeting of Commonwealth leaders discussed rising Indian nationalist sentiment, particularly among Indians living in African colonies. They passed a resolution, which South Africa refused to accept, calling for Indians citizenship rights to be recognized across the British Commonwealth. In July 1922, the prime minister of Australia,

[32] John Chesterman and Brian Galligan, *Citizens without Rights: Aborigines and Australian Citizenship* (Cambridge: Cambridge University Press, 1997), 85.

[33] Pat Stretton and Christine Finnimore, 'Black Fellow Citizens: Aborigines and the Commonwealth Franchise', *Australian Historical Studies* 25, 101 (1993): 521–35.

[34] Margaret Allen, '"A Fine Type of Hindoo" Meets "the Australian Type": British Indians in Australia and Diverse Masculinities', in *Transnational Ties: Australian Lives in the World*, ed. Desley Deacon, Penny Russell, and Angela Woollacott (Canberra: ANU E Press, 2008), 48–9.

[35] Indians were emboldened to ask for more political rights to reward the contribution of Indian soldiers (and Indian workforce) during the war.

Billy Hughes, wrote to the Indian nationalist Srinivasa Sastri, in a widely circulated public letter, committing his government to extending the franchise to Indians in Australia though nothing was subsequently done.[36]

When in 1924 an Indian, Mitta Bullosh, appealed against the interpretation that gave him a state vote but not a Commonwealth vote (and won), the cabinet dropped the High Court appeal that was started against him for fear that publicity of the case would encourage Aborigines to enrol and vote too. On 4 March 1925, the cabinet introduced a bill that made all Indians eligible to vote. Queensland and Western Australia, however, did not immediately amend their state legislation and only enfranchised Indians in 1930 and 1934 respectively.[37] There were only 2,300 recorded Indians living in Australia, and the White Australia policy prevented more Indians settling in the country, but the cabinet decided that giving into Indian political pressure was expedient. As Indians were given the vote, on the basis of their imperial citizenship, the broader issue of race and franchise rights in Australia was not discussed. It meant that Aborigines did not have powerful political allies in their demands for the vote, and Indians did not express any affinity with the plight of discrimination against indigenous peoples. The question of 'racial' solidarity or 'female' solidarity with disenfranchised groups in Australia was not one that Indians raised, despite colonial ties. Of course, Indians were subject peoples with little political leverage themselves. Possible parallels were not raised with caste and tribal distinctions in India. It was only in 1967 that all Aborigines were counted in the census in Australia and all became eligible to vote equally.[38]

Though only 22,822 Indians were living in Kenya, it was there that Indian female franchise was more directly addressed, albeit not intentionally, by Indian campaigners.[39] In 1920s Kenya, Indians were vocal in their demands for franchise rights but faced considerable opposition from the European community there. The 1921 Imperial

---

[36] Chesterman and Galligan, *Citizens without Rights*, 103–5.

[37] Chesterman and Galligan, *Citizens without Rights*, 115–16.

[38] Stretton and Finnimore, 'Black Fellow Citizens'.

[39] For more on Indians in Kenya (though there is no discussion of women at all), see Tinker, *Separate and Unequal*.

Conference had made it clear that British Indians should receive equal rights across the colonies, including East Africa. It was a cause that was taken up by Indian campaigners, especially V. S. Srinivasa Sastri, but Indian women were also concerned with this. The Surat branch of the WIA met in 1922 and resolved to recommend to the governor general that Indian claims for equality of status with other British subjects be recognized across East Africa.[40] Women in Madras also met to ask the Indian government not to exclude Indians resident in Kenya from the rights of citizenship.[41]

The campaigns for citizenship rights in Kenya, however, were based upon racial and communal distinctions. Indians asserted their superior right to the vote over black Kenyans, demanding parity with white voters. As a resolution of the Council of State in Delhi put it, in March 1923, Indians in Kenya wanted 'full and equal rights of citizenship with European settlers', not universal suffrage for all.[42] The Colonial Office had suggested that Indians be awarded a limited percentage of votes, but a convention of European Associations in Kenya passed a resolution in February 1923 disapproving of these measures, concerned that Indian votes, and therefore political power, would outnumber white representation.[43] An 'Englishwoman' wrote a letter of protest against Indian franchise rights to the *East African Standard*, fearful of the threat of Indian rule in Kenya. 'Do our sisters at home realize what it would mean?' she asked, explaining that British women wanted equality between the sexes but Indians treated women very badly through practices such as child marriage, polygamy, and poor treatment of widows.[44] These fears were echoed by the Kenya Women's Committee, based in London, who produced a pamphlet that was sent to potential sympathizers in Britain explaining that the ratio of Indians to Europeans was nearly three to one in Kenya and

---

[40] NMML, S. Muthulakshmi Reddi Papers, Subject Files, Mrs K. C. Mehta to Margaret Cousins, 11 April 1922.

[41] Herabai A. Tata, 'Indian Women's Enfranchisement', *The Vote*, 28 April 1922, 130.

[42] S. A. Waiz, ed., *Indians Abroad* (Bombay: Imperial Indian Citizenship Association, 1927), 53.

[43] Waiz, *Indians Abroad*, 51.

[44] Waiz, *Indians Abroad*, 138–9.

thus introducing a common franchise would place European women under 'Asiatic administration'.[45]

Following vocal opposition, defensive Indians increased their demands. Having previously been in favour of representative quotas, a mass meeting of Indians in Nairobi on 11 March 1923 called for full 'universal franchise'.[46] Implicitly, then, women were now included in this struggle in ways they had not been considered before. In 1924, Indians (men and women) were enfranchised in Kenya. The language in the ordinance was clear—no literary qualification was required and every 'Indian man and Indian woman in the Colony will now have the vote'.[47] The Devonshire Declaration, as it was referred to, extended the franchise to Indians on a communal basis; they were given five seats in the Kenyan legislature based on a separate electoral roll.[48] Indians were also excluded from the Kenyan highlands. This policy was met with great resentment by Indians in Kenya, who were concerned about the antagonism that could arise from separate political representation, as had been seen in India.[49] However, communal electoral rolls were common in other British colonies such as Fiji and Guyana.

The enfranchisement of Indian women in Kenya was reported with interest by Indian women's movements. At the same time as Indian women were being enfranchised in Kenya, Indian women were voting for the first time in Madras and Bombay. Margaret Cousins noted how the Kenyan case reflected that 'Indian women are responsible and trained citizens' with votes while 'the South African woman, white or colored, are still denied women suffrage' except in Rhodesia.[50] Interestingly, *The Vote* described the enfranchisement of

---

[45] BL, L/PO/1/6 (ii) East Africa: Kenya.

[46] Waiz, *Indians Abroad*, 51.

[47] *Kenya National Assembly Official Record*, 3 January 1924, 94, available at https://books.google.co.uk/books?id=oKmvefaweDoC&printsec=frontcover#v=onepage&q&f=false, accessed 7 August 2017.

[48] Daniel Gorman, *The Emergence of International Society in the 1920s* (Cambridge: Cambridge University Press, 2012), 134.

[49] Sana Aiyar, *Indians in Kenya: The Politics of Diaspora* (Cambridge, MA: Harvard University Press, 2015), 107–8.

[50] Margaret E. Cousins, 'Our Special Article: Women at Home and Abroad', *New India*, 10 November 1923, 4.

Indian women in Kenya as further incentive for white female suffragists in South Africa to secure their votes there.[51] As I am demonstrating here, suffrage victories and campaigns were interconnected,
especially within empire.

The fight for female (and male) franchise in South Africa was
more difficult, although Indians were technically allowed to be
enfranchised in neighbouring Southern Rhodesia. Over half of the
Indians living in South Africa in the early twentieth century lived
in Natal. Mohandas Gandhi had famously taken up a legal position
there in 1893, and the colony had a mix of Indians from indentured
labouring backgrounds as well as merchant and professional classes.
Several laws were passed from 1896 that restricted Indian immigration and their franchise rights in Natal, although Indian men who
had passed the property restrictions to be enrolled on voter rolls
before 1896 were able to vote until 1925. In the Cape 'coloured' men
(including Indians) who met property qualifications could also vote,
though this was an equally tiny minority. Upon delaying his return
to India, Gandhi spent a considerable amount of time, between 1894
and 1896, leading agitations against the 1894 Franchise Amendment
Bill which prevented the further addition of Indian voters to rolls
in Natal and appealing to Indians and Britons in South Africa, as
well as British politicians.[52] As Sukanya Banerjee and Goolam
Vahed have argued, Gandhi believed in the principle of imperial
citizenship during his time in South Africa (1893–1914), more so
than Indian nationalism, and thus argued that the status of Indians
as British subjects gave them leverage and rights in South Africa.[53]

---

[51] Margaret E. Cousins, 'Our Special Article: Women at Home and
Abroad', *New India*, 5 July 1924, 4.

[52] See, for example, M. K. Gandhi, 'Petition to Lord Ripon', before 14 July
1894, *Collected Works of Mahatma Gandhi (CWMG)*, vol. 1, 163–73; 'The Indian
Franchise', 16 December 1895, *CWMG*, vol. 1, 283–387, www.gandhiserve.org;
Marilyn Lake and Henry Reynolds, *Drawing the Global Colour Line: White
Men's Countries and the International Challenge of Racial Equality* (Cambridge:
Cambridge University Press, 2008), chap. 5.

[53] Banerjee, *Becoming Imperial Citizens*, chap. 2; Goolam Vahed, 'Race,
Empire and Citizenship: Sarojini Naidu's 1924 Visit to South Africa', *South
African Historical Journal* 64, 2 (2012): 321–2.

However, these agitations did not consider the position of Indian women.

Indian women rarely played a visible role in political agitation, especially relating to franchise, in South Africa until after the Second World War. Their most notable participation before this was in the 1913 passive resistance campaign.[54] The female suffrage movement in South Africa had been divided along racial lines, with some similarities with Australia. Suffrage agitation was relatively short lived following the formation of the Women's Enfranchisement Association of the Union (WEAU) in 1911, an organization that was exclusively white and followed constitutional methods of campaigning. The women asked to be enfranchised on the same terms as men, thus bypassing the issue of race, as it was only in the Cape that some non-white men were enfranchised. The call for equal franchise rights for women on the same terms as enfranchised men provides a parallel to the Indian women's movement in the 1910s and 1920s, which similarly only asked for franchise equality initially and did not consider disadvantaged, disenfranchised social groups along class or community lines. In 1909, Emmeline Pethick-Lawrence had noted that the protests in favour of enfranchising the 'coloured race' in South Africa had only discussed male enfranchisement, and, apart from notable exceptions such as Olive Schreiner, suffragists in South Africa did not consider political rights for black women.[55] When in 1930 the Women's Enfranchisement Bill passed by General Hertzog's government explicitly enfranchised only white women, there was no public opposition to the deliberate exclusion of other races. Women could, however, vote in municipal elections in Natal from 1914 on the same terms as men.[56] In 1924, Cousins had

---

[54] Waiz, *Indians Abroad*, 256–9.

[55] Emmeline Pethick Lawrence, 'Women or Kaffirs?', *Votes for Women*, 9 July 1909, 912, reproduced in Delap, DiCenzo, and Ryan, *Feminism and the Periodical Press*; Helen Dampier, '"Going on with Our Little Movement in the Hum Drum-Way Which Alone Is Possible in a Land like This": Olive Schreiner and Suffrage Networks in Britain and South Africa, 1905–1913', *Women's History Review* 25, 4 (2016): 536–50.

[56] BL, L/PJ/6/1323, file 3391, 1914 Ordinance of the Provincial Council of Natal extending the municipal franchise to women.

observed with surprise that Indian women's franchise rights were ahead of South African women's and that African women could not rely on the Labour Party to help secure their franchise rights.[57] In 1938, Cissy Gool set up the League for the Enfranchisement of Non-European Women, arguing that coloured women should be qualified to vote in the Cape as their male counterparts were, but this lacked a broad racial or geographical base and soon fizzled out.[58]

At the 1921 Imperial Conference, it was only the South African General Smuts who refused to grant equal franchise rights to Indians. In the aftermath of this conference, as Indians in Kenya became more agitated about their political rights, Sarojini Naidu was compelled by Gandhi to visit Kenya and South Africa in 1924 to offer support to the campaigns. In South Africa, Naidu lent her support to the agitation against the Class Areas Bill which would force Indians to live and trade in only certain locations. At a public meeting in Cape Town on 18 March, Naidu talked of the way the 'oppressed' black people of the world were linked together in their suffering and martyrdom.[59] In Pretoria, she noted that the land belonged to neither whites nor Indians but the black Africans, and thus that the white settlers should live equally to Indians.[60] At Durban, she spoke to the Indian Women's Association and called upon women to become involved and fight for equality in political status.[61] In her tour, Naidu not only urged women to become more politically active, and thus indirectly urge for franchise rights alongside other concerns, but she spoke about racial unity too. She encouraged Indian women to examine their relations with black South Africans, to dispel racial prejudice, and pursued the question

[57] Margaret E. Cousins, 'Our Special Article: Women at Home and Abroad', *New India*, 25 October 1924, 4.

[58] See Cherryl Walker, *Women and Resistance in South Africa* (London: Onyx Press, 1982), 21–3, 53–4, 105.

[59] *Indian Opinion*, 28 March 1924 quoted in Vahed, 'Race, Empire and Citizenship', 333.

[60] *Cape Argus*, 1 March 1924, quoted in Vahed, 'Race, Empire and Citizenship'.

[61] *Natal Mercury*, 10 March 1924, quoted in Vahed, 'Race, Empire and Citizenship', 335.

of the joint black struggle. Vahed argues that by emphasizing the South African identity of Indians, Naidu was disabusing the notion of imperial citizenship that Gandhi had favoured. In urging them to identify with Africa, rather than the British Empire, a new racial and 'global' identity was being framed by Naidu.[62] Certainly Naidu posited a broader racial awareness about the empire than was explicitly expressed by other Indian women in this period.

The fight for political equality for Indians (and other races) in South Africa was ongoing; it escalated after the Second World War, but was often beset by new political obstacles. It was only with the fall of the Apartheid regime that universal adult suffrage was introduced and all adult men and women could vote from 1994. Franchise was not the sole issue, or the most pressing issue, for a community that was curtailed economically and in their movement. However, some indication of the existing concern that Indian women had for the position of Indians in South Africa is evident in correspondence between the All-Indian Women's Conference (AIWC) and Dhanvanthi Rama Rau (living in South Africa from 1938 to 1941 as her husband was India's high commissioner there) and from the following telegram sent by the AIWC to the prime minister of the Union of South Africa in August 1939:

> The All India Women's Conference view with profound concern the disabilities imposed upon Indians resident in South Africa and earnestly urge the union government to take effective measures to remedy the grave situation.[63]

The interactions of Indian women's organizations with Indian women overseas, then, were not primarily concerned with their enfranchisement. This is especially relevant as Indian women overseas faced more pressing concerns on their liberty that needed to be addressed before their franchise rights could be brought into question. Indeed, the first Indian women's deputation to the viceroy was

---

[62] Vahed, 'Race, Empire and Citizenship', 341–2.

[63] NMML, AIWC Microfilm, Roll 13, File 207. Sukhthankar to Rama Rau, 30 August 1939. Note, however, that in Rama Rau's autobiography she says little about any agitations for women's rights in South Africa, but more generally about agitation against racial discrimination and segregation.

not the one on franchise in November 1917, but one in March 1917 on the issue of indenture. Led by Jaiji Petit, signed by Sarojini Naidu, Lady Meherbai Tata, Uma Nehru, Dilsahab Begam, and others, these Indian women had organized a petition for the abolition of indenture emigration. The Prayag Mahila Samiti, an Indian women's group founded in 1909, also held a conference on the issue in Allahabad in 1917 and were particularly concerned about the sexual exploitation of female indentured labourers in Fiji. Shobna Nijhawan has argued that the Indian women's compassion for plantation labourers was not merely based on shared 'sisterhood', as was so important for British feminist campaigners. The bond of imagined citizenship was also important, as the interests of diasporic Indians fed into Indian nationalist concerns about the honour of Indian women and the nation as a whole.[64]

British Dominions Women's Suffrage Union in London and Indian Members

On 9 July 1914, Harriet Newcomb and her partner Margaret Hodge set up the British Dominions Woman Suffrage Union (BDWSU) in London. They were both English educationalists who had lived in Australia for roughly 15 years.[65] The BDWSU was designed for Australian and New Zealand women to help Canadian and South African women win the vote. Since it had been exclusively set up for white women, Hodge and Newcomb did little to consider racial questions. They offered little opportunity to reflect on indigenous

[64] Shobna Nijhawan, 'Fallen Through the Nationalist and Feminist Grids of Analysis: Political Campaigning of Indian Women against Indentured Labour Emigration', *Indian Journal of Gender Studies* 21, 1 (2014): 111–33.

[65] Newcomb was 60 years old and Hodges 55; Kay Whitehead and Lynne Tretheway, 'Aging and Activism in the Context of the British Dominions Woman Suffrage Union, 1914–1922', *Women's Studies International Forum* 31 (2008): 30–41; Angela Woollacott, 'Australian Women's Metropolitan Activism: From Suffrage, to Imperial Vanguard, to Commonwealth Feminism', in *Women's Suffrage in the British Empire: Citizenship, Nation and Race*, ed. Ian Christopher Fletcher, Laura E. Nym Mayhall, and Philippa Levine (London: Routledge, 2000), 207–23 at 210.

Australian rights and did not challenge the White Australia policy, reflecting their fear of the First World War destroying the 'white race'.[66] Yet, though the BDWSU was designed for women in the settler colonies, it included Indian women in various ways from the outset. At the inauguration, the union had a special gathering at the International Franchise Club in Grafton Street where Sarojini Naidu spoke on the ideals of Indian women and the contribution they could bring to the women's movement.[67] Roy and Bhola Nauth, who had taken part in the Empire Pageant, were regular attendees and speakers at BDWSU in the 1910s. Naidu gave a speech at the 1914 BDWSU conference, and there was an evening meeting at the 1916 conference on the Indian women's movement, chaired by Lady Muir Mackenzie, though only Indian men (Sir Krishna Gupta, Mancherjee Bhownagree, Yusuf Ali, and Syud Hossain) were invited to speak.[68] As Gupta put it, the female suffrage issue had not yet been raised in India as men did not have the vote either, but he was cheered by the audience when he stated that he felt confident that were the franchise to be introduced in India it would be shared by men and women. Ali also noted that the suffrage question was not unknown to Indian women and girls, and they had the same ideals as women of 'England and its Dominions'.[69]

By 1917, the union had decided to make more formal provisions to include Indian women. The National Indian Association's journal, *The Indian Magazine and Review,* reported the following:

A desire has been expressed by women of the Overseas Dominions to come into touch with the women of India and to gratify it the British Dominions Woman Suffrage Union has arranged a series of 'Indian Teas' in London. At the first, which took place at the Minerva Cafe, 144 High Holborn, last month, there was a representative gathering of women from Australia, New Zealand, South Africa, Canada,

[66] Woollacott, 'Australian Women's Metropolitan Activism', 214.

[67] 'Hands across the Sea', *The Vote*, 17 July 1913, 209–10.

[68] Angela Woollacott, 'Australian Women's Metropolitan Activism', 214; JR, GB133 IWSA/3/141, 'Women's Place in the British Empire', *Christian Commonwealth*, 5 July 1916, 502.

[69] JR, GB133 IWSA/3/141, 'The Dominions Women's Suffrage Union', *India*, 14 July 1916.

and India. Mrs N.C. Sen read a short paper on Indian women from ancient to modern times, and an opportunity was afforded for social intercourse, which proved both enjoyable and enlightening.[70]

As reported in the *British Australian*, the BDWSU organized afternoon meetings so that ignorance on Indian matters could be corrected, and women from 'all the Empire may meet, and learnt to know each other': 'Possibly Australian and New Zealand women are more ignorant concerning the outlook of feminine India than are British women, and that is saying a good deal.'[71] Indians living in Britain including Sophia Duleep Singh, Mrs and Miss Bonnerjee (descendants of W.C. Bonnerjee, one of the founder members of the Indian National Congress) attended these meetings.[72]

In 1918, the union changed its name to the BDWCU to reflect the enfranchisement of British and Canadian women. India was well represented at the Third Biennial Conference of the Women of the Empire put together in London by the BDWCU in 1918 where an evening gala, dedicated to India, was put on.[73] Roy, Bhola Nauth, and Mrinalini Sen all spoke at the gala. They also brought a banner with 'India' in black letters upon yellow satin with them (evoking memories of the India banner at the Empire Pageant). According to *Jus Suffragii*, this 'bringing together of India and the self-governing British Dominions was perhaps one of the most notable achievements of the Conference'.[74] A commentator for *The Vote* remarked that the BDWCU was doing 'valuable service' in involving Indian women and 'awakening' their interest in Indian affairs.[75]

However, it was Miss Weatherly who spoke about the campaign for female suffrage in India, rather than any Indian women,

[70] 'From the Editor's Study: A New Entente', *Indian Magazine and Review*, 564 (December 1917), 214.

[71] Phyllis, 'In the Looking Glass', *British Australasian*, 18 October 1917, 18.

[72] Phyllis, 'In the Looking Glass', *British Australasian*, 1 November 1917, 18.

[73] 'Where East and West Meet', *The Asiatic Review*, 14, 39 (July 1918): 416.

[74] 'British Dominions Woman Suffrage Union Conference', *International Woman Suffrage News* 12, 10 (July 1918): 156.

[75] 'British Dominions Woman Suffrage Union', *The Vote*, 24 May 1918, 257–8.

perhaps because her focus was on the white campaign.[76] She discussed how the Mussoorie Suffrage Society had started in 1913 to win the vote for 'Anglo-Indian' women. Weatherly spoke of the social reform enfranchised women could bring about in India and how they should 'voice the inarticulate cry of their Indian sisters'.[77] The Mussoorie Suffrage Society had actually applied for affiliation with the BDWSU in 1914, but the union had been unable to facilitate work with India at that time.[78] As the conference was held a few days after the Imperial War Conference and members were aware of the pressing concerns of Indian rights within empire, the union opened a special department on Indian questions following the conference.[79] The BDWCU noted that regular meetings on India from 1917 had been successful attempts 'to give friends from the self-governing Dominions opportunities of meeting Indian women in pleasant social settings'.[80] The union was increasingly becoming interested in political issues of empire too.

In 1919, when the Tatas were touring Britain, they spoke at the union.[81] The BDWCU then wrote to the Joint Select Committee to urge that Indian women be enfranchised on the same terms as men. As Harriet Newcomb put it, with the exception of South Africa, the members were 'enfranchised citizens of the Empire', and though the self-governing dominions had no voice over other parts of the empire, women there were united in their support of enfranchising Indian women.[82] Indian women were being incorporated into this colonial feminist identity. The BDWCU had previously been

---

[76] 'British Dominion Woman Suffrage Union', *The Vote*, 7 June 1918, 277.

[77] 'The Woman's Suffrage Movement in India', *The Vote*, 28 June 1918, 301.

[78] British Dominions Women Citizens' Union. *Report of Work 1917–1918 and of the Third Biennial Conference, London 1918* (1918), 6.

[79] 'Facing the Future', *The Vote*, 14 June 1918, 284–5.

[80] British Dominions Women Citizens' Union. *Report of Work 1917–1918*, 6.

[81] 'Activities in Great Britain', *United India*, 26 November 1919, 143. See also 'The British Dominions Women Citizens Union', *British Australasian*, 20 November 1919, 23.

[82] TC, Newcomb to Jt Select Committee, 21 October 1919.

one of the signatories to an address written by the IWEA on female franchise sent to Lord Southborough at the end of 1918.[83] When the Joint Select Committee decided to leave the question of female franchise to provincial councils, Newcomb wrote on behalf of the union in protest. She explained to the prime minister, Lloyd George, that the women of the Overseas Dominions could not see the 'logical reason' to affirm the right for men to vote, but not women; she decried the government for upholding the view that women were 'merely the chattels of individual men': 'To support this view is a wrong done not only to the women of India but to women in every part of the Empire.'[84] Following the Government of India Bill, the BDWCU wrote to members of the legislative councils in India urging them to enfranchise Indian women, explaining that justice for women was in the highest interests of all.[85] The union also asked Lady Astor to add to her support for Indian female franchise by asserting the 'firm and growing conviction in the self-governing Dominions that the principle of sex equality in the councils of the nations is the best guarantee for the preservation and advancement of the British Empire'. News of BDWCU support for Indian women's franchise was reported back in Australia, through the Women's Service Guild.[86]

The depiction of the Indian women involved with the BDWCU was not without 'essentialised' attention to appearance. Margaret Hodge spoke about the aesthetic joy of the Indian presence at the BDWSU and how Indian women were 'conspicuous for the exquisite beauty of the colours and classic grace of her drapery'.[87] In an address in 1919, though, Hodge prevailed upon her colleagues of their duty to help Indian women, evoking not only notions of

[83] BL, L/PJ/9/8, Indian Women's Education Association to Lord Southborough, 12 December 1918.

[84] TC, Newcomb to Lloyd George, 26 November 1919. The same letter was also sent to Montagu.

[85] 'Colonial Support for Indian Women', *United India*, 3 March 1920, 363; TC, circular by Newcomb, 24 February 1920.

[86] 'Deputation of Indian Women', *The Daily News (Perth)*, 17 February 1920, 5.

[87] Margaret Hodge, 'Our Indian Sisters', *The Vote*, 27 June 1919, 238.

imperial comradeship but also obligations of 'Western' women to their 'Eastern sisters':

> Your Indian sisters are stretching out their hands to you across the vast ocean; asking you to give to them some of the privileges and some of the liberties that you have gained. Can you be so churlish as to refuse your help? They have given ungrudgingly of their best to the service of the Empire. Read the records of the magnificent work of the Indian troops in Palestine, in Egypt, at Gallipoli, and in Mesopotamia. Think of the anguish and self-sacrifice of the mothers, wives and sisters of these men, who suffered so cruelly and did so valiantly for a Western cause in these Eastern lands, and then complacently repeat to yourselves the smug and self-satisfied British patriots who will assure you that your Eastern sisters are as yet unfit for those liberties and privileges which are the undisputed possession of Western women.[88]

These concerns about 'Eastern' and 'Western' cooperation, not merely Commonwealth unity, continued to be expressed within the BDWCU the following year. At a meeting of the Indian section on 14 April 1920, at their usual meeting place (Minerva Café, Holborn), Elizabeth Abbott urged Indian women to attend the IWSA Congress in Geneva that was to be held in June. As the repercussions for provincial female franchise following the 1919 Government of India Act were being discussed concurrently in India, Abbott encouraged Indian members to take a more active part in public life, not only in India but also in international 'sisterhood'.[89] In July 1920, Margaret Hodge chaired a meeting of the WFL to protest the British and Indian government's responses to the Amritsar Massacre and the brutal treatment of Indian women in April 1919. The meeting demanded the recall of the viceroy and immediate enfranchisement of Indian women.[90] Dorothy Jinarajadasa then addressed the BDWCU in Holborn in November 1920 and discussed the Southborough Reforms and the long wait Indian women faced before the legislative councils worked

[88] Hodge, 'Our Indian Sisters', *The Vote*, 27 June 1919, 238.
[89] 'In Britain and India: British Dominions Women's Citizens Union', *Britain and India* 1, 5 (May 1920): 172.
[90] 'Our Indian Meeting', *The Vote*, 16 July 1920, 123.

in their favour.[91] In 1921, the union held a meeting at the Minerva Café to celebrate the enfranchisement of women in Madras, and the expected enfranchisement of women in Bombay. A resolution sending congratulations to Indian women suffragists was proposed by the South African Daisy Solomon, seconded by the Australian Vida Goldstein, and carried unanimously.[92] The position of Indian 'citizens' in the self-governing dominions was not discussed.

In 1922, the BDWCU merged with the British Overseas Committee of the IWSA. Interest in India and the Indian 'teas' continued, as did discussion about imperial and Commonwealth feminist ties. The new British Committee mounted a 'suffrage pavilion' at the British Empire Exhibition at Wembley in the summer of 1924. In February 1925, they convened a half-day conference on the franchise and citizen rights of women living in the British Empire. However, Indian women, or indeed any non-white women, were not included in this conference, and there was no discussion of any issues other than those pertaining to white women.[93] It was out of this, though, that the British Commonwealth Women's Equality League was set up in May 1925, and its name changed to the more manageable BCL by July. The BCL was to consider broader racial issues as it grew in scope over the years. It had been largely put together by the Australian feminists Marjorie Chave Collisson and Bessie Rischbieth, who was a Theosophist and friend of Dorothy Jinarajadasa.[94]

The British Commonwealth League

In the 1930s, organized Australian women were now publicly changing their attitudes towards Aborigine women. Having been silent about the rights of indigenous peoples, women in feminist organizations developed a new voice on this issue. The League of Nations'

---

91 'Indian Women of Today', *Indian Magazine and Review* (January 1921), 6.

92 TC, British Dominions Women Citizens Union Resolution, 2 May 1921; 'Women and Votes in India', *The Statesman*, 6 July 1921, 14.

93 Angela Woollacott, *To Try Her Fortune in London: Australian Women, Colonialism, and Modernity* (Oxford: Oxford University Press, 2001), 124–5.

94 Woollacott, *To Try Her Fortune*, 250n130.

guidelines on the rights of colonized peoples in mandated territories had heightened consciousness about minorities in Australia, and the WCTU in South Australia attempted to galvanize the country to revise their attitudes and policies, implicitly acknowledging their previous silence on these issues. Fiona Paisley argues that the BCL were one of the strongest critics of Australian Aborigine policy.[95] Papers on Aboriginal women were delivered at all BCL conferences from 1927, although no indigenous women were present to speak at these meetings.[96] Meanwhile, Patricia Grimshaw points to the 1933 national WCTU convention where Adelaide activist Constance Cooke spoke on 'Australia's Obligation to the Aboriginal Race' as a particularly momentous meeting. The convention agreed on a seven-point plan on the needs of Aborigines and passed a resolution calling on the Commonwealth Government to define the national status and rights of Aborigines as British subjects.[97]

In the 1930s, Australian feminists and the BCL became more actively concerned about Indian rights too. The 1927 BCL conference, for example, drew the ire of Dorothy Jinarajadasa and Hannah Sen (no relation to Mrinalini Sen), when Mrs Neville Rolfe, secretary general of the British Social Hygiene Council, suggested that Indian religions and the absence of social responsibility for the poor were largely to blame for prostitution and venereal diseases in India. In response to these criticisms, Rolfe was not allowed to move two resolutions later in the conference.[98] Two years later Eleanor Rathbone convened a conference on Indian women at Caxton Hall, which also drew the ire of Indian women, including Hannah Sen and Dhanvanthi Rama Rau, who were unhappy because Indian women had not been consulted.

[95] Fiona Paisley, 'Citizens of Their World: Australian Feminism and Indigenous Rights in the International Context, 1920s and 1930s', *Feminist Review* 58 (Spring 1998): 66–84; Fiona Paisley, 'White Women in the Field: Feminism, Cultural Relativism and Aboriginal Rights, 1920–1937', *Journal of Australian Studies* 21, 52 (1997): 113–25.

[96] Woollacott, *To Try Her Fortune*, 132.

[97] Patricia Grimshaw, 'Reading the Silences: Suffrage Activists and Race in Nineteenth-Century Settler Societies', in *Women's Rights and Human Rights: International Historical Perspectives*, ed. Patricia Grimshaw, Katie Holmes, and Marilyn Lake (Basingstoke: Palgrave Macmillan, 2001), 45–6.

[98] Woollacott, *To Try Her Fortune*, 130.

Marjorie Chave Collisson and the BCL supported the Indian delegates and had vocally criticized Rathbone's conference.[99]

Angela Woollacott argues that the inclusion of Indian women, and their ability to voice criticisms of the representation of Indian women, represented a politically progressive shift for the BDWCU and BCL. Despite the unequal relationships between white women, colonial white women, and non-white colonized women, the BCL, which had included the WIA from its inception in 1925, was more committed to racial equality than its predecessors had been. For example, the BCL took a clear stance on the *Mother India* debate (the controversial book by American Katherine Mayo).[100] They organized an evening conference in 1927 to hear Indian women's views on it, with three Indian speakers including Hannah Sen. Marjorie Chave Collisson went to India immediately afterwards to establish connections between the BCL and Indian women's groups.[101]

However, Angela Woollacott has also argued that 'Commonwealth feminism' (as opposed to 'imperial feminism') had given Australian women the authority to speak on behalf of 'women of colour'. They assumed that some women were inherently suited to lead, and that the enfranchised (white) women of the empire were responsible for their less fortunate imperial sisters.[102] Indian women involved in the BCL (and the BDWCU) made similar assumptions about the hierarchies of empire, happy to be privileged over women of other races such as Australian Aborigines or black Kenyans. In exploring Indian female interaction with these organizations, it is clear that they showed little public concern for or did little to demonstrate 'racial' solidarity with the unrepresented women of other races who were not given a voice in imperial settings. The rhetoric of 'colonial feminism', however, pervaded through the activities of the BCL in the late 1920s and 1930s and the Indian suffragettes connected with it, keen to exploit the broad networks of empire for Indian campaign support.

---

[99] Angela Woollacott, 'Inventing Commonwealth and Pan-Pacific Feminisms: Australian Women's Internationalist Activism in the 1920s–30s', *Gender & History* 10, 3 (November 1998): 439.

[100] For more on *Mother India*, see Sinha, *Specters of Mother India*.

[101] Woollacott, *To Try Her Fortune*, 130–1.

[102] Woollacott, 'Inventing Commonwealth and Pan-Pacific Feminisms', 438.

In July 1925, the BCL held a conference on 'The Citizen Rights of Women within the British Empire' at Caxton Hall. It included representatives from suffrage and women's groups from Britain, Australia, New Zealand, Canada, South Africa, Bermuda, and India (the WIA). The conference was dedicated to the 'special problems of equal citizenship within the Commonwealth'.[103] A number of Indian women were included in the programme to speak. Mrinalini Sen and Atiya Begum Fyzee Rahamin spoke in a session titled 'Political Equality', which included the British MP Ellen Wilkinson. Rahamin, a writer and music scholar, meanwhile, praised the conference for bringing together 'sisters of the vast Empire' 'irrespective of caste and colour' and 'begged the cooperation of the Western women' in facilitating the improvement of the position of Indian women.[104]

Lotika Basu spoke at a session on the 'Equal Moral Standard' chaired by Lady Astor. As Basu put it, the women's movement, which she argued had originated in the 'West', was 'great' because it was not concerned with one nation but with the 'whole world'.[105] Others involved included Miss Agjaonjar, Mrs Palit, and Lady Chatterjee (the British wife of Atul Chatterjee, the Indian high commissioner in the UK). The conference noted that Indian women had equality with Indian men in Kenya, but focused on the situation in India with a unanimous resolution on Indian female franchise. They called on the British government to amend the 1919 Government of India Act to allow women to be eligible for either election or nomination as members in the legislature and provincial councils.[106] As Chave Collisson put it to the secretary of state for India, it was a 'matter of serious dissatisfaction' for the committee that Indian women's eligibility was dependent upon the action of the British government.[107]

---

[103] 'The Citizen Rights of Women within the British Empire', *British Commonwealth League Conference Report* (London: British Commonwealth League, 1925), 5.

[104] 'The Citizen Rights of Women within the British Empire', 30, 32–3.

[105] 'The British Commonwealth League', *Stri Dharma* 8, 12 (October 1925): 185.

[106] 'The British Commonwealth League', 181.

[107] L/PJ/6/1878, Chave Collison to Secretary of State for India, 14 September 1925.

Where once Indian women were keen to appeal to British imperial responsibility, they now had support to start claiming their own rights outside of this imperial context and on the grounds of this national right.

The preamble for the 1927 conference report claimed that 'more than 200 millions of women of other than British race are governed under the British flag. Enfranchised women can no longer argue that they have no responsibility'. Members discussed their responsibility towards 'native' women, resolving that 'natives' should be treated equally before the law.[108] It is clear their conception of imperial responsibility was expanding while interest in Indian affairs continued. Avabai Wadia (née Mehta), a member of the London branch of the WIA, who had been educated at school in Britain and studied for the Bar in London in the 1930s, remembered the BCL as a popular organization, welcoming women from India and giving them a platform. She attended the BCL conference in 1929 with her mother, and then in June 1932, when she was 18, spoke on 'Women's Suffrage in India' in June 1932. In her memoirs, published in 2001, Wadia recalled that she had discussed opposition to Indian women's rights and then put forward arguments for adult franchise. She was congratulated for her 'brief, concise, convincing and well-informed arguments'.[109]

Members of the BCL also became good friends with their Indian counterparts. The BCL held a reception in London in May 1929 for Dhanvanthi Rama Rau on the 'Aims and Aspirations of Indian Women' at which Naidu was present. Rama Rau emphasized that Indian women did not want 'destructive criticism' but friendship through understanding of India's different culture and civilization.[110] Rama Rau also attended the BCL conference in 1929, where she was praised for speaking extempore. According to reports in *Stri Dharma*, she received public admiration from delegates from Australia and New Zealand, who were impressed with the 'amazing' work of Indian women and were conscious of their strong feeling of

---

[108] Woollacott, 'Inventing Commonwealth and Pan-Pacific Feminisms', 437–8.

[109] Wadia, *The Light Is Ours*, 62.

[110] 'Notes and Comments', *Stri Dharma* 12, 9 (July 1929): 383–5.

'kinship' with Indian women.[111] In 1938, when Rama Rau was leaving Britain with her husband to a new posting in South Africa, it was the BCL that organized a farewell party at the Economic Reform Club in London.[112]

The BCL also held a reception for the three women delegates (Naidu, Shahnawaz, and Subbarayan) at the Second RTC in 1931 (more on this in Chapter 5). Held at Miss Ruby Rich's house in Palace Gardens Terrace (not far from Kensington Palace), over 100 guests attended, including other Indians resident in the UK such as Lady Ali Baig, Sir Albion Banerji, Rameshwari Nehru, Dhanvanthi Rama Rau, Lady Sardani Ujjal Singh, Lady Shafi, Mrs Iyengar, and Kodanda Rao.[113] When Rajkumari Amrit Kaur stayed in London to discuss franchise at the Joint Select Parliamentary Committee, she was invited to an afternoon party alongside a number of 'overseas women' in September 1933.[114] Kaur had attended the BCL conference in June 1933 too. In a letter thanking Kaur for agreeing to attend, Daisy Solomon, the honorary secretary told her that she hoped the league would be able to 'do our share in helping the Indian women to obtain their franchise rights under the new constitution'.[115] In 1933, the BCL conference adopted suffrage resolutions for Bermuda, India, Malta, Palestine, and Quebec—more evidence of the expanding purview of the league and their continued interest in the suffrage question worldwide.[116] Here, Kaur made a statement about the demands of Indian women with regard to their franchise rights in the new constitution.[117]

---

[111] 'Notes and Comments', *Stri Dharma* 12, 10 (August 1929): 436–7.

[112] 'Mrs Rama Rau', *International Woman Suffrage News* 32, 7 (April 1938): 50.

[113] 'Round Table Conference Reception to Women Members', *The Vote*, 23 October 1931, 346.

[114] NMML, Rajkumari Amrit Kaur Correspondence Files, Todhunter to Kaur, 2 August 1933.

[115] NMML, Rajkumari Amrit Kaur Correspondence Files, Solomon to Kaur, 23 June 1933.

[116] 'Great Britain: British Commonwealth League', *International Woman Suffrage News* 27, 10 (July 1933): 78.

[117] H. M. Todhunter, 'British Commonwealth League Conference', *The Vote*, 23 June 1933, 198.

While the BCL was expanding, it was also enforcing and maintaining racial difference through language and through the structures of the conference. Una Marson, the Jamaican writer, broadcaster, and activist, attended and spoke at BCL conferences in the 1930s. She was a member of the League of Coloured Peoples, which was affiliated with the BCL from its inception. Marson spoke critically of the white women in the colonies who had no interest in the plight of native women, and spoke openly about racism in Britain as well as the colonies.[118] As Anna Snaith has argued, Marson's affiliation with the BCL and desire to support their struggle for universal rights for women was compromised by their 'racist terminology'.[119] Marson struggled with these contradictions, perhaps more so than her Indian colleagues. For example, the 1934 BCL conference covered the Dominions and India, as usual, with special parallel sessions for 'women of the colored races'.[120] It was evident in their language that Indians were given a higher, more 'equal' status to the white colonized women compared to their black counterparts. Reports of the 1934 conference reported on how, in addition to women from India, and now Burma, Palestine, Ceylon, and China, 'native Africans' were also present.[121]

From 1934 it is clear that the BCL was getting closer to the Indian women's movement, joining the Committee of Societies in the All-India Women's Conference Liaison Group in March 1934. The president of the BCL was now Margery Corbett Ashby, and it also appears that the BCL was becoming more closely allied with British feminist networks rather than 'Commonwealth' or colonial ones. For example, when Daisy Solomon, now secretary of the BCL, wrote to Kaur in March 1934 just after the Liaison Group had been set up, she thanked Kaur for the AIWC resolution that January which had appreciated the support of 'British women'.[122] It is clear then that now Indian women's groups were identifying the BCL with British women's

---

[118] Snaith, *Modernist Voyages*, 170–1.

[119] Snaith, *Modernist Voyages*, 32.

[120] 'Status of Women in the World', *The Daily News* (Perth), 28 March 1934, 8.

[121] Beetee, 'The Woman's World', *The Advertiser* (Adelaide), 16 August 1934, 8; 'Women's Problems at London Conference', *The Mail* (Adelaide), 11 August 1934, 17.

[122] NMML, AIWC Microfilm, Roll 6, file 59. Solomon to Kaur, 5 March 1934.

groups rather than the broader empire. In turn, in April 1934, when the members of the Liaison Group, including the BCL, sent a letter to the members of the Joint Select Committee, they described themselves all as British women's organizations.[123]

Despite the more 'British' affiliation, Indian women's groups, especially the AIWC, welcomed the interest and continued support of British and colonial women through these networks in their ongoing fight for suffrage. Maude Royden and Margery Corbett Ashby attended the annual AIWC at the start of January 1935 in India. Upon their return to Britain, a large meeting of welcome was arranged in London by the BCL in Friends House, for both to speak about their impression of India and to put forward the wishes of organized women as regards the new constitution.[124] At the 1935 BCL conference, it was resolved to demand that the principle of equality for women should be included in the Indian franchise proposals.[125] At the following AIWC conference over December 1935–January 1936, Daisy Solomon sent messages on behalf of the BCL and other women's groups. The BCL wished the AIWC success in their fight for the equality of status for women and assured them they were doing all in their power to make their point of view known in 'England and the Dominions'. Solomon had also recently returned from South Africa and relayed a message from the South African League of Women Voters sending their best wishes and expressing sympathetic interest. By this time the Government of India Act of 1935 had been passed and had increased the female franchise, but still on a limited basis. Solomon urged the AIWC to not be disheartened and to continue their work to educate women voters and take heart from the worldwide women's movement.[126]

At a BCL conference in March 1936, Grace Lankester, who was liaison secretary for the AIWC with British women's groups, spoke at length about the developments and campaigns regarding women

---

[123] NMML, AIWC Microfilm, Roll 5, file 50. British Women's Organisations to Joint Select Committee, 10 April 1934.

[124] *All-India Women's Conference, Tenth Session* (Trivandrum, 25 December 1935 to 4 January 1936), 58.

[125] 'Equality for Women', *Auckland Star*, 29 July 1935, 11.

[126] *All-India Women's Conference. Tenth Session*, 39–40.

in administration in India. Lankester explained that Indian women were realizing that the extended franchise and seats in the legislature would not give them enough voice in ameliorating social and political problems. She described the determination of the AIWC to have women ready to stand for election, although it was difficult to find suitable candidates not only because not too many of them met the property qualifications to vote but also because many Indian women refused to stand for reserved seats which were divided on communal lines. As Lankester put it, although women had been accorded reserved seats after 1932, these were limited to only 40 out of more than 1500 in the Provincial Assemblies and 6 out of 150 in the Council of State.[127] It was clear that the reform work of Indian suffragettes was going to continue, and the BCL would continue to have an interest in these developments.

Continuing 'Commonwealth' Connections

Antipodean interest in the Indian women's movement continued after Jinarajadasa's visit and independently of the work of the BDWSU and the BCL. For example, Jean Begg, national secretary of the Young Women's Christian Association (YWCA) in India, Burma, and Ceylon, spoke at a reception of women's groups in Auckland in 1935 where she discussed the work of the Indian women's organizations (AIWC, NCWI [National Council of Women in India], and WIA) and their opposition to the reservation of seats for women in the Indian legislatures. Begg described the women involved in these associations as natural leaders, as educated and cultured, and Begg remarked that 'we have to be on our mettle to keep up with them'.[128] In 1936 Joan McGregor returned to New Zealand, having worked in missionary service for 36 years in India. McGregor had worked at Pandita Ramabai's Mukti Mission near Poona and spoke about her work with child widows and orphans. She also discussed the enfranchisement of Indian women under the 1935 Government of India Act. Thus it was reported in the New Zealand press how Indian women could now qualify to vote through literacy qualifications and

[127] NMML, AIWC Microfilm, Roll 9, File no. 110, 1936 Important Correspondence by Hony Organising Secretary.

[128] 'The Woman's World', *New Zealand Herald*, 14 June 1935, 3.

not just property rights. As McGregor pointed out, in fact, some Indian women might be able to vote while their husband might not, which was perhaps a victory for 'feminism' in some way.[129]

Laura Bunting, meanwhile, produced a feature on Muthulakshmi Reddi, the first female legislator in Madras for the *Australasian* in 1927. During their interview, Reddi was keen to hear more about women in Australia and New Zealand from Bunting, explaining that she was not as familiar with their work as she was with developments in Britain and Europe.[130] Essentialized notions about Indian women in Australia continued to perpetuate though. An Australian paper in 1927 praised the political awakening of Indian women but also reminded readers that Indian women are the 'heart of the family' and would preserve ancient Indian traditions in the face of the 'evils of modern life'.[131] In 1935, when measures were introduced to expand the female electorate in India, an article for the *Daily News* in Perth proclaimed the 'wonderful advancement made by women of an Aryan race who have lived under a sex tyranny which is almost a religious fetish', bemoaning the fact that Australian women knew little of these successes.[132]

In 1937, Checha Eipe, vice-principal of the Women's College in Madras visited Australia. Eipe, a graduate of Madras University, had also studied in Canada and America. She spoke to the YWCA in Melbourne and women in Perth during her visit.[133] The Perth newspaper *West Australian* used her visit to produce a feature length article on Indian women, including photos of various 'types' of Indian women. Reflecting upon the advances for Indian women since 1917, the reporter explained that Indian women had achieved female franchise relatively quickly for a number of reasons including the 'national and international necessity that Indian women should be given as high a status as women in other parts of the Empire'.[134] When, in 1938, Radhabai Subbarayan was appointed as the first female member

---

[129] 'Ramabai Mission', *Evening Post (New Zealand)*, 14 December 1936, 11.

[130] Laura Bunting, 'Indian Public Woman', *Australasian*, 8 October 1927, 18.

[131] Quoted in 'Notes and Comments', *Stri Dharma* (May 1927): 98.

[132] 'Women of Modern India', *Daily News (Perth)*, 13 May 1935, 7.

[133] 'Good News for Co-Eds', *Queen's Journal*, 9 October 1928, 7; 'National YWCA', *The Argus (Melbourne)*, 19 January 1937, 3.

[134] Halsted, 'Women of India', *West Australian*, 10 March 1937, 4.

of the Central Assembly of India, and Vijayalakshmi Pandit as India's first female cabinet minister, an Australian paper remarked that Indian women appeared to be outstripping those of other countries whose 'pioneers for emancipation had blazed a trail very many years before it ever reached India'.[135]

* * *

Indian suffragettes projected themselves, when necessary, as colonized women and part of a broader network of women subjected by the British Empire. They used the networks at the peripheries of empire to gain inspiration from other suffragettes and to discuss common citizenship concerns and rights under British rule. They enjoyed the rhetoric of sisterhood and used these networks to help campaign for suffrage rights in India. They also used these webbed networks to engage with suffrage rights elsewhere, whether in Kenya, South Africa, or Australia, imagining a broader conception of Indian identity and citizenship rights that were not merely constrained to the territorial boundaries of British India.

Indian women were not being silenced by Australian and other colonial feminists. They were given the space to speak, to interact, and to put forward their demands and concerns in various imperial spaces, both in the imperial metropolis and various peripheries. Although the opinions and imagination of Indian women on Australia and other dominions is generally lacking in the archive, it is interesting that Indian women did not reject or criticize women in the white dominions for their imperialist feminism in the ways they did the British women they engaged with in the same spaces of London and at the same time. This is indicative of the ways in which they saw the wider empire, dominions, and Commonwealth as part of alternative networks to that of Britain. As David Featherstone has argued, solidarity can be liberating but it also entrenches the privileged position of some groups and the marginalization of others.[136]

---

[135] Quoted in 'Two Indian Women', *New Zealand Herald*, 2 February 1939, 4.

[136] Discussed in Caroline Bressey, 'Geographies of Solidarity and the Black Political Diaspora in London before 1914', in *Indigenous Networks: Mobility, Connections and Exchange*, ed. Jane Carey and Jane Lydon (New York:

This was evident in the colonial feminism that Indian suffragettes were engaging with, which did little to consider other racial or class-based inequalities.

It is important though to note, as Caroline Bressey has, the importance of personal geographies.[137] Whatever their sympathies might potentially have been, Indian women had almost no contact with Australian Aboriginal (or Maori or other indigenous peoples) at this time; they were not meeting them at the international conferences they frequented, they were not seeing them in London or India or Australia. Therefore, there were limits to their imagination and ability to reflect on speaking for them. This was less of an excuse for Kenya and South Africa. However, we should not assume that Indians and indigenous people would automatically create alliances or have a shared consciousness based on racial and gendered subjection in empire. They also had pressing domestic-facing concerns. The Indian suffrage fight was based on a conception of an electoral population which was largely viewed as racially homogeneous. Although the Indian population was, in reality, racially diverse, racial classifications based on 'colour' were not an issue for franchise campaigners. The issues of communal electoral rolls evident in other parts of the empire were transposed to different issues of communalism in India, based on religious lines. Therefore, where race did not enter debates about Indian citizenship specifically, though it was countered when discussing Indians overseas, Indian women were easily able to avoid contemplating these important issues, especially when their colonial 'sister' suffragettes were not raising them explicitly either. However, Indian suffragettes could not avoid facing stereotypical assumptions about Indian women. These became more apparent in broader international suffrage networks, which we turn to in the next chapter.

Routledge, 2014), 242. See David Featherstone, *Solidarity: Hidden Histories and Geographies of Internationalism* (London: Zed Books, 2012).

[137] Bressey, 'Geographies of Solidarity', 244.

3

Indian Suffragettes and International Feminist Networks

In 1946, a year before India gained independence, Hansa Mehta, member of the AIWC, served as a member of the United Nations subcommittee on the status of women. She was vice chair, with Eleanor Roosevelt, on the United Nations Universal Declaration of Human Rights committee. Mehta was instrumental in ensuring that the fundamental principle of equality for women was enshrined in that declaration. In 1949, when India introduced full adult suffrage, there were European countries (Greece and Switzerland) where full female enfranchisement had not been introduced. As Indian suffragettes had realized over the course of the interwar period, suffrage was not necessarily automatically awarded to women in the 'enlightened' countries of the 'West' and it was an ongoing global issue.

The fight for female suffrage had been internationally minded from the outset, extending beyond the British imperial world. Although initial suffrage networks for Indians had been based on imperial ties, it was inevitable that they would soon engage with the international movement and major international women's suffrage groups. As June Hannam has argued, although suffrage was an issue framed within a national context and directed against a particular government, the suffrage movement had always been internationalist because it was a common fight for women across most of the world.[1] Thus, Indian suffragettes soon engaged with women in non-colonial settings, engaging in similar fights for female enfranchisement and the recognition of women's political rights.

There are three main international women's organizations worth considering here. The ICW started in 1888, emerging out of the US National Woman Suffrage Association. Conservative and elitist, according to Leila Rupp, the council set up an Indian branch (the NCWI) in 1925. By 1925, the ICW could claim to represent 36 million women members worldwide.[2] In 1902, suffrage campaigners met in Washington, frustrated that the ICW did not focus on suffrage enough; thus, the International Woman Suffrage Alliance (IWSA) was founded in Berlin in 1904, with its initial headquarters in London. Dominated by women of 'European heritage', the IWSA held meetings every three years. Indian women began to attend these meetings from 1920. American hands were also involved in the foundation of the WILPF in 1915. Founded by the American campaigner Jane Addams in the Hague, this was an organization formed to unite women on the issue of peace, during the First World War, but also took on other women's rights issues. All three associations were internationally minded, requiring membership through affiliate 'national' organizations, and were dominated by European and American women. However, as the enfranchisement of women in Europe gathered pace in the 1910s, and as they looked to continue and expand their campaigns, these organizations began to expand their definition of the 'international'. Previously having failed to recognize 'non-nations',

---

[1] Hannam, 'International Dimensions of Women's Suffrage: "At the Crossroads of Several Interlocking Identities"', *Women's History Review* 14, 3–4 (2005): 543–60.

[2] Leila J. Rupp, *Worlds of Women: The Making of an International Women's Movement* (Princeton: Princeton University Press, 1997), 15, 20.

these Western reformers increasingly began to recognize the right of colonized women to have a place in these international settings.[3]

Engagement with women from diverse backgrounds and with different agendas was always likely to lead to misunderstandings and conflict. Leila Rupp has argued that conflict was a necessary process by which women came together to create a sense of belonging. The international women's movement was formed out of exclusivity, but women found ways to unite over their struggles for equality and international understanding. However, despite pronouncements on universality, there were clear obstacles to the equal participation of all groups of women. Participants in international conferences needed to take lengthy and expensive trips to attend meetings, and so not only did they need money but also free leisure time. This meant that the women members were generally of an older age. There was also a domination of English speakers (although French and German were also popular), but this was not much of a disadvantage for Indians. Rupp argues that international women's associations, dominated as they were by women of European origin, also tended to be Christian in nature, using Christian phrases and mottos and peddling orientalist assumptions about women in the 'East'.[4] It was with these challenges and assumptions that Indian women had to find a place and voice in international spaces to discuss their own suffrage concerns and campaigns.

Indian women started attending these international women's conferences from 1920; the WIA became member of the IWSA in 1923. *Jus Suffragii: International Woman Suffrage News*, the newspaper of the IWSA, published in London, regularly provided articles on Indian suffrage achievements and activities. Indeed, according to Marie Sandell, India received the most attention out of all the 'Eastern' countries in the *IWSN* and *ICW* bulletin, probably because of its close connection to Britain.[5] As discussed in the first chapter, Carrie Chapman Catt had described Britain as the storm centre of the women's movement.

---

[3] In 1921, for example, WILPF changed the name of the 'India (British)' section to just the 'Indian Section' (Rupp, *Worlds of Women*, 79).

[4] Rupp, *Worlds of Women*, 6, 51–8.

[5] Marie Sandell, *The Rise of Women's Transnational Activism: Identity and Sisterhood Between the World Wars* (London: I. B. Tauris, 2015), 62.

This centrality had some advantages for Britain's imperial subjects, but Indian women were increasingly rejecting subordinate roles. They were keen to place India's achievements in an international context. Suffrage was seen as part of a modernizing agenda, and Indian women could refer to their own campaigns to justify their place in international settings. This is why Indian women exhibited such pride when provincial votes began to be awarded in the 1920s, keen to publicize these victories internationally, often contrasting the speed of reforms in India to that in parts of Europe which were still to enfranchise any women.

Although European powers continued to hold empires and subject peoples around the world to colonial oppression in this era, imperialism was becoming internationalized and decentralized in the early twentieth century, especially after the First World War. This new outlook, as Daniel Gorman has argued, was exemplified by the foundation of the League of Nations, but also evident in the increased number of international NGOs and the expansion of transnational civil society.[6] In the interwar years, as the international suffrage movement's centre shifted away from western Europe and North America towards the Middle East, Asia, and Latin America, delegates from these parts of the world were increasingly encouraged to attend the regular meetings organized by these associations.[7] Despite many social and political differences, Indian women were able to identify with other women across national borders through these new networks, learning about and from other campaigns, all feeding into their activities back in India.

International feminist organizations had more egalitarian aims than the imperial or Commonwealth associations Indians had more natural connection to. Indian suffragettes were thus eager to find new roles within international, global networks of feminism not bound

[6] Daniel Gorman, *Emergence of International Society in the 1920s* (Cambridge: Cambridge University Press, 2012), 3, passim.

[7] Hannam, 'International Dimensions of Women's Suffrage'. See also Ellen DuBois, 'Woman Suffrage around the World: Three Phases of Suffragist Internationalism', in *Suffrage and Beyond: International Feminist Perspectives*, ed. Caroline Daley and Melanie Nolan (Auckland: Auckland University Press, 1994), 252–74.

by their colonial predicament. In the following chapter, I will explore these Indian connections and experiences at these international conferences. I will consider how Indian women expressed themselves in international contexts, though they were bound by colonial identities and in tension with the European and American women who led these organizations. I will also discuss suffrage campaigners' interactions with the League of Nations and local and national organizations in the United States. My focus is, as ever, on how discussions on Indian suffrage featured in these settings, and also, more broadly, on how Indian women were conceptualizing 'international sisterhood', and the ways they located their activities within the international 'feminist' movement.

Indian Suffragettes and International Women's Organizations in Europe

Indian women actively engaged with the IWSA in the interwar period, and it is through these interactions that they most clearly identified their suffrage struggle with other movements around the world. They were keen to use the stage given to them in this international organization to publicize and add international pressure on the British and Indian governments as franchise negotiations continued in this period. Meanwhile, the leaders of the IWSA were keen to expand the membership of the organization beyond its Western core. By encouraging women from the Middle East and Asia to join the IWSA, the organizers were able to demonstrate the universal 'sisterhood' of women and also take on roles as 'teachers' to newly emerging women's movements. Although the IWSA was removed from imperial structures, in its Western dominance and the language and attitude towards non-Western women it carried many imperialist and orientalist overtones. Although Western feminists encouraged women around the world to demand equal suffrage, the IWSA balked from demanding national independence for colonized countries. There was an inevitable paradox in some of these campaigns where women were encouraged to demand equal citizenship in political systems that were inherently undemocratic because of imperial rule, and yet these tensions were never fully explored by the Western leaders of the IWSA and its counterparts, which led to inevitable fractures by the 1930s.

The American Carrie Chapman Catt was one of the main founders of the IWSA and was evidently interested in the international dimensions of the suffrage movement. In 1912, Catt visited India and, in an article published in *Jus Suffragii*, noted that women in Bombay already had the municipal vote and efforts were underway to get more Indian women on electoral rolls. Though she did not discuss wider suffrage concerns in India, especially as no legislative assemblies existed yet, Catt remarked that the main outcome of her trip was introducing the Alliance to a 'number of sympathetic feminists whose names were unknown to us before', and she hoped that an organization would grow in time in India through these connections. She also hoped that an Indian woman could be found to attend the Budapest Congress in 1913.

> Some of the women I have met are so sweetly charming, so individually emancipated that I long to meet them again and to have our delegates know them and love them as I do. After all, our movement will never be truly international until it counts the oriental woman in its list of members.[8]

No Indian women attended the 1913 IWSA Congress in Budapest. Indian women did not travel to attend any IWSA (or ICW) meetings before the First World War and the IWSA did not meet during the war. At the next meeting in Geneva in 1920, Indian women, now with legislative assemblies in place, did attend.

1920 Geneva Congress

Following their activities in Britain at the end of 1919, Herabai and Mithan Tata remained in Britain and continued to engage with women's organizations. As Herabai told Jaiji Petit in March 1920, the IWSA pressed her 'very much' and 'a lot' to attend their conference in Geneva in June. As she considered going, Herabai told Petit that she would go as a representative of women in Bombay and was especially eager to meet the Chinese and Japanese representatives who

---

[8] Carrie Chapman Catt, 'India', *Jus Suffragii*, 6, 11 (15 July 1912): 101. See also Margot Badran, *Feminists, Islam, and Nation: Gender and the Making of Modern Egypt* (Princeton: Princeton University Press, 1995), 71.

had been invited.[9] The IWSA was, however, keen that more Indian women than just the Tatas attend.

The British campaigner Elizabeth Abbott, of the IWSA, had been impressed by the campaigning activities of the Tatas in 1919 and started to demonstrate interest in Indian suffrage and Indian women.[10] In her efforts to engage more Indian women in the Geneva Congress, Abbott corresponded with Mrs Gray in Bombay to discuss other Indians residing in India who could represent different communities and who might be willing to attend the Geneva convention. She was concerned that the confirmed representatives at the start of January 1920 were not religiously diverse.[11] Abbott asked Pinja Powallah, a student at Lady Margaret Hall College in Oxford, if she could suggest names of suitable Indian women. As Abbott explained to Powallah, the first IWSA conference after the war would have to focus on unenfranchised countries and, most importantly, 'the women of the East'. As an international alliance, their work was not complete unless and until they included and considered the plight of all women around the world, and not just the European and American founding members.[12] Abbott made a strong appeal to Indian women at a meeting of the BDWSU at the Minerva Café in April 1920 to get involved with the IWSA. She explained that it was important that Indian women take on a more public role, especially as the provincial councils in India were still considering whether or not to enfranchise women. As it was the first conference to be held since the war, Abbot had a keen sense of the importance of drawing women from around the world together in 'sisterhood'. Following her exhortations at this meeting, Sarojini Naidu, Herabai and Mithan Tata, and Mrinalini Sen all agreed that they would attend the conference in Geneva.[13]

    [9] TC, Herabai to Petit, 10 March 1920; 28 March 1920.

    [10] In August 1919, Abbott also asked Besant to supply her with information on Indian campaigns for *Jus Suffragii* (JR, IWSA/2/3, Abbott to Besant, 20 August 1919; IWSA/2/12, Abbott to Mrs Gray, 8 October 1919).

    [11] IWSA/2/12, Abbott to Gray, 1 January 1920.

    [12] IWSA/2/25, Pinja Powallah to Abbott, 13 October 1919; Abbott to Powallah, 25 November 1919.

    [13] 'British Dominions Women's Citizens Union', *Britain and India* (May 1920): 172.

In publicity for press purposes, before the Geneva conference began, the Alliance provided an information sheet which noted that it would be the first time that women from the East, of 'other races', would attend, giving 'expression to the solidarity of the women's movement.... It will perhaps surprise many Europeans who are in the habit of thinking of Indian women as living secluded from the world to know that there is a strong demand for the suffrage, amongst the women of India'. The information sheet discussed the example of Bombay, noting that Herabai Tata would be attending the conference, and also reiterated the argument put forward by Indian women that enfranchisement was a process of recovery for Indian women, who had historically enjoyed equal rights before successive waves of colonization. 'Hence the demand of the women of the East for a direct share in political power is not so surprising as it seems at first sight.'[14]

In the end 10 Indian delegates went to Geneva in June 1920. Naidu, the Tatas, and Sen were joined by Hansa Mehta, Lolita Roy, Meenarkshi Devi, Mrs Hameed, Mrs Dharamsy Thacker, and Mrs L. Ram.[15] According to Herabai's report on the conference to Jaiji Petit, 89 countries were represented. Key speeches were made on the vote for women, the need for women members in parliament, as well as equal wages, educational reform, child welfare, maternity care, and prostitution. India was not an affiliated member of the IWSA, as membership only came through an organizational affiliation. Thus, the Indian women there had no right to vote in business meeting; they were present as invited guests rather than delegates.[16]

Chrystal Macmillan, a Scottish suffragist and one of the founders of WILPF, in her introduction for the report of the congress, eagerly pointed out that it was the first time that women from India and Japan had attended an IAW meeting. She was glad that they would be able to tell delegates about the beginnings of organized movement among

[14] League of Nations Archives, Geneva (hereafter LoN), Women's Questions, File 4377/Series 3554, *Eighth Congress of the International Woman Suffrage Alliance, Information for Press Purposes*, May 1920.

[15] SSC, International Alliance of Women, Box 2, Folder 1, *Report of Eighth Congress, Geneva, Switzerland, June 6, 7, 8, 9, 10, 11, 12, 1920* (Manchester: Percy Brothers, 1920), 15.

[16] TC, Herabai to Petit, 29 June 1920; 'Indian Suffragettes', *Young India* (August 1920), 172.

'women of the East'. She acknowledged that the difficulties of travel to Europe had prevented more women from beyond Europe to attend the gathering. However, Macmillan was happy that the addresses by Japanese and Indian women had shown 'how similar are the difficulties of the women both of the East and of the West', and how it was essential for the Alliance to fulfil its aims to be international to urge more women from around the world to attend and speak at these meetings.[17]

These women from the 'East' (India, Turkey, and Japan) addressed a public meeting at the conference. Mrinalini Sen was one of the speakers, with a speech entitled 'Indian Women and Their Part in the Future'. Appreciative of the invitation extended to Indian women to attend the Alliance's congress for the first time, Sen did point out that Indians had good claims to have been invited before 1920. She explained that India had a 'highly developed' past and the largest female population outside of China. Sen also invoked her sense of the international solidarity of women, asserting that they were 'women first' and then Indian, French, Swiss, Japanese, or other, explaining that there was little difference between nations. Further invoking an internationalist identity, Sen argued that women's rights should be the same all over the world as the life responsibilities of women were the same: 'I feel myself only a woman amongst women I see here one universal womanhood personified in all of us present here.'[18] Meanwhile, Herabai gave a history of the Indian female suffrage movement at the meeting. It was clear, though, that Naidu felt some frustrations at the activities of the IWSA. In a letter to her son, she criticized the impersonal, academic nature of the conference that did little to consider the 'humanity' behind the problems they were discussing. Naidu also criticized the European women delegates for imitating men in their organization instead of realizing, and drawing upon, the sanctity and special strength of womanhood, although she did not elaborate further on how she would change the organization.[19]

---

[17] *Report of Eighth Congress*, 23, 26.

[18] Sen, *Knocking at the Door*, 12.

[19] Makarand Paranjape, ed., *Sarojini Naidu: Selected Letters 1890s to 1940s* (New Delhi: Kali for Women, 1996), 146; Sarojini Naidu to Jaisoorya Naidu, 16 June 1920.

The IWSA report noted that 'Eastern' women had different traditions and old civilizations but were producing feminist movements,
which shared similarities and differences with the Euro-American
movements. These differences were not articulated beyond the
allusion to different traditions; although the report did mention
that some of the ideas from these women were a 'little vague and
illusive'.[20] On the other hand, Regine Deutsch, a German member
of the IWSA who wrote its history in 1929, remarked upon how the
inclusion of Eastern delegates at Geneva emphasized differences.
Deutsch recalled that the delegates from India, Turkey, and Japan
had 'proved in their speeches how like and yet unlike their women's
aims were to our own'. Despite the 'forward movement' among
Eastern women, Deutsch believed that there was still work to do
and she noted: 'It is difficult to arrive at a full understanding with
these women, more bound by tradition and faith than us.'[21] Using
the terminology of East and West clearly indicated that these differences were ingrained in the perceptions of the Alliance. This terminology would continue to be used for more than a decade, as we shall
see in the next chapter.

Margaret Hodge (one of the founders of the BDWSU) had
attended the Geneva Congress too and provided a report for *Britain
and India*, the monthly journal published in London by Theosophist
Josephine Ransom. Remarking that Geneva was renowned for its
cosmopolitan nature and international meetings, Hodge supposed
that this was the first time women from different Eastern countries
shared the same platform. Impressed with the power, bearing, and
speeches of these women, Hodge explained that they had dissipated
any preconceived notions of the subjection of women and she was
confident that they would lead their own political emancipation. She
described Sen as 'looking like a girl' and her rose-coloured robe;
unfortunately this focus on clothing detracted from Sen's discussion
on the women's movement in India. Hodge also described the eloquence of Naidu, who was noted for her strength in public speaking

[20] 'The Eighth Congress of the I.W.S.A.', *The Woman's Leader*, quoted in
Report of Eighth Congress, 40.
[21] Regine Deutsch, *The International Woman Suffrage Alliance: Its History
from 1904 to 1929* (London: IWSA, 1929), 25.

and who had received enormous applause at the congress.[22] A report for *Independent Hindustan*, a paper produced in San Francisco by the Indian revolutionary Gadar Party, used similar descriptions about the clothing of the Indian delegates who were 'clad beautifully in draped sari' and the renowned eloquence of Naidu. The newspaper also mentioned that Herabai had told the conference that Indian men fully supported Indian women and she did not foresee difficulties for Indian women to obtain franchise rights.[23] Herabai's optimism had not yet been tempered by the harsh realities of unsuccessful votes in some parts of India nor had she reflected sincerely upon existing deep-set Indian patriarchal attitudes; she clearly wished to suggest that India's attitudes towards women were in advance of some other countries to present Indians as modern and thus having the right to be present at the IWSA.

The Indian visitors had had the opportunity then to discuss their campaigns on an international stage and meet women they might otherwise not have had the opportunity to meet. It was expected that they would continue to build upon these networks and attend future congresses. The visit to Geneva was a chance for Indian women to see new sights and traverse through new spaces.[24] During their visit to Europe, Herabai and Mithan Tata also met the Indian revolutionary Madame Cama in Paris. Cama was an ardent Indian nationalist. She had unfolded an Indian tricolour flag at the 1907 International Socialist Congress in Stuttgart and published a journal *Bande Mataram* from 1909 in Paris. Though she has been described by some twenty-first-century commentators as a suffragette, Mithan's recollections of this visit paint a different picture.

> She asked us why we had come to England and what I was studying there. On being told that initially we had come to England to ask for Votes for Indian women before the Southborough Committee on

[22] Margaret Hodge, 'Women's Congress at Geneva', *Britain and India* (July 1920): 241–2.

[23] 'Indian Women Suffragists at Geneva', *Independent Hindustan* (September 1920): 21.

[24] In the photo collection collated by the IAW there is a picture of the two Tatas beside a British policewoman in front of the conference building (TWL, 2IAW/1/J/1/02, Triennial Congress, Geneva 1920).

Indian Reforms, she just shook her head rather sadly and stated—
'"Work for India's freedom and Independence". When India is
independent women will get not only the Votes, but all other rights'.[25]

Thus, while some Indian women were thinking about using imperial and international networks to further the suffrage cause, Cama
was adamantly more nationalist in her approach, and less concerned
about women's votes, than her contemporaries.

Following the Geneva meeting, the IWSA, and Catt in particular,
continued to express interest in the activities of Indian suffragettes.
In September 1920, Catt sent a letter to the 'progressive men of India'.
Aware that the legislative councils were considering Indian women's
franchise, Catt pointed out that since the end of the war, 'most'
'nations of the world' had enfranchised women, listing Great Britain,
Canada, New Zealand, Australia, British East Africa, Rhodesia, the USA,
and various European countries. She urged Indian men to spare
their women from the 'pain and toil of a long struggle to secure the
vote' and to acknowledge the worldwide recognition of the capaci-
ties of women for public affairs. Catt also appealed to sentimental
notions of India, describing it as the 'cradle of all civilization' and
an 'old civilization', congratulating Indians for the self-government
they would enjoy through the reformed legislative assemblies and
hoped they would keep pace with the 'democratic trend of modern
times'.[26] Again this points towards the ways in which the suffrage
movement was being presented in internationalist modern comparative contexts.

Indian suffragettes also continued to engage with the IWSA
outside of the biennial conferences. In May 1921, Margaret Cousins
asked Elizabeth Abbott of the British section of the IWSA for financial help for the Indian cause. As the British section was responsible for India too, Cousins asked for help for the campaigns to
enfranchise women in the provinces and to run the WIA journal
Stri Dharma. Cousins noted that apart from herself, Jinarajadasa,
and Besant, all the other suffrage campaigners were Indian and
they needed the practical help of Western suffrage societies at this

---

[25] Lam, 'Autumn Leaves', chap. X.
[26] TC, Carrie Chapman Catt circular to Progressive Men of India,
30 September 1920.

time.[27] In response, the issue was passed on to Catt who wrote to Jinarajadasa sending $500 (2,094 rupees) from the IWSA's Leslie Woman Suffrage Commission, and continued to send $500 again to the WIA every year from 1923 to at least 1928.[28] Although other sources of financial help are not obviously recorded, it is evident that Indian suffragettes would not have been able to network internationally without money.

1923 Rome Conference

The next IWSA conference took place in Rome from 12 to 19 May 1923. A call for Indian delegates was published in the Calcutta-based journal *Modern Review* in March 1923.[29] However, India also became affiliated—through the WIA—with the IWSA in 1923 and sent delegates through official channels. The Indian delegates were Herabai and Mithan Tata, Dorothy Jinarajadasa, Malati Patwardhan, and Ramdulari Dubé. Jinarajadasa, Patwardhan, and Dubé were accompanied by their husbands.[30] Chinese, Japanese, and Egyptian women were also represented in Rome.[31] The Indian delegates, now that they were full members, were able to join in the administrative side of the IWSA. For example, India was among the countries who nominated Rosa Manus from Holland, Miss Sterling from the UK, and Frau Schreiber-Krieger from Germany to the new Board of Officers. Herabai Tata was also nominated, solely by Uruguay, but she did not get enough votes to join the board.[32]

The Alliance celebrated the establishment of equal suffrage, since the last conference, in USA and Ireland, and also suffrage victories

---

[27] Reddi, *Margaret Cousins*, Margaret E. Cousins to Mrs Abbot, 19 May 1921, 29–31.

[28] Reddi, *Margaret Cousins*, 38–9; 54–5.

[29] 'Ninth Congress of the International Woman Suffrage Alliance', *Modern Review* (March 1923): 398–9.

[30] 'Women in India', *Auckland Star*, 20 October 1923, 20; International Woman Suffrage Alliance, *Report of Ninth Congress Rome, Italy, May 12th to 19th 1923* (Dresden: B. G. Teubner, 1923), 13.

[31] Helen Fraser, 'The Women's Suffrage Congress', *Manchester Guardian*, 25 May 1923, 14.

[32] *Report of Ninth Congress*, 69–70.

in the provinces and states of Bombay, Madras, Travancore, Jhalwar, and Burma, described as 'the first Eastern countries to give votes to women'.[33] Margery Corbett Ashby was elected the new president of the IWSA in Rome (replacing Catt). In her outgoing presidential address, Catt referred to Indian and Burmese suffrage successes. Despite her visit to India in 1912 and correspondence and encounter with Indian women, she used stereotypical images of India— welcoming delegates 'for the second time from that far-away mystical country'. Catt congratulated Indians for their franchise successes in several provinces, but was ashamed that these victories came in advance of some Western countries, for 'the ancient Indian civilization with modern democratic aspirations has shamed more youthful nations in generous justice to its women'.[34]

The franchise successes in India were remarkable points of celebration at Rome then, though the Bombay paper *New India* (edited by Annie Besant) was disappointed that the IWSA organ *Jus Suffragii* failed to discuss the activities of Indian delegates in its post-congress report. Jinarajadasa had addressed the congress and, of course, the enfranchisement of women in Madras, Bombay, the United Provinces (UP), and Burma had been celebrated, but the report in *New India* hoped that the expanse of the Indian franchise question might have been discussed in more detail at Rome. The Indian paper noted that the population covered by the provinces that had enfranchised women was over 150 million, many times larger than the population of Great Britain (though the paper neglected to acknowledge that 150 million Indian women were not actually enfranchised). However, emphasizing that Indian women were enfranchised on the same terms as men, and not on differential qualifications based on age as in Britain, *New India* concluded in clear internationalist perspective: 'We know that the world sisterhood has been sharing in the pride of our Indian representative in this matter.'[35]

Following the Rome Conference in May, Jinarajadasa attended the European Theosophical Society Congress in Vienna in July. She gave an address titled 'The Emancipation of Indian Women', in which

---

[33] *Report of Ninth Congress*, i.

[34] *Report of Ninth Congress*, 31.

[35] 'India at the Women's International Suffrage Congress', *New India*, 22 May 1923, 4.

she discussed franchise developments in India since 1919. She explained that Indian women had been inspired during the Great War by the public role women took in the West. However, she was keen to note that having worked in the English suffrage movement the remarkable difference in India was the support of Indian men. Simplifying and obfuscating the level of male opposition to female suffrage in India, Jinarajadasa told her Theosophical Society colleagues that Hindu men realized that there was no separation of sex and they positively supported the enfranchisement and election of Indian women in legislative bodies.[36] On the international stage, Indian suffragettes emphasized modernity and the successes rather than all the realities of franchise struggles in India.

The links between the IWSA and Indian suffrage campaigns was evident beyond attendance at European conferences. Towards the end of 1923, the president of the overseas committee of the IWSA sent a message of congratulations to the Maharaja of Mysore, with regard to the enfranchisement of women in that princely state. *Stri Dharma* saw this message as evidence of 'increasing ties of sisterhood that are being felt all over the world', cementing 'friendship between East and West'.[37] A pattern had now been set where the WIA would send Indian representatives to the triennial conferences of the IWSA, all based in Europe so far, where Indian women could publicize the franchise advances in India and also engage in cementing India's position as internationally minded.

1926 Paris Conference

In 1926, the IWSA changed its name to the International Alliance of Women for Suffrage and Equal Citizenship (IAWSEC). This reflected how many members had achieved suffrage in their countries, but broader political rights were still a battle. While many women were becoming enfranchised in Europe and beyond, particularly after the

---

[36] Dorothy Jinarajadasa, 'The Emancipation of Indian Women', *Transactions of the Eighth Congress of the Federation of European National Societies of the Theosophical Society held in Vienna July 2st to 26th 1923*, ed. C. W. Dijkgraaf (Amsterdam: Council of the Federations, 1923), 82–8.

[37] 'International Sisterhood', *Stri Dharma* (December 1923): 17.

First World War, the French demands for suffrage had not been met by the time of the conference in Paris. Indeed, French women would have to wait until 1945 to vote in their first general elections. Jennifer Anne Boittin has argued that French women found it difficult to watch women become enfranchised elsewhere and especially resented the enfranchisement of women in the British colonies of Kenya and India.[38] These sentiments, though, were not evident in official responses to or by the Indian women at the Paris Conference. In the call for this tenth congress sent out by Corbett Ashby and Catt, the Alliance noted with pleasure that three more provinces (United Provinces, Assam, and Bengal) had enfranchised women in India, as had the princely states of Cochin and Mysore, since the last Congress.[39]

As ever, the Calcutta journal the *Modern Review* was keen that 'responsible women leaders of India' should visit Paris and represent Indian women from all parts of India.[40] Afterwards, the *Modern Review* explained how important it was for Indian women (and men) to have contact with people from around the world and avoid isolationism.[41] In the end there were eight delegates representing India. They were Mrs Drysdale, Miss Barry, Mme Dr Monod (from Pondicherry), Muthulakshmi Reddi, Rukmini Lakshmipathi, Mrs Sen, Mrs Swaminadhan, and Mr M. Vakil.[42]

Attendance at the conference had consequences back in India, in terms of rhetoric and activity. Reddi mentioned the Paris conference and discussions of European franchise when she spoke to a group of new graduates in India in August 1930. She used this example

[38] Boittin, *Colonial Metropolis*, 179–80.

[39] International Alliance of Women for Suffrage and Equal Citizenship, *Report of Tenth Congress Paris, France, May 30th to June 6th, 1926* (London: London Caledonian Press, 1926), ii.

[40] 'The International Society for Women's Suffrage', *Modern Review* (February 1926): 237.

[41] 'Indian Women at Paris Women's Congress', *Modern Review* (August 1926): 219.

[42] NMML, S. Muthulakshmi Reddi Papers, Correspondence, Cousins to Muthulakshmi, 31 January 1926. Although their first names are not given, I assume that Mrs Sen was Mrinalini Sen and that Mrs Swaminadhan was Ammu Swaminadhan, but I may be mistaken.

to explain that the Indian women's movement sought to widen its sphere beyond the home, city, and country through 'international friendship and cooperation' to bring about 'better health and happiness' for all nations.[43] Another delegate, Lakshmipathi, incorporated a visit to other parts of Europe and Britain in the trip and attended the BCL conference soon after.[44] In 1935, Congress put forward Lakshmipathi as a candidate in a by-election for the Madras Legislative Council. Reflecting on this achievement, Cousins recalled this visit to Paris in 1926 and how contact with women from other lands had fanned the flame of Lakshmipathi's 'patriotism'. Cousins noted that Lakshmipathi and her contemporaries had worn high heels and spoke English before they went abroad, but returned wearing nothing but sandals and endeavoured to speak in their mother tongues in public.[45] If so, it appears that Lakshmipathi and colleagues rejected the dominant European culture at international conferences and were keen to assert their 'national' identity in the face of these homogenizing tendencies.

Though the programme did not indicate that any Indian women would be delivering addresses during committee meetings, a public meeting on Monday, 31 May in the amphitheatre of the Sorbonne chaired by Corbett Ashby was an opportunity for women of all affiliated nations, including India, to speak.[46] The first resolution adopted at Paris was one of congratulations to the places which had obtained parliamentary and municipal franchises including those mentioned in India. This resolution also included a congratulatory message to Travancore for electing their first woman member of parliament.[47] This was followed by resolutions urging equal franchise for women in

---

[43] NMML, S. Muthulakshmi Bound Speeches and Writings, 'Advice to New Graduates', 22 August 1930.

[44] NMML, Rukmini Lakshmipathi Papers, Acc. no. 1036, Lakshmipathi to 'Kakka', no date.

[45] Margaret E. Cousins, 'Mrs Rukmini Lakshmipathi', *Modern Review* (June 1935): 644.

[46] See Zohreh T. Sullivan, 'Eluding the Feminist, Overthrowing the Modern? Transformations in Twentieth-Century Iran', in *Remaking Women: Feminism and Modernity in the Middle East*, ed. Lila Abu-Lughod (Princeton: Princeton University Press, 1998), 230.

[47] *Report of Tenth Congress*, 105.

various countries including Great Britain. The Alliance then resolved to work with the League of Nations; they passed various resolutions relating to issues such as equal pay, employment, nationality of married women, and trafficking of women, indicating the increasingly broadened interests of the association.

It was decided in Paris that the British Overseas Committee for the Alliance should organize a pavilion for the British Empire Exhibition to be held in Wembley in 1924 but that the committee should disaffiliate from the Alliance.[48] This became the BCL (as discussed in the last chapter). The BCL reflected not only the ways in which the IAWSEC encouraged women delegates to form new associations out of the networks created at the international congresses, but also the way in which the Alliance would only allow membership through association rather than as individuals. The Indian women who attended these conferences then were linked to the WIA and supported the WIA's official line regarding franchise in India. The 'masses' were not being invoked at these meetings, but Indian suffragettes were able to visualize the place that Indian women had in an international network, learn from other campaigns, and think beyond their national predicament. Thus, they continued to invoke international interest and pressure upon the British and Indian governments to listen to their demands.

1929 Berlin Congress

In 1928, Helen Archdale of the women's group Equal Rights International (based in Geneva) traced international developments in the woman's movement for 'Current History'. This article was discussed in *Indian Review*, which, in turn, was quoted in the *Indian Ladies' Magazine*. Archdale had explained that the demands for equal suffrage had been enlarged to encompass equal citizenship.[49] This clearly resonated with the Indian women's movement which was concerned not only about franchise but also about political representation and

---

[48] *Report of Tenth Congress*, 54.

[49] 'The Woman's Movement', *Indian Ladies' Magazine* (January 1929): 336–7. The *Indian Ladies' Magazine* was edited by Kamala Satthianadhan in Madras.

legal equality. At the 1929 IAWSEC Congress in Berlin then the resolutions began with restating the policy of the organization and confirming that suffrage remained the chief aim of the Alliance. It was also recognized that though many women were enfranchised on equal terms with men around the world, franchise requirements based on property were often disadvantageous to women and work needed to be done to ensure their full enfranchisement. However, Congress was also interested now in issues of peace, economic rights, 'moral' rights, and legal rights.[50]

Sarojini Naidu attended the IWSA Congress held in Berlin in June 1929 (see Image 3.1). In a letter to M. K. Gandhi from Berlin, she used the terminology of the 'East' that was often used to describe delegates, keen to tell Gandhi that women from Egypt, Turkey, Japan, China, and Persia were present, and that the Indian flag was flying for the first time.[51] However, Naidu's sister-in-law Kamaladevi Chattopadhyay, who also attended the congress, later criticized the IWSA for lacking an 'international character' and suggested that only India and Egypt were the non-Western countries present. Aware of India's colonial position while at the conference, because Indians had to stand under the Union Jack, Kamaladevi had complained to organizers that there was no Indian flag at the conference. The night before the opening, the Indian delegates cut up fabric from their saris to make up the tricolour which was flown alongside the others. Having felt 'statusless', Kamaladevi was proud of this achievement and the oratorical ability of Naidu to sway the Berlin audience and thus highlight Indian issues.[52] In 1921, Kamaladevi had also visited Naidu's brother, Virendranath 'Chatto' Chattopadhyay, a revolutionary in exile in Europe, in Berlin. In 1929, when Kamaladevi, as secretary of the AIWC, had arranged to visit Berlin again for the IWSA, she was refused a passport. She thus became aware of British suspicion of her activities, though she only

---

[50] International Alliance of Women for Suffrage and Equal Citizenship, *Report of the Eleventh Congress Berlin June 1th–22nd 1929* (London: IAWSEC, 1929), 308–9.

[51] Makarand Paranjape, ed., *Sarojini Naidu: Selected Letters 1890s to 1940s* (New Delhi: Kali for Women, 1996), 229, Naidu to Gandhi, 18 June 1929.

[52] NMML, Kamaladevi Chattopadhyay Papers, file 97, undated reminiscences of 1929 European tour.

IMAGE 3.1   International Woman Suffrage Alliance Conference, Berlin,
June 1929
Source: From the LSE Library's collections, 2IAW/1/J/1/5/01

intended to attend the women's conference. This experience may have
clouded her own perceptions of the value of the IWSA afterwards.[53]

In November 1929, Kamaladevi wrote about the Berlin conference for the *Indian Ladies' Magazine* and was critical of the ways in
which Indian delegates and India had been demeaned and dimin-
ished. 'India hardly had any place in the international gathering', she
claimed, 'the Indians simply did not matter, so little was India known,
so little had she asserted herself'. Although Indian delegates had been
invited for years, they were not allowed to speak in the main proceedings. 'It came as a surprise to many of the people there that Indian
delegates were able to follow and partake in proceeding', Kamaladevi
observed, 'and that they were accustomed to such huge gatherings
in their country'.[54] It was these feelings of being slighted that may

[53] NMML, Kamaladevi Chattopadhyay Papers, file 137, 'Activities of a [*sic*]
Indian Freedom Fighter Abroad' (undated).

[54] 'The International Woman's Congress: Mrs Chatopadhyaya's Impressions', *Indian Ladies' Magazine* (November–December 1929): 218.

also have influenced Lakshmipathi to reject Western clothing and languages after the 1926 conference.

The other Indian delegates were Dorothy Jinarajadasa, Dhanvanthi Rama Rau, Miss Krishna (a student in Paris), and Mrs Matthai. Miss D. M. Gunasekara was a delegate from Ceylon. In her memoirs published in 1978, Rama Rau made various mistakes about the conference, suggesting it took place in 1932 and describing it as the first time that Indians had been invited to attend the conference. However, she recalled: 'The subject before the conference concerned Western women only, for India had not yet begun to play an active part in international conferences. We were supposed to be only observers and could not introduce questions of suffrage and equal citizens' rights that concerned India.'[55] Rama Rau, the wife of an Indian diplomat, was, however, invited to become a member of the board of the Alliance. Having attended the 1929 Berlin Congress, she had also gone to a meeting at Marseilles in 1933. The Alliance was keen to appoint a non-European and as Rama Rau lived in Britain, it was very convenient for her to attend regular meetings.[56]

The Berlin conference had been the first international gathering of women Rama Rau had attended and her board membership naturally gave her experience of international work for women's rights; she later attended board meetings in Paris and Amsterdam. In a letter to *Stri Dharma* on the Berlin conference, Rama Rau wrote of how encouraging it was to see the 'snow-white heads' of all the 'great women who have fought in the women's cause for the past 25 years'.[57] In March 1933, Rama Rau spoke about the Marseilles meeting to a group of women at the Minerva Café in London. She told the audience that Indian women had to deal with the same problems as women in the West, even though the differences between East and West appeared insurmountable. She explained that Indian women had insisted that their representative be sent to Marseilles because they recognized the value of international organization. They had also invited the Alliance

---

[55] Dhanvanthi Rama Rau, *An Inheritance: The Memoirs of Dhanvanthi Rama Rau* (London: Heinemann, 1978), 179.

[56] 'The Alliance Board', *International Woman's News* (May 1933): 61.

[57] 'India's Triumph at the Berlin Congress', *Stri Dharma* (August 1929): 439.

to hold its next conference in India.[58] In her memoirs later, Rama Rau reiterated this sense that, to the other women, Indian society, culture, and issues seemed 'almost unimaginably remote', though her membership gave her the opportunity to raise Indian problems for discussion.[59] Rama Rau and her counterparts found it difficult to substantially (or quickly) alter international perceptions about Indian women, but were keen to keep on trying.

Meanwhile, members of WILPF such as Jane Addams and Agnes Smedley had been corresponding with Indian women from 1921, keen that Indian women form a branch and attend their international conferences. Their focus was not on suffrage, and it was clear that on the broader issue of peace and international relations Indian women were less forthcoming about involvement. In 1929, the organization offered £20 to cover the travel and accommodation within Europe for a 'moderate nationalist' to attend the Prague Conference in August.[60] Kamaladevi Chattopadhyay and Shakuntala Paranjpe took up the invitation to attend. Yet Kamaladevi was fairly critical of the WILPF in a piece for *Stri Dharma* upon her return. She commended the league for their good intentions but likened them to a 'drawing room affair' whose members lacked enough appropriate awareness of international relations. Kamaladevi told her Indian readers that she and Paranjpe had taken up the opportunity to speak in Prague as India was always keen to put her case before the European public. 'The West is so tragically ignorant of India', Kamaladevi opined, and she criticized the 'villainous propaganda' spread by the British about India in the European press. Kamaladevi spoke to the WILPF about the subjection of India by British rule.[61] This was a platform where Indian women could present themselves in an international context, to discuss the consequences of imperialism, asking for moral support from women

[58] 'International Feminism', *The Vote*, 21 April 1933, 122.

[59] Rama Rau, *An Inheritance*, 179.

[60] SCPC, WILPF India Section, International Secretary to Lady Chatterjee, 4 July 1929.

[61] Kamaladevi Chattopadhyaya, 'The International Congress of the Women's League for Peace and Freedom', *Stri Dharma* (November 1929): 563–4. Kamaladevi's surname was spelt in two different ways, depending on publications—either 'Chattopadhyay' or 'Chattopadhyaya'.

from other non-imperial countries. Following her tour of Europe, which had included a visit to the League against Imperialism in Frankfurt, Kamaladevi did have one positive suggestion; she returned to India eager for the AIWC to improve its election process for office-bearers and present a more modern and outgoing climate.[62]

At the same time (1928 and 1929), Cousins toured various countries and obtained messages of goodwill for Indian women. The executive council of WILPF had met in Lyon and passed a resolution in support of the demand made by Indian women for self-government. Similar resolutions were passed by branches of the league in America including Philadelphia, the inter-racial branch in New York, Detroit, Cleveland, Pittsburgh, Boston, Chicago, New Haven, Swarthmore, San Francisco, and Winnipeg.[63] Cousins was particularly happy that during her international tour she was able to disabuse women of the notion of the backwardness of Indian women, delighting in telling audiences of the franchise equality that Indian men and women enjoyed (neglecting to discuss the low proportion of enfranchised Indian women). Like Kamaladevi, Cousins suggested that British viewpoints, as well as those of Christian missionaries, had allowed exaggerations and untruths about India to spread in the Western world. Cousins was also especially keen to draw the favourable comparison between enfranchised Indian women and unenfranchised women in France and Switzerland.[64]

At a public meeting in London in October 1933, Rajkumari Amrit Kaur, Shareefah Hamid Ali, and Sarojini Naidu told the audience that India had to develop a 'co-operative international mind' to obtain real freedom and secure her 'proper place in the world'.[65] Despite growing nationalist sentiments, Indian women realized the value of engaging with internationalist thought and placing their suffrage campaigns within this broader internationalist movement.

[62] NMML, Kamaladevi Chattopadhyay Papers, file 97, undated reminiscences of 1929 European tour.

[63] 'Notes and Comments', *Stri Dharma* (November 1929): 1.

[64] Margaret E. Cousins, 'World Sisterhood', *Stri Dharma* (November 1929): 10.

[65] TWL, 3AMS/C/5/16, Meliscent Shepherd Correspondence, Shepherd to Miss Neilans, 1 November 1933.

So Indian women continued to meet at European conferences in the 1930s. In 1930, eight female delegates representing India— Dr Norona, Mrs Sahani, Miss Rustomji, Mrs Srivastava, Mrs Patel, Lady Meherbai Tata, Dorothy Jinarajadasa, and Mrs Jackson—attended the ICW conference in Vienna.[66] The WIA had asked the council to support the claim for Indian self-government, but the resolution was not brought forward at the conference.[67] Mrs Maneklal Premchand led a delegation of ten Indians to the 1934 ICW in Paris. Each delegate was assigned a particular responsibility and it was Rama Rau who attended the suffrage standing committee.[68] At the 1936, ICW conference in Dubrovnik, Dr Kashibai Navrange led the Indian delegation. However, she only attended the finance and child welfare meetings and it does not appear as though franchise was a concern at this Yugoslavian conference.[69] In 1936, Maneklal Premchand became one of the vice-presidents of the ICW. In 1939, the board included Kunwar Rani Maharaj Singh from India as the fourth vice-president (described as a charming, capable woman by Rosa Manus).[70]

In 1936, WILPF turned down the request for affiliation from a British-headed peace organization in Calcutta as they wanted the Indian section to be led by Indian women.[71] Meanwhile, the Equal Rights International association was keen to expand membership and open a branch in India. Their chair, Helen Archdale, wrote a number of letters to Indian women, such as Rama Rau, Reddi, Hamid Ali, and Shahnawaz, in 1933 and 1934, hoping they would be able to form a branch for international work on the equality of sexes.[72] There was

---

[66] *Stri Dharma* (August 1930).

[67] 'The Indian Delegation at Vienna', *Indian Ladies' Magazine* (September 1930): 110.

[68] LoN, Legal, General, Status of Women, Correspondence with All-India Women's Conference.

[69] LoN, Social, General, File 9668/Series 9668, *National Council of Women in India, 6th Biennial Report, 1936–7*, 48.

[70] Mineke Bosch, ed., *Politics and Friendship: Letters from the International Woman Suffrage Alliance, 1902–1942* (Columbus: Ohio State University Press, 1990), 250.

[71] Rupp, *Worlds of Women*, 79.

[72] TWL, 5ERI/1/A/09, Equal Rights International, Correspondence with India.

little enthusiasm for another international women's organization though from Indians who were already chafing at the management of the IASWEC and ICW. As Margot Badran has argued using the example of Egyptian women, the IAW ignored colonial realities, trying to amalgamate national and imperial feminisms under the umbrella of international feminism. These universalizing tendencies felt oppressive to women who wished to discuss their particular struggles.[73] Although Indian women were thinking internationally and were eager to place their suffrage campaign within an international setting, they were happier in personal transnational networks and interactions than in the kind of organizations that resembled the domineering imperialism or Eurocentrism they were trying to break free from. After Berlin in 1929, the IAWSEC did not meet again in congress till 1935 in Istanbul. I will discuss this and subsequent meetings in Chapter 4 (as well as the 1936 joint ICW and NCWI meeting held in Calcutta), when the focus of Indian suffragette attention turned more obviously towards Asia and the 'East' rather than the broad, homogenizing international space of these earlier meetings that are the focus of this chapter.

Indian Suffragettes and the League of Nations

The League of Nations, founded in 1920 and based in Geneva, was not designed to interfere with 'domestic' issues such as suffrage, political equality, or self-determination. However, it was an organization designed to support peace and intervene for the welfare of human beings. In May 1921, Dorothy Jinarajadasa, on behalf of the WIA, wrote to the League of Nations regarding women in Vilna, Lithuania. The WIA expressed concern and opposition to the news that women would not be able to vote in a proposed Polish–Lithuanian plebiscite and urged the league to ensure the principle of equality was observed. Claiming that women were of 'equal importance in any community' and suggesting that Europe was not observing the principle of sex equality that had been acknowledged recently in Madras, the WIA clearly felt that the League had a role in ensuring not only the plebiscite, but also ensuring, more broadly, that women enjoyed

---

[73] Badran, *Feminists, Islam, and Nation,* 108–9.

political equality.[74] Indian women, then, began to engage with the League of Nations on the issue of suffrage from the outset, clearly agreeing with the international women's organizations that suffrage was an international, and not merely national, issue.

During the 1930s, Indian women, mainly through the AIWC, began to demand more Indian female representation at the League, particularly on the committee relating to child welfare and the trafficking of women. This was related to ongoing demands for greater female political representation in India. Radhabai Subbarayan, Begum Shahnawaz, and Shareefah Hamid Ali all became consecutive members of this committee, visiting Geneva for meetings. Indian women were also interested in, and became members of, the committee related to the nationality of married women from 1931 (as I will discuss in the next chapter). In September 1933, while Reddi, Kaur, and Hamid Ali were meeting the Joint Parliamentary Committee (JPC) on constitutional reforms in London, their attention was also drawn to the League. An Indian women's deputation (Kaur, Hamid Ali, Keron Bose, Ammu Swaminadhan) submitted a note to the president of the Council of the League of Nations on the lack of representation of Indian female opinion in the council. They suggested that Indian women constituted one-fifth of the world's women and that they were 'systematically studying the problems connected with the position, rights, and duties of women and could, therefore, co-operate to international advantage' with the League.[75] This engagement with the League typifies Indian women's desires for recognition of their worth on the international stage.

In addition, from 1934 to 1938, the AIWC sent their annual reports and resolutions to the League of Nations for their information. These included resolutions such as that in 1934 for full adult franchise and the improved representation of Indian women on political bodies, including the League of Nations.[76] Much of this correspondence was with appropriate members of League committees including Erik

---

[74] LoN, Political, File 12306/Series 1226, Jinarajadasa letter, 25 May 1921.

[75] LoN, General and Miscellaneous, File 7025/Series 7025, Note to President of the Council of the League of Nations, 27 September 1933.

[76] LoN, Social, General 11A, f. 9668, All-India Women's Conference Sessions. Amrit Kaur to A. C. Chatterjee, 25 January 1934; Agatha Harrison to E. Ekstrand, 28 January 1934; Amrit Kaur to E. Ekstrand, 13 February 1935.

Ekstrand, who was director of the social questions section from 1931. Princess Gabrielle Radziwill, from Lithuania, was responsible for maintaining relations with voluntary and women's organizations. She corresponded with a number of Indian women, including Shareefah Hamid Ali, then treasurer of the AIWC, in 1935. Hamid Ali had met Radziwill in London and Geneva during her visit in 1933, and early in 1935 sent Radziwill copies of the recommendations of the Indian women's associations' franchise committee. In response, Radziwill asked Hamid Ali if the women's associations would be happy to send free copies of *Stri Dharma* for the League library. The League kept all these records of memoranda and meetings regarding the Indian female franchise question as they were sent to them, expressing interest although refraining from any kind of intervention. These Indian female leaders clearly felt that their suffrage rights were an international matter, one that should be considered as much by the League of Nations as by international women's associations.[77]

In 1935, the League undertook a survey on the status of women worldwide. Governments were invited to complete questionnaires relating to the political, civic, and economic status of women in their countries. Within this remit, governments were invited to include information on the enfranchisement and political representation of women. The Government of India complied with a breakdown of women voters in the provinces of British India although they made it clear that 'this is a domestic concern of peculiar complexity in view of (1) the close connection between religious and social custom in India, and (2) the variety of religions and races in the country'. Further, the secretary of state asserted that the League of Nations would not be able to intervene in alleviating existing inequalities relating to suffrage and political representation as domestic leaders were aware of the problems. He argued that outside intervention would not help the gradual process of solving them in India.[78]

---

[77] LoN, General and Miscellaneous, File 7025/Series 7025, Shareefah Hamid Ali to Princess Radziwill, 1 February 1935; Radziwill to Hamid Ali, 4 March 1935; Hamid Ali to E. Ekstrand, 10 February 1936.

[78] LoN, Legal, General, File 25904/Series 18243, Status of Women, Communications from Governments and Women's International Organisations (A.33.1936.V.), 6 April 1936, 19.

The IAWSEC and ICW also decided to provide information to the League, undertaking their own surveys from members, including information on India's female enfranchisement. They were keen for the League of Nations to intervene for unenfranchised women. The ICW hoped for an international convention based on the principle of equality of rights for both sexes. Arguing that increasing the number of women voters worldwide would be highly influential in promoting peace and security, the ICW discussed the benefits that women had accrued by visiting other countries where women already had the experience of suffrage. 'The constructive work done by women's international organizations in bringing women of many nationalities together at meetings and congresses, and keeping up contacts by letter, must be reckoned as a considerable factor in the peace propaganda of our time.'[79]

The League of Nations differed from international women's groups, because of its wider remit, its more overtly political nature, and its membership of men and women. Though the League of Nations ultimately decided that they could not and should not intervene on the issue of women's political rights, Indian suffragettes enjoyed the opportunity to correspond with the League and present their suffrage rights as a matter of international concern. In engaging with the League, the question of Indian national self-determination also became more pressing as Indian women were keen that their voice and opinions on their domestic struggles were heard equally on the international stage.

Indian Suffragettes in the United States of America

It was relatively easy for Indian suffragettes to visit international meetings and conferences in Europe as they followed well-worn shipping routes from India to Britain via Suez and the Mediterranean. The majority of Indian suffragettes attended these European gatherings via the imperial metropolis. Many of the European countries they visited (notably France) also held empires at this time. Therefore, their

---

[79] LoN, Legal, General, File 25904/Series 18243, Status of Women, Communications from Governments and Women's International Organisations (A.33.1936.V.), 25 May 1937, 73–4.

European experiences were often mediated through experiences in Britain and navigation of imperial and colonial feminist networks. However, these international feminist organizations had a large number of American delegates too, without obvious imperial ties; leading feminists of this era included American feminists such as Carrie Chapman Catt and Jane Addams. Indian engagement with American suffragists encouraged Indians to think more internationally and globally in the depth and breadth of their engagement with questions of international suffrage and feminism.

As with the rest of the world, Indian connection with Americans and migration to America was longstanding. However, in an experience similar to that of Indians overseas in imperial colonies, there was little engagement with the suffrage rights of Indians who lived in America. Between 1908 and 1922 at least 69 Indians gained US citizenship through 'naturalization' by claiming legal whiteness. These claims to belong ethnically to the 'Caucasian' race through racial and caste distinction reveal the ambiguities towards racial identity that some Indians were able to exploit. However, after the 1923 case *The United States v. Bhagat Singh Thind*, when the Supreme Court ruled that to be Caucasian did not mean to be 'white', the government denaturalized the majority of Indians who had previously been awarded citizenship rights.[80]

However, just as the issue of race and racial hierarchies was important, though often hidden, in the suffrage rights of Indians living in other countries in Australasia, Africa, and the Americas, it is important to consider the racial makeup of the American suffrage movement and how this had an effect on relations between American and Indian suffragettes. The American women who attended the IWSA conferences were generally racially 'white' and race was not discussed. The African American Mary Church Terwell attended the

[80] See Nico Slate, *Colored Cosmopolitanism: The Shared Struggle for Freedom in the United States and India* (Cambridge, MA: Harvard University Press, 2012), 28–31. See also Harold A. Gould, *Sikhs, Swamis, Students, and Spies: The India Lobby in the United States, 1900–1946* (New Delhi: Sage, 2006), 266–72; Joan M. Jensen, *Passage from India: Asian Indian Immigrants in North America* (New Haven: Yale University Press, 1988), chap. 12. It appears that the Indians involved in these citizenship cases were mainly men.

1904 ICW in Berlin and the 1919 WILPF in Zurich, but because she had 'pale skin' her racial background did not seem to be remarked upon.[81] The celebrated successes of American suffrage in this period failed to overtly discuss—in an international setting—the ways in which African American women (and men) were excluded from the franchise as a result of voter registration restrictions (which were in place until 1965). That is not to say, unlike the Australian case, that there were no African American suffragists. Black American women were involved in the suffrage fight from the nineteenth century. Indian women also engaged with African American women on other political issues, especially through the International Council of Women of the Darker Races (founded in 1920) and later through the National Association for the Advancement for Colored People (NAACP).[82] However, there is little evidence of any close relationship between Indian and African American suffragettes. Nor were any parallels on the issue of enfranchisement, based on racial subjection, drawn explicitly between these groups.

Indian nationalists had been organizing in the space of America since the 1910s, and so bringing in discussion of Indian female suffrage to an American audience was not absurd. In 1921, the *Independent Hindustan*, the organ of the Gadar Party in San Francisco, published an interview with Lila Singh conducted by Agnes Smedley, partner of Virendranath Chattopadhyay. She described Singh as an Indian suffragist. Educated in Calcutta, Singh was married to an educationalist, Deep Narayan Singh, whom she was accompanying on a tour of the United States. Fluent in English, Singh had met a number of American women through her travels and was particularly keen to discuss the need to improve educational provisions for women in India. Singh suggested that India's isolation from the rest of the world was one of the reasons behind poor educational records in India, but she pointed to the successes and role models in women such as Naidu, the Tatas, and Mrinalini Sen. Therefore, she not only issued a demand for equal educational opportunities for men and

[81] Christine Bolt, *Sisterhood Questioned? Race, Class and Internationalism in the American and British Women's Movements, c. 1880s–1970s* (Abingdon: Routledge, 2005), 77.

[82] Slate, *Colored Cosmopolitanism*, 91, 138.

women in India, but also insisted women take a more active part in public life. Additionally, she demanded 'self-government and equal political rights.[83]

As Indian women slowly became enfranchised during the 1920s, reports of their achievements reached American audiences through the pages of the NWP organ *Equal Rights*. Before this, in 1920, the American weekly paper the *Literary Digest* had reported on the failures of the 1919 Government of India Act to enfranchise women and the deep disappointment of many Indians at this.[84] For *Equal Rights*, Cousins sent in accounts of Indian women at the polls in 1923.[85] Kamaladevi Chattopadhyay's election speech in 1926 was reproduced, even though the paper knew she had lost the election by then.[86] In 1923, a barrister, Indu Bhushan Sen, wrote an article, 'The Hindu Woman', which discussed various advances for Indian women including municipal enfranchisement.[87] Reports on franchise successes were also produced in 'Current History' and the *Literary Digest*.[88] These reports all showed that there was international interest in Indian suffrage and that news was being circulated outside of the environs of the Indian subcontinent.

In 1924, Dorothy Jinarajadasa visited America and spoke about the work of the WIA in over 30 cities.[89] It is clear that the rhetoric of American women's organs differed from those in India. In an

[83] Agnes Smedley, 'Women and New India', *Independent Hindustan* (May 1921): 10–11.

[84] 'Suffrage Denied Indian Women', *Equal Rights*, 20 March 1920, 35.

[85] 'Indian Women at the Polls', *Equal Rights*, 22 December 1923, 354; 'Indian Women at the Polls', *Equal Rights*, 8 March 1924, 26. See also 'Progress in India', *Literary Digest*, 10 January 1925, 378.

[86] 'India's Needs', *Equal Rights*, 25 December 1926, 365.

[87] Indu Bhushan Sen, 'The Hindu Woman', *Equal Rights*, 22 September 1923, 251. He then had a letter to the editor published the following year in which he discussed how *Equal Rights* was being read in India and how women were agitating for the legislative vote in his province of Bengal ('Correspondence', *Equal Rights*, 15 December 1924, 319).

[88] See 'Women's Progress in India', *The Literary Digest*, 22 January 1927, 20; 'India's Two Kinds of Women', *The Literary Digest* 30 March 1929, 17.

[89] Women's Indian Association, *Reports for the Years 1924–5, 1925–6* (Adyar: Women's Indian Association, 1926), 10.

editorial in *Equal Rights* entitled 'Congratulations to the Orient', in June 1926, Indian women were congratulated for resolutions that now allowed them to be elected to public office in all legislatures. This was seen as 'indication of the spread of Feminism in India', even though 'feminism' was not a popular term among Indian campaigners.[90] With greater contact, through Indian visits to America, these comparisons in achievement and terminology would be brought to light more clearly.

Over 1928 and 1929, Cousins and Naidu both visited America and addressed a large breadth of women's clubs. Cousins was pleased to report on the successful response to Naidu's addresses at dozens of these clubs.

> It was a great happiness to me to see the triumphant effect she made, not for herself but for India, on a Luncheon audience of 1,700 people in New York under the auspices of the Foreign Policy Association. Sarojini Devi is a member of the world sisterhood of whom every woman may feel proud. She and I can bear testimony to the unstinted kindness and hospitality shown to us by every type of American woman.[91]

The *New York Times* heralded Naidu's visit in October 1928 by describing her as sponsor and leader of the feminist movement. The report was also keen to point out that the Indian suffrage movement was not merely populated by 'intelligent commoners of high caste' but that princesses and rulers had also taken up the cause.[92] In February 1929, Naidu and Cousins addressed the NWP in Washington. Naidu told her audience that Indian women did not have the time to be feminists while they campaigned for both national freedom and political equality.[93] She also told audiences, 'I do not like what you call feminism', describing it as a bad inferiority complex, aiming to be like men.[94]

---

[90] 'Congratulations to the Orient', *Equal Rights*, 19 June 1926, 149.

[91] Cousins, 'World Sisterhood', *Stri Dharma* (November 1929): 12. See also 'Woman, Bombay Ex-Mayor, Tells Her Own Story Here', *Chicago Daily Tribune*, 29 October 1928, 31.

[92] 'India's Poetess to Visit America', *New York Times*, 14 October 1928, 14.

[93] 'News from the Field', *Equal Rights*, 23 February 1929, 24; 'Indian Feminist Movement', *Equal Rights*, 2 March 1929, 28–9.

[94] *The Woman's Journal* (1929) quoted in Bolt, *Sisterhood Questioned?*, 64.

During her trip Naidu reflected on the international women's movement as well. She visited Canada and clearly enjoyed this North American trip. To her daughter, in April 1929, Naidu pondered on the positive responses she had received from audiences abroad. 'I can rise to greater heights in international gatherings abroad than in India. It is the *quality* of the audiences and environment that makes all the difference.'[95] As she was also visiting the USA in the aftermath of the publication of Katherine Mayo's *Mother India*, Naidu was keen to counter some of Mayo's stereotypical comments about India; she also spoke at numerous African American and Jewish organizations, drawing links with Indian struggles.[96] In 1931 Naidu told the *New York Press* that there was no difference between Eastern and Western women. She argued that women all over the world were united by a 'truly mystical sisterhood', but equally that women of one nation did not owe any debt to women of another. 'The longer I have talked to my Western sisters, here or in America, the more I have been impressed by the similarity of thought and ideal.'[97]

Malati Patwardhan, secretary of the WIA and editor of *Stri Dharma*, visited America in 1930. She spoke to the NWP in Washington too, and discussed the social and political movements that women were involved in India. Patwardhan graced the cover of the NWP organ *Equal Rights* on 5 July 1930, shaking the hand of Mrs Paul Linebarger of the NWP. As the paper pointed out, Patwardhan said, 'I refuse to be a Feminist' and then 'promptly proved that she is one because of her firm conviction that men and women should work together on a basis of equality'.[98] However, it was clear that American and Indian ideas and use of the term 'feminism' still varied in the 1930s.

---

[95] Paranjape, *Naidu Selected Letters*, 226, Sarojini Naidu to Leilamani Naidu, 7 April 1929.

[96] W. E. B. DuBois presided over a reception to Naidu in Brooklyn and described her as India's 'greatest woman' ('Entertain India's Greatest Woman', *Chicago Defender*, 19 January 1929, 11 quoted in Sinha, *Specters of Mother India*, 103).

[97] 'Women of Orient and West Alike in Ideals', *Indian Ladies' Magazine* (January 1932): 299.

[98] 'Women in India', *Equal Rights*, 28 June 1930, 165.

Indian women continued to perceive the term to imply sex division rather than understand the term in its broadest sense. Though they were engaged in feminist campaigns for equal rights and opportunities for men and women, they did not recognize that they could easily appropriate the term 'feminism' for their activities.

In 1931, Cousins complained to Hanna Sheehy Skeffington that though she believed that the NWP were the 'most vital women' they 'are not interested in either Ireland or India in a way to help them get political freedom'.[99] However, American interest in Indian suffrage campaigns, through the paper *Equal Rights*, was growing during the 1930s. In 1931, Dr Kalidas Nag spoke about 'Women in India' to an audience at the Ohio home of NWP member Mrs Valentine Winters. He gave a glowing account of the progress that Indian women had made in the past 50 years. Winters had met Naidu at a conference in Washington in 1930 and was keen to corroborate Nag's observations that Indian women were gaining political recognition and responsibility in many ways in advance of American women.[100]

During 1931, *Equal Rights* published a number of articles reflecting on Indian franchise demands. This included a report on the activities of Indian women (Shahnawaz and Subbarayan) at the RTC in London, demanding enfranchisement and representation.[101] In July 1931, an article written by Bhagat Ram from the Punjab discussed the demands being made to Congress to not only recognize the need to enfranchise women on the same terms as men, but also to modify property laws so that women could inherit and own property in their own right.[102] Cousins was then back in America and addressed an audience at the Cosmos Club in Washington in August 1931 in which she talked about her own experiences in the Indian women's movement.[103]

---

99 NLI, Sheehy Skeffington Papers, MS 41,177/12, Cousins to Hanna Sheehy Skeffington, 31 December 1931.

100 'Women in India', *Equal Rights*, 4 April 1931, 69.

101 'Feminist Notes', *Equal Rights*, 25 April 1931, 95. See also 'Indian Women Want Full Equality', *Literary Digest*, 22 October 1932, 14.

102 Bhagat Ram, 'Women's Place in the Future Constitution of India', *Equal Rights*, 11 July 1931, 183–4.

103 'Close-up of Indian Feminism', *Equal Rights*, 5 September 1931, 245.

In September 1932, Mayadevi Gangulee addressed the NWP in Washington on the women's movement in India. Gangulee's husband was made Commander of the British Empire; she had worked with Gandhi since 1929, and was visiting America for a year at the invitation of the American branch of the Indian National Congress. Gangulee was eager to explain to the NWP that the Indian demand for franchise equality was not born out of a 'modern feminist slogan' but was a demand for the re-entitlement of rights that Indian women had enjoyed in the past, noting that Indian women had once reigned with equal sovereignty alongside men. She discussed the solidarity of Indian women who did not wish to be divided electorally into communal sections. Gangulee described the successful tactics that Indian suffrage campaigners had already employed in peacefully picketing electioneering campaigns and polling booths. She closed her address by invoking her hope to create an Indo-American Women's Fellowship League during her visit.

On the morning of her talk, Gangulee laid a wreath at the suffrage monument in the Capitol. At the busts of Susan B. Anthony, Lucretia Mott, and Elizabeth Cady Stanton, Gangulee thanked 'America's foremost sisterhood' (the NWP) for inviting 'its sisters of India' here. She thanked American women for their sympathies towards the aspirations of Indian women, which gave them spiritual incentive in their fights for equal rights for all women. 'I fervently hope and pray that the natural indivisibility of women, as a whole, will come to be realized, not merely as an abstract belief,' she asserted, 'but in the earnest endeavor to draw them closer together, in unsectarian spirit, to promote an universal recruitment of their service for the sake of human welfare.'[104]

Interviewed by the *Brooklyn Daily Eagle* in August 1932, Gangulee was described as being famous in India for her work on women's suffrage and her alliance with Gandhi. In addition to her work with the American branch of the Indian National Congress, Gangulee told the paper that she wished to observe American elections during

[104] 'The Woman Movement in India', *Equal Rights*, 8 October 1932, 283–4; SCPC, WILPF, US Section, Correspondence, India: Text of address by Mayadevi Gangulee before the National Woman's Party in Washington, 28 September 1932.

her visit. She explained that she had become an 'ardent feminist' (note her willing use of the term) when an Indian editorial had declared that Indian women should be classed electorally alongside the 'depressed caste' (note her evident caste prejudices). She further wondered, as universal suffrage was unlikely to be introduced in India yet, whether a compromise solution would work with female-only electorates to elect women candidates.[105] In a letter to Jane Addams in November 1932 from New York, Gangulee admitted her astonishment and appreciation of the warm sympathy she had experienced in favour of Indian women in spite of the 'virus injected' by 'British agents' against Indians in the minds of the American public. She asked Addams if she could urge WILPF to support Indian women in their demands for equal political rights, as they were being made at the RTCs in London. 'Since the WILPF stands for and aims to unite women in all countries,' Gangulee argued, 'I think, the cause of the women of India is deserving of your generous treatment.'[106]

Gangulee also approached Richard Gregg in Boston, asking if a campaign could be started in the USA in support of women's franchise as it was being discussed at the Third RTC in London. She wanted the support of American voices not only in favour of equal rights for women but also to protest against communal representation, and urged the International Women's League and NWP to send statements to the US. 'It would be a wonderful gesture on the part of the American women's bodies, who avow the policy of international interest in behalf of the women's cause, all over the world.' Gregg discussed the matter with Martha Elliott of the WILPF about whether it would be appropriate to intervene in this matter as it was being considered by the British government. He told Elliott that it would be good for the British government to learn that American public opinion was interested in Indian women's suffrage and hoped an intervention would stimulate mutual sympathy between American and Indian women's

[105] 'Fill Jails to Win, Urges Hindu Woman', *Brooklyn Daily Eagle*, 25 August 1932, 7.

[106] SCPC, WILPF, US Section, Correspondence, India: Mayadevi Gangulee to Jane Addams, 3 November 1932.

organizations.[107] Although these interventions did little to change policy, Gangulee was successfully engaging Americans and ensuring that the Indian suffrage fight was becoming an international issue and not merely an imperial one.

In 1933, Muthulakshmi Reddi visited America and attended the ICW conference in Chicago. The subject of the conference was 'creative citizenship' and Reddi was able to draw upon her experiences in the Madras Legislature for her speech. Welcomed and appreciated at the conference, Reddi was also invited to speak at various other parties and events, including a visit to New York, with all her American travel expenses paid for by the National Council of Women in America. She recalled how American audiences were enthralled by her fluency in English and her saris. For her part, she was interested to meet African American women at the congress. Reddi appreciated the interest that American women had in the Indian women's movement and their awareness of her own achievements, particularly proud that she was referred to as the 'Jane Adam of India' [sic]. She believed that she received genuine appreciation from American women: 'Even though I discovered that spirit in the cultured and enlightened womanhood of every country and nation, the American woman seemed to possess it immensely.'[108]

Indian suffragettes were clearly enjoying the interest some American women had in their suffrage fight. This was especially important to them in the face of Mayo's criticisms of Indian practices in her 1927 book *Mother India*. In the USA, Indian visitors were able to discuss Indian successes and debate the nature of feminism. Naidu was most vocal about her dislike for the term 'feminist', but she did celebrate the international woman's movement and the common rights of humanity that women around the world were able to assert together.[109] Intersections of racial subjection and the needs of the labouring classes, within the international women's movement,

[107] SCPC, WILPF, US Section, Correspondence, India: Mayadevi Gangulee to Richard B. Gregg, 28 October 1932; Richard B. Gregg to Martha Helen Elliott, 29 October 1932.

[108] NMML, S. Muthulakshmi Bound Speeches and Writings, handwritten undated notes on trip to USA.

[109] Sinha, *Specters of Mother India*, 205.

however, were not addressed as clearly. Indian fights for citizenship, as they were presented on the world state, were based on suppositions of a monolithic Indian identity that was unable to draw out the complexities of the ways in which women could be disenfranchised in India.

* * *

As India approached independence in 1947, universal adult suffrage had still not been introduced in India, and Indian women continued to engage with international organizations and travel. In 1947, the IAWSEC conference was held in Interlaken in Switzerland, and Konda Parvathy Devi attended on behalf of India with the Maharani of Vijayagram. In her report for the AIWC journal, *Roshni*, Parvathy Devi hoped that the dominance of European ladies would soon be usurped by women from Eastern and Pacific countries.[110] Thus, though Asian women were beginning to assert themselves in regional associations, as we shall see in the next chapter, there were still frustrations with the definition of the 'international' as India stood on the verge of independence. In the meantime, the United Nations had been set up in 1945, replacing the League of Nations at the end of the Second World War. Indian women were actively engaging with this new international body, where the issue of citizenship and equal rights was discussed. Shareefah Hamid Ali attended the first session of the Status of Women Commission in 1947, as a representative of the Government of India. This was held in the USA, and Hamid Ali pressed very hard for the inclusion of the right of adult franchise to be included in the new charter. She noted that it was British and American delegates who were most opposed to including this principle at face value for all countries, urging the need for education before franchise rights.[111] Her colleague Hansa Mehta went on to play a major role in ensuring that the United Nations Universal Declaration of Human Rights recognized that all human

[110] Konda Parvathy Devi, 'The Fourteenth Congress of the International Alliance of Women', *Roshni* (March 1947): 28–32.

[111] Shareefah Hamid Ali, 'My Visit to America II', *Roshni* (August 1947): 16–22.

beings, rather than just all men, were born free and the rights to equality did not have distinction based on sex.[112] There is little evidence of Indian suffragettes engaging with international socialist women's groups on the issue of suffrage. There were definite ways in which Indian women worked with socialist and communist groups, seen in the activities of Madame Cama in Paris, Kamaladevi in India and Europe, and Indian students at British universities such as Renuka Ray, who engaged with underground communist reading groups. However, in these struggles on the broader questions of universal social equality and the fight for Indian independence, concerns about Indian female franchise were subsumed by debates on the nature of the Indian state. As socialist campaigners realized, national independence was a priority first. International women's organizations such as the IWSA naively failed to acknowledge this necessity.

The comparisons Indian suffragettes made between their campaigns and international ones remained powerful throughout the interwar period. In 1934, an Assamese female politician remarked upon the need for women in India to be as 'free as their sisters in the West'. She pointed out that, apart from France, women had the vote in the majority of European countries, in the British Dominions, and the United States. Although women had the ability to be enfranchised in India, there was still large social inequality in franchise rights and obstacles to election of women to Indian legislatures.[113] It was clear that Indian women had to continue to organize and mobilize on this matter, and take heart and inspiration (directly and indirectly) from international successes. Just as British suffragists had campaigned for the right to vote in order to influence imperial politics, Indian women could begin to justify the need for a vote to influence India's place and relationship with world politics, exhibiting a clear international identity, engaging as they did with a range of international women's organizations and the League of Nations. However, as Madame Cama

---

[112] Susan Deller Ross, *Women's Human Rights: The International and Comparative Law Casebook* (Philadelphia: University of Pennsylvania Press, 2013), 548.

[113] 'Demands of Women', *Indian Ladies' Magazine* (September and October 1934): 189.

put it: 'I have nothing against American or English sisters [but] to establish internationalism in the world there must be nations first.'[114] Engagement with these international networks emphasized further to Indian suffragettes their imperial subjection and the need for equal citizenship within an independent state. Ultimately, the only way to win these citizenship rights was within a local and anti-colonial movement in India that ideally spoke to and for all Indian women, and that would hopefully create the bedrock of equality for women within a newly created national constitution.

---

[114] Quoted in Bolt, *Sisterhood Questioned?*, 88.

4

Indian Suffragettes and Asian, Oriental, or Eastern Networks

Indian suffragettes had been involved in various international feminist networks, but these were primarily with 'Western' or 'white' women, including Euro-American dominated organizations such as the IWSA and WILPF or colonial organizations such as the BDWSU and the BCL. Though Indian women expressed their loyalties to the colonial or global sisterhood, as international and local outlooks merged, they also looked to their more immediate vicinity and geographic region for female solidarity and inspiration. With growing interest in Indian nationalist ideas of pan-Asianism, they sought out networks based on similar experiences with women from other parts of Asia. Indian women had special relationships with their closest neighbours—women in Ceylon and Burma—but also looked to suffrage successes in countries slightly further afield such as Japan and China. This desire to solidify networks of Asian sisterhood was evident through the foundation of the AAWC in 1931. Indian suffragettes were also forming broader coalitions of 'Eastern' women, or 'Oriental' women, with whom, they argued, they shared stereotypically Asian interests in family, domesticity, tradition, and spiritualism in the pre-industrial 'Orient', thus perpetuating certain notions of Asian femininity and the place of suffrage and citizenship struggles within Asian contexts.

Western feminists commonly assumed that they were best placed to provide global leadership for women, accentuating difference such as, in the Indian case, literacy levels or the purdah system. It was the assumptions made about 'Eastern ways' by these organizations, which they had used to justify Western leadership, which eventually led women in 'Eastern' countries to insist that they could represent themselves and confront feminist Orientalism. Fiona Paisley has shown how non-Western women began to occupy the public office of transnational women's groups, demonstrating international feminism's progressive discourses, but she also showed how they continued to be regarded as objects of the civilizing mission.[1] We have seen this to some extent with Rama Rau. Although Elisabeth Armstrong has argued that Asian women consolidated their long-standing critique of Western feminism and developed feminist solidarity along a South–South axis in the 1940s and 1950s, Indian suffragettes were involved in assertions of Asian solidarity well before decolonization.[2]

However, in much of their rhetoric about Asian networks, Indian suffragettes were guilty of using 'self-Orientalizing' language and stereotypes about 'Eastern' women to accentuate their distinctiveness. They portrayed the experiences of Asian women as homogeneous, when, in fact, their social and political experiences and outlooks were often very different. Sultan Jahan of Bhopal, in her opposition to full female franchise in 1919, had argued that as an 'Asiatic', and a Muslim, woman, it was clear that the Western franchise did not necessarily fit the 'peculiar conditions of the East'.[3] Thus, in many ways

[1] Fiona Paisley, *Glamour in the Pacific: Cultural Internationalism and Race Politics in the Women's Pan-Pacific* (Honolulu: University of Hawai'i Press, 2009), 6–7.

[2] Elizabeth Armstrong, 'Before Bandung: The Anti-Imperialist Women's Movement in Asia and the Women's International Democratic Federation', *Signs: Journal of Women in Culture and Society* 41, 2 (2016): 306.

[3] Bodleian, Southborough Papers, MSS Eng c.7355, Sultan Jahan of Bhopal to IWEA, 10 April 1919.

Indian suffragettes allowed for a perpetuation of ideas and language about Orientalist differences between women and justification for Indian suffrage to become less of a priority than Western campaigns. Yet, their interaction with Asian networks were examples of the ways in which Indian suffragettes were rejecting Western-dominated feminist networks and ties of imperial solidarity, while asserting themselves in new ways by establishing new connections on the international stage. I will explore this range of connections, and the language Indian suffragettes used to describe themselves—invariably as Eastern, Asian, or Oriental—in this chapter. How useful was 'Asian' identity in forging new bonds of female campaiging in the suffrage fight in India?

The desire to form pan-Asian feminist connections was indicative of the new internationalism of the interwar period. While Indian women were engaging with international organizations, including the League of Nations, simultaneously many men and women looked to form new alliances that decentred global networks away from the West. Asian networks related to suffrage campaigns existed before the 1930s. The WCTU, as I mentioned in Chapter 2, was particularly successful in forging branches and connections in Asia. The WCTU had formed branches in Burma, China, India, Japan, and Korea in the 1880s. Indeed, the WCTU had been influential in establishing connections between India and Japan through the visit of Indian reformer Pandita Ramabai to Japan in 1889. However, suffrage was not on the agenda for Indians at this time; though DuBois argues that the WCTU heritage was important for Asian suffrage as many of its protégés emerged as leaders in the 1920s and 1930s.[4] While Indian suffragettes looked to new Asian connections and identities, there were other attempts to organize women along regional lines in this period. These were designed to compete with the triennial conferences convened by the IAWSEC and included the 'Eastern Women's Congresses' in 1930 and 1932 in the Middle East.[5] In 1928, the first Pan-Pacific Women's Conference was held in Honolulu, out

---

[4] Ellen DuBois, 'Woman Suffrage: The View from the Pacific', *Pacific Historical Review* 69, 4 (2000): 547.

[5] Ellen DuBois and Haleh Emrani, 'A Speech by Nour Hamada: Tehran, 1932', *Journal of Middle East Women's Studies* 4, 1 (2008): 111.

of which the Pan-Pacific Women's Association (PPWA) was born in 1930.

Indian men were engaging concurrently with Asian networks, which probably provided some inspiration to Indian women. For example, the Japanese Pan-Asian Society convened a Pan-Asian Conference in 1920 and there was an Afro-Asian Conference held in Delhi in 1929.[6] Influenced by the organizational reach of the Comintern, Jawaharlal Nehru and the Indian National Congress attempted to cement Asian bonds through the League against Imperialism, and Indian trade unions organized together through associations such as the Pan-Pacific Trade Union and the Asiatic Labour Congress, while ideas about an all-Asian army were put forward by men such as the revolutionary nationalist Raja Mahendra Pratap.[7] The influence of Indian nationalist ideas about Asia and rejection of traditional imperial and Western networks was evident in the activities of Indian suffragettes in the 1930s and 1940s. It is particularly evident in the example of the AAWC in 1931 (the main focus of this chapter), the IAWSEC conference in Istanbul in 1935, and various other conferences, meetings, and dialogues in the build-up to and aftermath of the Second World War that I will discuss here.

Asian Identities

The AAWC, organized by Indian women, was actually the most successful Indian attempt in this period to foster Asian solidarity through a federation format. Birendra Prasad has argued that the

---

[6] Thomas Davies, *NGOs: A New History of Transnational Civil Society* (London: Hurst & Company, 2013), 98–9.

[7] Caroline Stolte and Harald Fischer-Tiné, 'Imagining Asia in India: Nationalism and Internationalism (ca. 1905–1940)', *Comparative Studies in Society and History* 54, 1 (January 2012): 65–92. See also Caroline Stolte, 'Bringing Asia to the World: Indian Trade Unionism and the Long Road towards the Asiatic Labour Congress, 1919–37', *Journal of Global History* 7, 2 (July 2012): 257–78; Caroline Stolte, '"Enough of the Great Napoleons!" Raja Mahendra Pratap's Pan-Asian Projects (1929–1939)', *Modern Asian Studies* 46, 2 (March 2012): 403–23.

idea for an Asiatic federation came directly out of Indian nationalist thought.[8] However, the inspiration for Indian women did not solely come from domestic, imperially inflected experiences. As we have seen, Indian women had been attending international suffrage conferences since at least 1920. They had observed how focus was often on their appearance or clothing rather than other cultural attributes. Their dependence on British women became evident in international meetings, owing to their lack of national independence. Indian suffragettes were looking at ways to assert themselves on a global stage. It was this 'embattled and precarious national consciousness' that had galvanized a drive towards internationalism and regionalism in a new direction.[9]

Margaret Cousins, who was so influential to India's suffrage movement, had a particular interest in Asian networks. Cousins was eager, as Catherine Candy has argued, that Indians should consolidate Asia as a cultural bloc by promoting their spiritual natures as a counter to Western modernity.[10] In 1922 Cousins published *The Awakening of Asian Womanhood*. In this book she discussed the symbolic unity of Asian womanhood in their desire for 'freedom', in their self-determination, and their independent initiative. Inspired by Theosophical teachings, she believed Asian women had a special spiritual affinity, although she acknowledged that there was little intercommunication between women in Asia, suggesting that Indian women knew more about the activities of British and American women than Chinese.[11] Despite conceptions of Asian commonality, Cousins privileged Indian experiences over other Asians. As some Indian women had been granted the right to vote in 1921, Cousins was optimistic that 'one day the women of India will lead the women of the East in all public movements'. Despite acknowledging

[8] Birendra Prasad, *Indian Nationalism and Asia (1900–1947)* (Delhi: B. R. Publishing Corporation, 1979), 174–6.

[9] Mrinalini Sinha, Donna J. Guy, and Angela Woollacott, 'Introduction: Why Feminisms and Internationalism?', *Gender & History* 10, 3 (1998): 351.

[10] Catherine Candy, 'Mystical Internationalism in Margaret Cousins' Feminist World', *Women's Studies International Forum* 32 (2009): 29–34.

[11] Margaret E. Cousins, *The Awakening of Asian Womanhood* (Madras: Ganesh and Co., 1922), 1–3.

that Burmese women had been granted the right to vote, that Chinese suffragettes had been involved in militant activities, and that Japanese women had started a branch of the International Women's League for Peace and Freedom, Cousins portrayed Indian women as natural leaders in the region, inspired by her own experience with the Indian women's movement in the past five years.[12]

During the 1920s, Cousins published regular articles in a series titled 'Women at Home and Abroad' in *New India*, an English-language newspaper published in Bombay and edited by Annie Besant. In August 1923 Cousins congratulated Burma for electing a woman to the Burmese Municipal Council and Central China for securing female suffrage and the seat for Wong Chang-Koo in parliament.[13] In November 1923 Cousins discussed 'Asia's contribution to World-Sisterhood' with similar remarks to those in *The Awakening of Asian Womanhood*: 'There is very little international knowledge and real friendship between the various Asian peoples'. She noted that Asian people had once been linked through Buddhism and were now able to communicate through the English language. Acknowledging the work of the League of Asian Peoples, and the Young Men's Christian Association (YMCA) and YWCA in bringing together Asian women, Cousins mentioned the work of the Russian Madame de Manziarly, who was travelling through Asia at the time, 'bringing the message of Asian Sisterhood and World Sisterhood to the women in every large city', having spent time in India and linking Indian women with women in Tokyo, Kyoto, Seoul, Peking, and Shanghai. A 'time must soon come', posited Cousins, 'when the needs of Asia as the exponent of Eastern civilisation will force her peoples ... into much closer friendly relationships with one another', suggesting that women in particular would be pivotal in these collaborations.[14]

In 1929, as an international representative of the WIA, Cousins collated messages of goodwill for Indian women following visits to various countries. She visited Tokyo and obtained a letter

[12] Cousins, *The Awakening of Asian Womanhood*, 8–12.

[13] Cousins, 'Our Special Article: Women at Home and Abroad', *New India*, 18 August 1923, 4.

[14] Cousins, 'Our Special Article: Women at Home and Abroad', *New India*, 24 November 1923, 4.

congratulating Indian women on their suffrage successes. It was signed by the principal of the Women's Medical College in Tokyo, members of the WCTU, the journalist Miss Shigi Tokenaka, Miss Ichikawa from the Women's Suffrage League, and others including Miss Casey from the Theosophical Society.[15] Cousins suggested that Indian women could influence Japanese women more wisely 'and more in accordance with their oriental nature' than American women whom, Cousins feared, Japanese women were imitating too slavishly. It was the gifts of 'the spiritual life' which Cousins decreed Indian women possessed that should be used for the 'enrichment of world sisterhood'.[16]

The spiritual value of the Indian subcontinent recurred through Cousins' dealings and writings. In 1927 she wrote to Muthulakshmi Reddi asking her to raise money to help Cousins go on pilgrimage from Srinigar to the Cave of Amarnath explaining that 'whatever benefit I get from the pilgrimage and journey through the high Himalayas you know will be shared with you + used for the good of India'.[17] Avabai Wadia, a Theosophist, remarked in her memoirs on the spiritualism of Besant and Cousins, and how this helped in their roles in the Indian women's movement. She explained how Besant and Cousins were 'deeply embued not only with the culture but the religious heritage of India', and so how they worked for, and with, Indians not as 'teacher' but as 'fellow seeker of truth and peace'.[18] Cousins was also keen to emphasize the distinctiveness, as she saw it, of an 'Asian' identity for women. In 1935 Wadia visited Geneva (aged 22) as the AAWC representative on the committee relating to the nationality rights for women. As she continued her work in this area, she received a letter from Cousins: 'I know from first hand how necessary it is that the Asian view of things should be retained in

[15] 'Notes and Comments', *Stri Dharma* (November 1929): 2.

[16] Margaret E. Cousins, 'World Sisterhood', *Stri Dharma* (November 1929): 14.

[17] NMML, S. Muthulakshmi Reddi Papers, Correspondence, 6 June 1927 Cousins to Reddi.

[18] Avabai B. Wadia, *The Light Is Ours: Memoirs and Movements* (London: International Planned Parenthood Federation, 2001), 27.

these international matters.... We thank you cordially for keeping the Asian flag flying.'[19]

The language about Asia and the Orient was evident in other women's organizations. The PPWA held its first conference in Hawai'i in 1928. Emerging out of work between American feminists and various ethnicities that were found in Hawai'i, the PPWA opened out to Polynesians, Japanese, and Chinese women beyond Hawai'i.[20] Paisley has argued that the success of the PPWA lay in the involvement of a broad range of non-Western women and the self-conscious internationalism and anti-racism they invested in, though there were inevitable fractures.[21] Its focus was primarily related to the struggles women of various races and ethnicities had with American 'imperialism'. Through Theosophical Society connections Indian women were invited as special guests (not as members of the PPWA) because, though they resided outside of the Pacific region, they were seen as a major element of the 'Orient'.[22] Burmese women were also invited to attend.[23] In 1933 the PPWA invited Kaur and Rajwade to attend the 1934 conference, expecting them to represent the women of India, Burma, and Ceylon, equating them together.[24] Although Indian women did not attend the PPWA conferences, the PPWA would prove a useful model and ally for Indian suffragettes during the 1930s and 1940s.

Five years after the publication of *The Awakening of Asian Womanhood*, Cousins was instrumental in the foundation of the

[19] Cousins to Wadia, 17 November 1937 in Wadia, *The Light Is Ours*, 67.

[20] Rumi Yasutake, 'The Rise of Women's Internationalism in the Countries of the Asia-Pacific Region during the Interwar Years, from a Japanese Perspective', *Women's History Review* 20, 4 (2011): 521–32. See also Paul F. Hooper, 'Feminism in the Pacific: The Pan-Pacific and Southeast Asia Women's Association', *The Pacific Historian* 20, 4 (Winter 1976): 367–78.

[21] Fiona Paisley, *Glamour in the Pacific: Cultural Internationalism and Race Politics in the Women's Pan-Pacific* (Honolulu: University of Hawai'i Press, 2009), Introduction.

[22] Paisley, *Glamour in the Pacific*, 52.

[23] IOR, Mss Eur D1230/3, NCWB Third Annual Report 1928.

[24] NMML, AIWC Papers, Microfilm 3, file 35, Georgina Sweet to Kaur and Rajwade, 7 November 1933.

All-India Women's Education Conference in January 1927. In 1926 Cousins sent circular letters to women across India, suggesting they organize local conferences to discuss educational issues. By 1928 the organization dropped the 'education' element from its title as members realized that educational issues could not be removed from social disabilities too. Although the AIWC decided to remain apolitical, many of its members (including key Gandhi allies Naidu and Rajkumari Amrit Kaur) were intimately involved in the nationalist movement.[25] As we shall see in the next chapter, the AIWC played a leading role in nationalist debates about female political participation and their political identity in the lead-up to, and after, the 1935 Government of India Act. The AIWC also played a leading role in the organization of the AAWC. However, there were concerns about the ethnic 'identity' of Indian suffragettes too. Despite Cousins's integral involvement in the AIWC, in 1936, some members were keen to dissociate from her because she was not racially Indian and they were unhappy with her appointment as honorary president that year.[26] However, after her death in Adyar in 1954, the AIWC named its national library in Delhi after Cousins.

Suffragettes in Burma and Ceylon

One of the issues Indians had with international feminism was the ongoing 'Orientalization' of all 'Asian' women. Even when Western feminists acknowledged that Asian women were not homogenous, they still assumed superiority. For example, as Lucy Delap has demonstrated, Western feminists portrayed Burmese women as modern (and especially more modern than their Indian counterparts), but failed to allow Burmese women any opportunity to participate in debates

[25] Geraldine H. Forbes, 'Caged Tigers: "First Wave" Feminists in India', *Women's Studies International Forum* 5, 6 (1982): 529; Geraldine H. Forbes, *Women in Modern India* (Cambridge: Cambridge University Press, 1998), 78–82. See also Aparna Basu and Bharati Ray, *Women's Struggle: A History of the All India Women's Conference 1927–2002*, 2nd ed. (Delhi: Manohar, 2002).

[26] Forbes, *Women in Modern India*, 78–83.

about feminism, especially before the First World War.[27] Burmese women had a close relationship with Indian women, compelled in many ways by their political relationship as Burma was governed as a province of British India until 1937. Rameshwari Nehru, editor of the Hindi women's journal *Stri Darpan*, was invited to Rangoon in the 1910s to help establish women's organizations.[28] In 1919, when the Government of India Bill was passed and the right to enfranchise women was delegated to the provinces, Burma quickly used this ability to enfranchise women on the same terms as men, although women could not run for election.[29] However, Maung Pu argued in *United India* that the new bill actually meant that Burmese women lost their previous right to vote in rural areas.[30] This argument about Burmese exceptionalism in terms of 'traditional' gender equality recurred continuously through Burmese suffrage debates.

The fight to allow Burmese women to be elected to political positions was not as straightforward. A motion was put forward in February 1927 to remove the sex disqualification for Burma electoral rules, but there was noticeable opposition. The home member argued that Burmese women had not 'progressed as far as her sister from the West' to be eligible to take up positions in representative institutions and suggested delaying a decision until 1932. On the other hand, during the debate, U Maung Gyee pointed out that some Indian women already had the right to be elected but that Burmese women had a stronger claim to political equality than Indian women because of historical claims to equality.[31] The motion

---

[27] Lucy Delap, 'Uneven Orientalisms: Burmese Women and the Feminist Imagination', *Gender & History* 24, 2 (August 2012): 389–410.

[28] Vir Bharat Talwar, 'Feminist Consciousness in Women's Journals in Hindi, 1910–1920', in *Recasting Women: Essays in Indian Colonial History*, ed. Kumkum Sangari and Sudesh Vaid (New Brunswick: Rutgers University Press, 1990), 216.

[29] See Chie Ikeya, *Refiguring Women, Colonialism, and Modernity in Burma* (Honolulu: University of Hawaiʻi Press, 2011), chap. 3.

[30] Maung Pu, 'The Position of Women in Burma', *United India*, 24 December 1919, 200–1.

[31] L/PJ/6/1848, Extract from *Rangoon Times*, 3 February 1927 and related memos.

was defeated. As a result, Burmese women came forward publicly to demand political rights; they argued that they had assumed they would have automatically received these equalities because of historical rights but now saw the need to be more vocal and active on this issue.

In 1926 the National Council of Women in Burma (NCWB) was set up as an affiliate of the NCWI, itself a unit of the ICW, and membership consisted of European, Burmese, and Indian women living in Burma. Members of the NCWB were represented on the central executive of the NCWI.[32] The NCWB organized a demonstration in support of the resolution in 1927 to allow women to become members of the legislature. Members marched to the legislative council building in Rangoon. About a hundred women, of various ethnicities, carried banners including ones with the names of Nancy Astor and Muthulakshmi Reddy emblazoned on them, as examples of women who sat on legislative bodies in Britain and India respectively and were an inspiration to them.[33] As this was a last-minute demonstration, it had little effect upon the debates, and it was not until 1929 that women could take up seats in the Burmese legislatures.

When Dorothy Jinarajadasa visited Rangoon in 1926, she spoke to the NCWB, remarking on the spread of branches of the National Council of Women around the world. She showed concern that Asian women seemed reluctant to start national associations and encouraged Burmese women to understand the value of international cooperation. Jinarajadasa reprimanded Burmese women for not lobbying for political positions for women despite having won the vote in 1921, as Indian women had done in gaining posts on municipal councils and as magistrates. Invoking the 'divine force' of women, she explained that women all over the world had a natural interest in other women and emphasized the spiritual background of the women's movement. Differing from Cousins, in that she

---

[32] BL, IOR, Mss Eur D1230/1, Papers of Sybil Mary Dorothy Bulkeley, National Council of Women in Burma 1927.

[33] Daw Mya Sein, 'Towards Independence in Burma: The Role of Women', *Asian Affairs* 3, 3 (October 1972): 296–7.

observed this spirituality beyond Asia, Jinarajadasa claimed that 'with the spiritual power that women could give to all kinds of work, she thought that salvation was going to come'.[34] One of the NCWB members who sat on the NCWI executive in 1927 was May Oung. Also known as Daw Mya Sein, Oung attended the AAWC at Lahore in 1931 and presided over a session. She was appointed secretary of the Liaison Committee that was formed afterwards to engage with the League of Nations and international organizations. She was then appointed by Cousins to represent the AAWC at the League of Nations in July 1931, as an alternative to Muthulakshmi Reddi, on a Women's Consultative Committee on Nationality. The other AAWC representative was Dr Rosa Welt Straus from Palestine, a member of the Palestine Jewish Women's Equal Rights Association.[35] Oung was also a member of the Equal Rights International organization, and was vice-chair in 1934.[36] She consistently argued that Burmese women had always enjoyed economic equality with men.[37] At the Burmese Round Table, which she attended in London in 1931, she further asserted that Burmese women enjoyed greater social and economic independence than Indian women.[38]

[34] NMML, S. Muthulakshmi Reddi Papers, Subject File 5. 'Women's National Council', *Rangoon Gazette*, 11 September 1926.

[35] LoN, 3E/Legal, Codification of International Law, file 25712/Series 25640, Nationality of Married Women: Consultation of Feminist Organisations, (Council) Resolution of 24 January 1931. See also NMML, All India Women's Conference Papers, Microfilm 1, Oung to Reddi, 19 April 1931.

[36] TWL, 5ERI/1/A/08, Equal Rights International Correspondence, Newsletter of the Six Point Group, March 1932; 5ERI/1/A/06, Equal Rights International letterhead, 8 May 1934.

[37] Daw Mya Sein, 'The Women of Burma: A Tradition of Hard Work and Independence', *Atlantic Monthly* (February 1958), http://www.theatlantic.com/magazine/archive/1958/02/the-women-of-burma/306822/ (accessed 7 August 2017); Mya Sein, 'Towards Independence in Burma: The Role of Women', *Asian Affairs* 3, 3 (October 1972): 288–99.

[38] 'Mya Sein's Speeches at the Burma Round Table Conference 1931', in *Myanmar Literature Project. Working Paper No. 10:18. Two Books on Sex and Gender*, ed. Hans-Bernd Zöllner (Druck: Universität Passau, 2011), 67. My thanks to Jonathan Saha for this reference and copy of the working paper.

The appointment of Oung at the Burmese Round Table had not been without its difficulties. In this, there were some parallels with the appointment of women to the Indian RTC, which we will encounter in the next chapter. On 29 September 1931 the government announced the 20 Burmese delegates who would be attending the conference. They included representatives from different political parties and minority groups, but no women. After the announcement various British women from British and international women's organizations, including the WFL, the BCL, the Six Point Group, Equal Rights International, and the St Joan's Social and Political Alliance, sent letters to the secretary of state, Sir Samuel Hoare, hoping it was not too late to include one or more women. In particular, the name of Oung was put forward because she was conveniently already in London. As Emmeline Pethick-Lawrence pointed out in a letter sent to Hoare on 29 September 1931, women in Burma had enjoyed an equal franchise with men since 1922 and so should be included in the conference. She also argued that as Oung had been educated at Oxford University she understood the 'English mind and point of view' as well as that of her own people. Burmese women, who had held a mass meeting in Rangoon, pointed out that two Indian women had been delegates to the Indian RTC (even though Indian women did not enjoy equal franchise) so at least two Burmese women should be sent as representatives at this conference.[39]

However, the governor of Burma, Sir Charles Alexander Innes, did not wish to appoint Oung. In various telegrams to the secretary of state in October 1931, the governor suggested that May Oung's Aunt, Mrs Hla Oung, who was vice president of the Burmese Women's Association, would be a better candidate. Hla Oung insisted that she would need Oung to accompany her on account of her age and language difficulties, but Innes believed that May Oung was too young and that the Burmese men would not approve of her appointment. He also did not want two women delegates who would be in favour of separation of Burma from India, as that would upset the political balance of the delegation. Innes agreed to compromise

39 IOR: L/PO/9/3. Burma Round Table Conference: Notes on Groups Represented at Burma Conference. Emmeline Pethick-Lawrence to Samuel Hoare, 29 September 1931.

by allowing Oung attend the conference as her aunt's advisor, but not to be named as a formal delegate. This suggestion was not well received, leading to a standoff. Hla Oung insisted on two women delegates and threatened to arrange a boycott by the whole Burmese delegation.[40]

British and international women's organizations petitioned the India Office once more for the inclusion of May Oung on the delegation. As Winifred Mayo of the Equal Rights International put it, the women of Burma had enjoyed equality in the past with men and it would be unfortunate to exclude them at a time when 'Eastern, as well as Western women are coming into their own'. Sir Seton also noted that Burmese women were, on the whole, 'more advanced' than Indian women so it was odd to exclude them.[41] Finally, the male Burmese delegates themselves, on their arrival in London in November 1931, sent a letter to Hoare asking that Oung be included in their delegation. Innes eventually relented after getting written assurance from the Burmese Women's Association that they would be happy with one delegate. On 20 November 1931, Oung was formally invited to attend the Burmese RTC. She accepted the invitation.[42] Oung had to promise not to take sides on the separation issue.[43]

Sarojini Naidu was in Britain at the same time for the Second RTC. In her private correspondence she was rather disparaging about Oung, describing the way Oung had 'wangled her way on the Committee'.[44] Though Western commentators were guilty of essentializing Indian feminists by descriptions of their colourful dress, Naidu was just as guilty in describing the opening of the conference. Not only did she describe the 'Mongolian faces' and 'slant eyes' of the delegates and the 'gorgeous rose, pinks, primrose yellows, forget-me-not blues and glowing plums and petunias of the Burmese delegates'

---

[40] L/PO/9/3.

[41] L/PO/9/3, Winifred Mayo to Samuel Hoare, 23 October 1931; note by Sir M. Seton, 28 October 1931.

[42] L/PO/9/3, Burmese delegates to Samuel Hoare, 10 November 1931; telegram 19 November 1931; May Oung to Croft, 22 November 1931.

[43] Mya Sein, 'Towards Independence in Burma', 298.

[44] Sarojini Naidu to Padmaja and Leilamani Naidu, 25 November 1931, in Paranjape, *Naidu Selected Letters*, 260.

costumes, their lungis and head-dresses', she also focused on Oung's flowers in her hair and the way she had 'put away her accustomed dowdiness and rowdiness and arrived in the old Court Costume of a tight fitting white silk jacket and a curve-sweeping rose brocaded lungi skirt'.[45]

Following the Burmese Conference, international organizations such as the BCL and the IWSA continued to argue, in correspondence with the India Office, that Burmese women enjoyed equal economic and legal rights to property as Burmese men and that the franchise should be extended for them. Suggestions were made to the effect that as men and women were generally joint owners of property in Burma, the wives of enfranchised men should be automatically enfranchised too.[46] Contrasts were made with the lower position of Indian women. As Shobna Nijhawan has argued, in the case of Rameshwari Nehru, Indian women proposed a sisterhood between Indian and Burmese women marked by cultural affinity and shared experiences of colonialism, drawing upon nationalist accounts that described the 'high status' of Burmese women. However, as with Western feminists, they did not engage in the writings of Burmese women, nor acknowledge the ethnic strife that was emerging in the country.[47] Thus, this regional network was used to assert Indian women's rights (and notions of superiority) in the face of unfavourable comparisons with Burmese women's experiences, rather than an equal relationship of feminist solidarity.

India's other near neighbour was Ceylon (modern-day Sri Lanka) and there were close links between Indian and Ceylonese suffragettes. Ceylonese women were also engaging in broader international networks. The Theosophical Society had strong links and influences on the island. Mary Rutnam, a Canadian married to a Sri Lankan,

45 Naidu to Padmaja and Leilamani, 27 November 1931, in Paranjape, *Naidu Selected Letters*, 261.

46 IOR, M/1/181, Status of Women under New Constitution (1933), Chave Collison to Samuel Hoare, 20 December 1933; Corbett Ashby to Hoare, 20 December 1933.

47 Shobna Nijhawan, 'At the Margins of Empire: Feminist–Nationalist Configurations of Burmese Society in the Hindi Public (1917–1920)', *The Journal of Asian Studies* 71, 4 (2012): 1013–33.

helped set up the Ceylon Women's Union in 1904, the Tamil Women's Union in 1909, a branch of the WCTU, and the Women's Franchise Union in 1927. These organizations were the forerunners of the Lanka Mahila Samiti founded in 1930, which used the Indian terminology for a women's group, but was based on the model of the Canadian Women's Institute.[48]

While there is clear evidence of the influence the British suffrage movement had on Indian women, there was little evidence of this influence on Sri Lankan women. The Ceylon National Congress was not engaged in public demonstrations of nationalist agitation against the colonial government, unlike the Indian counterpart. Parliamentary franchise had been introduced between 1910 and 1912, but initially only 0.15 per cent of the population (and only men) were eligible to vote. The male electorate was increased between 1920 and 1923 to just 4 per cent of the population. In 1919, Dr Nallamma Murugesu passed a resolution in the Ceylon National Congress in favour of female suffrage but this was not passed and there was no organized Ceylonese suffrage movement at the time. In 1923 when E. R. Tambimuttu, a member of the legislative council for Batticaloa, proposed removing the sex disqualification there was little support. However, in 1925, Aseline Thomas proposed at a general session of the Ceylonese National Congress that there should be a limited female franchise. It was seconded by Agnes De Silva and passed with only three opponents. De Silva was Dutch by descent and the secretary of the Ceylon Women's Franchise Union.[49]

The Women's Franchise Union of Ceylon was founded in December 1927 and gave evidence before the Donoughmore Commission in January 1928 demanding the rights of women to vote.[50] One of the members of the commission looking into Ceylon's constitution was

[48] Chandra de Silva, 'A Historical Overview of Women in Sri Lankan Politics', in *Women and Politics in Sri Lanka: A Comparative Perspective*, ed. Sirima Kiribamune (Kandy: International Centre for Ethnic Studies, 1999), 27.

[49] de Silva, 'A Historical Overview', 31.

[50] Chulani Kodikara, 'The Struggle for Equal Political Representation of Women in Sri Lanka', *Report for UNDP* (2009), 11, http://www.lk.undp.org/content/dam/srilanka/docs/governance/WPE%20FINAL%20PDF.pdf, accessed 7 August 2017.

Dr Drummond Shiels, a Labour Party member who had been a keen supporter of the British suffrage movement and had encouraged women to form the Women's Franchise Union of Ceylon.[51] The union produced its own journal, *Prabuddha Stri*, and was presided over by Lady Bandaranaike (mother-in-law to the world's first female prime minister). Initially the union had only asked for a limited franchise, believing that any more would be impossible to achieve.[52] The Donoughmore Commission actually recommended that all women aged over 30 be enfranchised, which emboldened the union to ask for franchise on the same terms as men, who were to be enfranchised at the age of 21. In 1929, the legislative council recommended enfranchising men and women over 21, as long as they met literacy qualifications.[53] By 1931, universal adult suffrage had been introduced in Ceylon for all men and women over 21.

As the Indian journalist, St Nihal Singh, put it for the American women's paper *Equal Rights*, it appeared as if 'votes came swiftly to Ceylonese women'. However, he explained that enfranchising women in Ceylon was a 'sign of the times in the Orient' and 'Asian lands'.[54] When the colonial government had initially left women out of the franchise there had been no noticeable protest or public discontent, and the demand for women's enfranchisement was only about two years old. Proximity with India had some influence, though other global influences had been circulating through Ceylon for years. It was clear that Ceylon was a very different case to that of India, but in 1929 the Women's Franchise Union of Ceylon did apply for affiliation with the IAWSEC.[55]

In May 1929 Muthulakshmi Reddi addressed the Young Men's Buddhist Association in Ceylon where she congratulated the Women's Franchise Union. She noted that Ceylon and India were tied

51 De Silva, 'A Historical Overview', 31.

52 St Nihal Singh, 'Votes Came Swiftly to Ceylonese Women', *Equal Rights*, 13 April 1929, 77.

53 'Ceylon's Women's Movement', *Equal Rights*, 24 August 1929, 228–9.

54 St Nihal Singh, 'Votes Came Swiftly to Ceylonese Women', *Equal Rights*, 13 April 1929, 77.

55 'Women's Franchise Union of Ceylon', *Indian Ladies Magazine* (April 1929): 509.

by Buddhist and Hindu mythology, but also used the opportunity to praise Indian men for giving Indian women the vote 'ungrudgingly'. Thus a lecture congratulating Ceylonese women's successes was linked back to Indian rights.[56] In 1930 Bandaranaike wrote to the secretary of the WIA to thank the association for their congratulations on achieving the female franchise in Ceylon. 'Our thanks are largely due to you for was it not you who gave us all the necessary help and guidance?' Looking back, Bandaranaike traced much of the developments to her visit to Madras and getting in touch with the 'right people' for the Ceylon Union's work.[57] Following the success in Ceylon, the WIA continued to maintain interest and provide advice. *Stri Dharma* criticized the Women's Political Union of Ceylon for not putting forward their own female candidates for the 1931 elections, but noted the success of another female candidate, Mrs Melamure, who was elected to the Ceylonese legislative council that year.[58] Thus, Indian suffragettes had some loose connections with Burmese and Ceylonese campaigners, which might be described as almost maternal, but during the 1930s they started to look further afield for broader familial 'Asian' networks of solidarity.

The All-Asian Women's Conference in Lahore

In January 1931 the AAWC was convened in Lahore—the result of a suggestion initially presented by Cousins through the WIA. Cousins visited the PPWA conference in 1928 following a trip to America, and felt disappointed by the lack of 'spiritual ascension' visible in the conference, which inspired her to mobilize for an All-Asian equivalent.[59]

[56] NMML, S. Muthulakshmi Reddi Papers, Bound Speeches and Writings, 'Women Today and in History', *Ceylon Observer*, 15 May 1929.

[57] 'Ceylon Women's Movement', *Stri Dharma* 8, 7 (May 1930): 294.

[58] Reprinted in 'Universal Adult Franchise in Ceylon', *Indian Ladies' Magazine* 5, 6 (January 1932): 299–300.

[59] Catherine Candy, 'The Inscrutable Irish-Indian Feminist Management of Anglo-American Hegemony, 1917–1947', *Journal of Colonialism and Colonial History* 2, 1 (2001): para 32. I have also discussed the AAWC in Sumita Mukherjee, 'The All-Asian Women's Conference 1931: Indian Women and their Leadership of a Pan-Asian Feminist Organisation', *Women's History Review*, 26, 3 (2017): 363–81.

Cousins had put out various feelers to parts of Asia in 1929 to ensure there was interest, and on 12 March 1930 a circular was issued suggesting the dates of January 1931. These dates were chosen so that it could take place in the off year, between the two Pan-Pacific Women's Conferences being held in Honolulu in August 1930 and China in 1932, and to immediately follow the AIWC meeting in January 1931. It was decided to hold the AAWC in the same location as the AIWC gathering to help with issues of organization and availability. Fourteen Indian women, including Sarojini Naidu, Lady Abdul Quadir, Rajkumari Amrit Kaur, Lakshmibai Rajwade, and Rustomji Faridoonji, signed the circular inviting Asian women.[60] Though Cousins often emphasized 'Asian' spirituality, she was keen that Indian women assert themselves in this case, while retaining their distinctness in contrast with the 'over-westernized Western woman'.[61] Thus, though she had a leading role in the initiation of the AAWC, Cousins wanted Indian women to take charge, to sign the letter inviting other delegates, and to lead the local organization of the conference.

Invitations to the AAWC had extended to women from 33 Asian countries, as it had been defined by the conference. This included Georgia, Palestine, Iraq, and Syria, as well as Malaya, Indo-China, Siam, and Hawai'i. Though the conference was conducted in English, provisions had been made for it to be supplemented by Arabic, Urdu, and French.[62] Though advertised widely, only 19 delegates attended in addition to 17 Indian delegates and 9 foreign visitors (including Cousins). These were women from Afghanistan, Burma, Ceylon, Japan, and Persia and visitors from America, Britain, Java, and New Zealand (see Image 4.1). There were a total of 45 official participants. Despite Sandell's assertions that regional women's

[60] James H. Cousins and Margaret E. Cousins, *We Two Together* (Madras: Ganesh & Co., 1950), 538–9.

[61] Catherine Candy, 'Relating Feminisms, Nationalisms and Imperialisms: Ireland, India and Margaret Cousin's Sexual Politics', *Women's History Review* 3, 4 (1994): 588.

[62] *All Asian Women's Conference Report* (Bombay: Times of India Press, 1931), 11, 57; 'Women and India: All Asian Women's Conference', *Pax International* 6, no. 2 (December 1930). Note that there are copies of Cousins' letter and invitation in the Japanese Women's Library, Fusae Ichikawa Center for Women and Governance, Tokyo.

All the Asian Delegates.

IMAGE 4.1   All the Asian delegates at the All-Asian Women's Conference, Lahore, January 1931
Source: From the Elmina Rose Lucke Papers, Sophia Smith Collection, Smith College (Northampton, MA, USA).

associations, such as the AAWC, were better at integrating women from the non-West than the Euro-American-centric women's organizations, this conference was extremely limited in its Asian reach.[63] The American women's paper *Equal Rights* while reporting on the conference failed to realize the lack of equal representation, claiming that it was 'attended by outstanding women from every country in Asia'.[64] Ruth Woodsmall, an American Christian surveyor, however did identify the disparity, remarking that the conference was 'not truly representative of Asia, since China was not represented and Japan only by a young student' though she was hopeful that it marked the

---

[63] Marie Sandell, '"A Real Meeting of the Women of the East and the West": Women and Internationalism in the Interwar Period', in *Internationalism Reconfigured: Transnational Ideas and Movements between the World Wars*, ed. Daniel Laqua (London: I. B. Tauris, 2011), 175–6.

[64] 'Justice for Women Urged in Far East', *Equal Rights*, 2 July 1932, 174.

beginning of future collaborations.[65] Cousins, meanwhile, was most disappointed by the lack of delegates from 'Western Asia'.[66] Despite Cousins' leadership, she was not the only person interested or invested in the AAWC. As mentioned earlier, it was Indian women who had put their name to the circular invitation that was subsequently publicized across the world. This letter suggested that it was time for 'Oriental women' from 'our common Continent' to develop a 'spirit of Asian sisterhood' to preserve and review their common heritage in the face of 'tides of Western influence'.[67] Although the letter explained that they would also look to discriminate the best features from outside Asia as well, the organizers were keen to accentuate Orientalist understandings of Asia as ancient and spiritual. They may have been looking forward to modern political and economic change, in relation to suffrage rights and education, but at the same time they presented Asian women as inherently culturally different and less 'modern' than Western women. Once the location and dates had been confirmed, a bulletin published in November 1930 set out the six objectives for the conference. Their objectives included the promotion of consciousness among Asian women of their 'common oriental culture' and preservation of certain Oriental qualities (simplicity, philosophy, art, cult of the family, veneration for motherhood, spiritual consciousness). The conference was essential to share experiences and also to discuss appropriate Occidental influences Asian women should take on (education, dress, freedom of movement, cinema, machinery). The bulletin signed by the Indian committee also acknowledged that there were specific issues for Asian women that they needed to discuss and combat (ill-health, illiteracy, poverty and underpayment of labour, infant mortality, marriage customs).[68]

---

[65] Ruth Frances Woodsmall, *Eastern Women Today and Tomorrow* (Boston: The Central Committee on the United Study of Foreign Missions, 1933), 90.

[66] Cousins, 'Women in Conference: the All-Indian and All-Asian Conferences Contrasted', *Modern Review* (March 1931): 326.

[67] *New India*, 3 April 1930, in Centre for Modern Indian Studies, Göttingen, Monthly Reports of India Branch of International Labour Organisation, April 1930.

[68] *AAWC Report*, 8.

A preview of the conference in the *Indian Magazine and Review,* a British journal edited by Jessie Duncan Westbrook, provided a supportive view of pan-Asian womanhood, inspired by the circular letter of invitation. Pointing out that 'Oriental women' were influenced by various Western relationships, the journal suggested that the women of Asia should continue to meet together to discuss their unique problems and thus by highlighting their 'fundamental difference from women of other lands' come to solve their difficulties.[69] The invitation circular had explained that the '"oriental" best expresses the quality of Asia', including its quietness, simplicity, and reliance on agriculture as opposed to the industrial attributes of the West, and that Asian women were inherently concerned with the family, children, and their vocation as 'race nourishers'.[70] And so, despite the potential for progressiveness, commentary within and on the AAWC failed to recognize the dynamic, transnational activity of female campaigners in the region and remained constrained within the language of East-West binaries.

Naidu had been appointed president of the AAWC. In May 1930, before entering jail for her role in the civil disobedience movement, she wrote to Cousins unaware that she would end up missing the conference owing to her continued incarceration: 'I am looking forward to it, and I hope I shall be free to attend it and to preside over it also.'[71] In private, however, she expressed concern about the timing of the conference, the fact that it had been agreed upon merely so that it could coincide with the AIWC. She did not think there was any political urgency to hold such as an Asian gathering, as she believed civil disobedience in India was more pressing.[72] As Naidu was not present, the conference had different presidents for each session. Lady Bandaranaike from Ceylon, Mrs Kamal-ud-din from Afghanistan, May Oung from Burma, Mrs Shirin Fozdar from Persia, and Miss Hoshi from Japan presided over events in addition to two Indian women, Reddi and Hamid Ali.

[69] All-Asian Women's Conference in India, *Indian Magazine and Review,* 678 (November 1930): 136.

[70] *AAWC Report,* vii.

[71] Cousins and Cousins, *We Two Together,* 538.

[72] Sarojini Naidu to Padmaja Naidu, 15 January 1931 in Paranjape, *Naidu Selected Letters,* 242.

Though there were non-Indian presidents, many of these women had previous connections to Indian women. Fozdar was born in India. In her address to the conference, Bandaranaike remarked that India was the point of origin for the Ceylonese and the birthplace of the Buddha, thus asserting India's cultural right to host and dominate the proceedings. Mrs S. W. Ilangakoon from Ceylon presented a focus that assumed India was representative of the rest of Asia. Explaining that the 'matriarchal system' was the essence of the East and that family was prioritized as opposed to the individualism of the West, Ilangakoon used her speech to criticize the American Katherine Mayo's book *Mother India* to assert that Indian women were not chattels. Mustafa Khan from Persia drew upon pan-Islamic experiences to discuss the issues of purdah and early marriage.[73] There were attempts by other women to draw the conversations away from Indian examples. Concerns about inheritance rights and polygamy were brought up, along with other issues such as health, labour, education, and, of course, franchise, which were not problems unique to Asia.

The rani of Mandi, daughter of the ruler of Kapurthala State, gave a welcome address at the AAWC that called on delegates to take the best qualities from both the Oriental civilization and the West, and to reject the perception that women in Asia were mute or helpless ornaments. She explained that Asian women shared similar domestic and social conditions, shaped by their own customs and traditions, and shared a longing for change.[74] As Lakshmibai Rajwade, a trained medical doctor and honorary organizing secretary of the conference, put it in her preface to the conference report, the organizers felt the conference was necessary to bring about a 'keener realisation of their cultural unity'. Echoing Cousins, Rajwade mentioned the 'self-realization' and 'common awakening' that was taking place in the Orient. She talked about Asia coming into her own and the spiritual and peaceful attributes of the region, beyond national borders. This homogenizing idea of Asian spirituality and cultural unity was at odds with the nationalist dialogues of various countries within the region, and merely echoed the language and imagery of mainstream Indian nationalism, which

[73] *AAWC Report*, 28, 38, 41.
[74] *AAWC Report*, 22–4.

had strong religious and spiritual underpinnings. The preliminary letter sent out to gauge interest had discussed how India was the 'foster mother' of Asia's cultures, hosting Islam, Buddhism, and Aryans. The AAWC conference opened with a Vedic hymn and it presented a vision of Asian spirituality, most closely allied with Buddhism, certain strands of Hindusim, and non-violence, but it neglected to consider the 'spiritual' diversity of the region beyond India.[75]

There was no evidence of anti-imperialist rhetoric or rejection of Western institutions during the AAWC. They were not united by the common enemy of imperialism nor by the common racial subjection that unified equally composite organizations such as the Pan-African Congresses or PPWA. There was also little consideration of the variation in structures and institutions that the different Asian members had to deal with to enact the kind of social reform the conference was concerned with. One of the main resolutions passed by the AAWC, through the insistent communication from Alice Paul of the US-based NWP to Margaret Cousins, was to urge Japanese and Persian delegates sitting at the League of Nations in Geneva to support reform to grant married women the same nationality rights that existed for unmarried women and men.[76] According to Cousins, it was the resolution on the nationality of married women and engagement with the League of Nations that attracted the interest of the press towards the AAWC, perhaps not only because it demonstrated the reach of the conference beyond Asia, but also because of the input the American NWP had in the resolution.[77] Although Naidu told Reddi in private that she did not see the relevance of this agitation to Indian concerns, the AAWC continued to send delegates (all of them Indians apart from Oung in 1931) to the aforementioned Women's Consultative Committee on Nationality at the League of Nations until at least 1935.[78] Alice Paul praised the AAWC for sending

---

[75] *AAWC Report*, i–ii, viii.

[76] Cousins, 'Asian Women Influence League of Nations', *Times of India*, 24 February 1931, 4.

[77] Cousins, 'Asian Women Influence League of Nations'; 'The All-Asian Conference', *Equal Rights*, 5 September 1931, 245.

[78] NMML, AIWC Papers, Microfilm 1, file 11, Reddi to Rajwade, 6 July 1931; Microfilm 7, file 89: All-Asian Women's Conference.

these telegrams, writing in both the *New York Herald* and *Equal Rights* that now 'the women of Asia have taken their place in the ranks of the most advanced women of the Occident'.[79]

The comment by Paul exemplifies the supposition underlining the AAWC that Asian women were inherently less advanced than those in Western countries. However, an editorial by Edith Houghton Hooker for *Equal Rights* in July 1932 reflecting on the publication of the AAWC report was more circumspect.

> The report shows that the problems confronting the women of the Far East are identical with those with which their sisters of Europe and the Americas are preoccupied. As Americans we are rather inclined to complacently assume that we are in the vanguard of progress. It is therefore quite pleasantly disillusioning to discover that our sisters in Burma have outstripped us in the race to secure Equal Rights.[80]

In the same issue, an article on the report also mentioned the 'striking similarity' in the problems that 'confront the women of the East and West' and reflected that 'Feminism, it seems, is not an exclusively European or American manifestation'.[81] Hooker in her editorial continued to commend the 'high standing' of the delegates—doctors, social workers, poets, writers, and heads of ruling families—failing to acknowledge the social disparity of the region that was not represented. Finally, however, she expressed her admiration for the idealism, nobility, and 'deep spirituality' that pervaded the conference, suggesting that 'discussions were maintained on the high plane', harking back to the spiritualist stereotypes of pan-Asianism.[82]

It was the sixth session of the conference, presided over by Hamid Ali, which was dedicated to the issue of franchise and government. Reddi traced the history of enfranchisement of women in India for the delegates, while Ilangakoon explained how women in Ceylon had organized to demand, successfully, for female franchise. Rustomji Fardoonji took the opportunity to raise the point that married women

79 *New York Herald*, 27 January 1931, quoted in Cousins, 'Asian Women Influence League of Nations'; 'Asian Women Demand Equality', *Equal Rights*, 14 February 1931, 12.

80 'East Is West', *Equal Rights*, 2 July 1932, 170.

81 'Justice for Women Urged in the Far East'.

82 'East Is West'.

were at a disadvantage as few could exercise the right to vote, as property was usually in the name of their husbands, and so asserted her desire for adult franchise. It was then that Cousins reflected on the franchise more broadly, noting that Javanese women did not have the right to vote but hoped that the AAWC would help them in their self-expression, which was confirmed by the Javanese delegate Miss Sunaryati. Cousins also suggested that though the property qualifications in India and Burma were inadequate, she was not in favour of full adult suffrage, when only 3 per cent of the population were literate. When Reddi argued that possession of property did not mean that the voter was literate, Cousins refused to be drawn into discussing the details further.[83] Ultimately, the AAWC did pass a resolution on the equality of status of men and women which included a clause in favour of equal adult franchise. A permanent committee was set up consisting of Oung (Burma), Rajwade (India), Bandaranaike (Ceylon), Fozdar (Persia), Kamal-ud-din (Afghanistan), Hoshi (Japan), Reddi (India), and Naidu (India).[84] At the end of the conference it was decided that a second would be held in either Japan or Java in 1935, but no future conference ever took place.[85]

The Aftermath of the the All-Asian Women's Conference and Other Conferences

Rajwade, organizing secretary of the AIWC and AAWC, was keen to continue the work of the committee after the first conference, but found that there was little support from colleagues such as Naidu. Besides, she was overworked with domestic concerns. She was also concerned that the committee was not representative enough of Asian, and indeed Indian, experiences.[86] In a letter written to the American writer Ruth Woodsmall in January 1932, Rajwade asked her for impressions of the women's movement in Japan, suggesting that 'the Japanese are far in advance of us, but I always feel that they

---

[83] *AAWC Report*, 134–5, 138–9.

[84] SCPC, WILPF India Section, AAWC Interim Report, 6 February 1931.

[85] Cousins and Cousins, *We Two Together*, 540.

[86] NMML, AIWC Papers, Microfilm 1, file 11, correspondence between Reddi and Rajwade 1931.

have taken the West as their standard in many things'.[87] Woodsmall, a member of the YWCA and the United Study of Foreign Missions was an apt correspondent as she had shown a great deal of interest in 'Eastern' women. Woodsmall had worked as a member of a commission on Higher Christian Education in Japan, and a Laymen's Commission conducting a number of interviews with women in Japan, China, Burma, and India from 1930 to 1931. Her publications included *Eastern Women: Today and Tomorrow*, published in 1933, and *Moslem Women Enter a New World*, in 1936. Woodsmall had attended the AAWC too and delivered an address at the public meeting put on for the non-Asian visitors on 22 January in which she talked about the 'romance' of India for Americans and the awakening of women in the Middle East. She also brought greetings from women in Geneva who recognized a 'promise of necessary self-conscious element in the federation of the world and the establishment of unity in diversified world sisterhood'.[88]

Perhaps, as Woodsmall suggested, the involvement of Asian women in international organizations was remarkable as it had only been recently that they had broadened their conceptions beyond the family to local and national organizations.[89] Woodsmall also highlighted the sea-change she had observed in international conferences that had formerly been populated by Western women who spoke about Eastern situations; by the 1930s Eastern women were representing themselves at these gatherings. She commended the Indians for sending women to the RTCs and was very keen on the success of the AAWC. As she put it: 'The fact that women of thirty-three countries of Asia, the Near East, Middle East and Far East were invited, shows the unexplored possibilities of future relationship among the women of Asia.'[90]

There were other networks of 'Eastern' women, especially centred on the activities of feminists in Turkey. *Stri Dharma* was keen to point

---

[87] SSC, Ruth Frances Woodsmall Papers, correspondence box 15, folder 44, Rajwade to Woodsmall, 23 January 1932.

[88] *AAWC Report*, 117.

[89] Woodsmall, *Eastern Women Today and Tomorrow*, 82.

[90] Ruth Frances Woodsmall, *Moslem Women Enter a New World* (London: George Allen and Unwin, 1936), 370, 372.

out some of the similarities in outlook between Indian and Turkish women in 1928. Turkish women were fighting as part of a nationalist revolution, as well as for women's rights within Turkey. They were enfranchised in 1935.

> Judging from the social revolution in Turkey and the awakening in India, the emancipation of the women of the East does not seem to have involved much noise and clatter.... Unlike the West our fiercest battle will rage, not round the employment bureaus or qualifying academies, but round the domestic hearth.[91]

A clear connection between Indian and Turkish suffragettes was evident through the figure of Halidé Edib. She had been involved in the Turkish resistance movement but later forced into exile for her opposition to Mustafa Kemal. She lived in Britain and France in the 1920s and 1930s. In 1929, on a tour of the US, Edib met Naidu. In 1935, she visited India for three months meeting various Indian feminists including Naidu, Kamaladevi Chattopadhyay, and Begum Shahnawaz. In memoirs published in 1937, Edib recalled the thrill it gave to 'every Eastern woman' when Naidu had presided over the 'Indian parliament' (presumably referring to the Indian National Congress), and described Naidu as the 'best known Eastern woman in politics'. However, Edib also remarked upon Naidu's perfect English and described most of the Indian men and women she met as speaking and thinking in the same terms as intellectuals 'bred in Oxford', noting the strength of British influence on Indian culture and possibly on India's future.[92]

Indian women, then, were involved in 'Oriental' and 'Eastern' networks. In 1930, Indian women were invited (via the WIA) to a conference held by the Oriental Arab Feminist Academy in Damascus.[93] In 1932, Cousins intended to visit a women's conference in Baghdad, which she wanted to bring into contact with the AAWC.[94] Egyptian

---

91 'Notes and Comments', *Stri Dharma* 11, 11 (September 1928): 249.

92 Halidé Edib, *Inside India*, ed. Mushirul Hasan (New Delhi: Oxford University Press, 2002), 16, 25.

93 'Notes and Comments: Arab Women's Conference', *Stri Dharma* 13, 7 (May 1930): 293.

94 NLI, Sheehy Skeffington Papers, MS14, 177/12, Cousins to Hanna Sheehy Skeffington, 13 October 1932.

interest in India was keen. Naidu had visited Egypt in 1929 and the weekly Wafdist paper *al-Balagh al-Usbu'i*, which included regular articles on India, published an article on Naidu and then two articles on 'The Indian Woman' in June 1930.[95] Madame Hoda Charouie Pasha of Egypt, who had first attended the IAW in Rome in 1923, was a popular leader not only in the Arab world but also among Indian women. Egyptian women were invited to the 1939 AIWC, though none were able to attend. However, Kamaladevi Chattopadhyay did visit Egypt and meet with Egyptian women in 1939, where she argued for the need for closer cooperation between Indian and Egyptian women.[96] By the time of Pasha's death in 1948 she had been vice-president of the IAW, president of the Egyptian Women's Union, and president of the Pan Arabic Union of Women. Upon her death, Avabai Wadia remarked in *Roshni* (the AIWC journal) that Pasha had brought about a 'new era in the Asian world by fighting for women's equality with men on the basis of human rights'. She was thus an 'Asian' role model, and there were clear links drawn between the work she did to abolish the purdah system in Egypt and the issues that Indian women faced. However, at the time of her death, Egyptian women did not have the vote, not even in a limited form.[97]

The IAWSEC conference held in Istanbul in April 1935 was perhaps the culmination of the sea change in 'Eastern' involvement in Euro-American women's conferences. Woodsmall described it in the following way:

> Three women from India (as it happened all three were Moslems), a young woman from Teheran, a number from Egypt, both Moslems and Copts, a large delegation of Syrian women, representing Christians and Moslems, and also a group of students from the American Junior College in Beirut—all these Eastern delegates together with a group of very active Turkish delegates, the total number of Eastern women

[95] Noor-Aiman I. Khan, *Egyptian–Indian Nationalist Collaboration and the British Empire* (New York: Palgrave Macmillan, 2011), 200n12.

[96] NMML, AIWC Papers, Microfilm 13, file 207, *Bulletin of Indian Women's Movement*, no. 20 (January 1939); Mlle Hamza Bey, 'Srimati Kamaladevi's visit to Egypt' (no date).

[97] A. B. W., 'In Memoriam: A Great Woman of Asia', *Roshni* 3, 2 (March 1948): 24.

constituting perhaps half of the Congress, gave one the very definite impression of the active participation of women of the East in international life.[98]

Women from 30 countries attended the triennial conference presided over by Margery Corbett Ashby, who visited India that same year. Alongside the expected resolutions related to equality of status such as those connected to labour, suffrage, and nationality, the conference included a resolution entitled 'East and West in Co-operation'. Keen to dispel the notion of difference, despite using the terms 'East' and 'West', the resolution called for greater unity and co-operation between women across the world.[99] With greater participation of Asian women in larger international conferences, women did not need to use the artificial 'Asian' collective identity to give voice to their concerns. They had more opportunity to speak of their own individual activities, but the 'Eastern' identity did remain powerful.

Shareefah Hamid Ali, treasurer of the AIWC, was one of the Indian delegates at the Istanbul conference and delivered a speech with the same title as the resolution, 'East and West in Co-operation'. In contrast to the short resolution, Ali talked of 'Asia' as a unified entity, of the solidarity of the 'women of the East', and emphasized the spirituality of the 'East' in her speech: 'For centuries Asia has been the cradle of religions—of spiritual knowledge—of philosophy which gives life a deeper significance.' She explained that 'Oriental Civilisation' was defined by its simplicity and spiritual consciousness, arguing that this simplicity was something Asian women could offer in their international collaboration. She also warned European and American women against any 'arrogant assumption of superiority or patronage' or undue pressure on their religion, government, or economic spheres of influence.[100]

[98] Woodsmall, *Moslem Women*, 370–1.

[99] International Alliance of Women for Suffrage and Equal Citizenship, *Report of the Twelfth Congress, Istanbul, April 18th–24th 1935* (London, 1935), 19.

[100] SSC, International Alliance of Women Papers, box 3, folder 2, Shareefah Hamid Ali, 'East and West in Co-operation' (1935). For further discussion on the Orientalizing tendencies of the IWSA, see Charlotte Weber, 'Unveiling Scheherazade: feminist Orientalism in the International Alliance of Women, 1911–1950', *Feminist Studies* 27, 1 (2001): 125–57.

The *Catholic Citizen* viewed Hamid Ali's interventions slightly differently in their report of the Istanbul meeting. Focusing on her appearance, the periodical described her 'attractive figure in her beautiful robes'. Though noting that Hamid Ali described herself as representing not only India but the whole continent of Asia, the Catholic paper focused on Hamid Ali's gratitude to women's organizations such as St Joan's Alliance which 'had done so much to awaken the women of the east'.[101] Hamid Ali offered her personal reflections in a report she produced for the AIWC. Particularly impressed by the modernity of the Turkish women and the Ata Turk regime, she wrote much about the affinity the Asian, African, and Jamaican delegates had with each other, less so about Western women. Thinking about Asia, Hamid Ali remarked that it was 'a thousand pities that neither China nor Japan Burma nor Ceylon were represented as we were looking forward with great interest to come into contact with Chinese and Japanese women'. However, with the other delegates, 'we felt the strength of our unity with a great surge of pride and we knew that without pacts and treaties we could rely on the Unity friendship and joint action of the women of Asia'.[102]

The other two Indian delegates at Istanbul were Begum Ikbal-u-nissa (Mrs Hussain) and Begum Kamaluddin, thus all three women came from Muslim families. The conference in Istanbul was also notable for its inclusion of the first woman of African descent. The Jamaican Una Marson attended the conference and even penned a poem about it entitled 'To the IAWSEC'.[103] Marson discussed, among other things, the brutality of lynching in America. However, a number of Western delegates, in response, tried to explain away the provocations because of 'Negro' attacks on white women. Representatives from the Middle East rose in protest against these unjustified attacks on blacks, drawing from their own experiences of living with and among them for centuries. India supported them and Hamid Ali praised this 'solidarity of Asiatic women's attitudes against any assumptions of

[101] 'Foreign Periodicals', *Modern Review* (August 1935): 203.

[102] NMML, AIWC Papers, Microfilm 8, file 96, Shareefah Hamid Ali, *Report on the International Congress of Women, 12th Session*.

[103] Anna Snaith, *Modernist Voyages: Colonial Women Writers in London, 1890–1945* (Cambridge: Cambridge University Press, 2014), 171–2.

racial superiority by any nation'. It was felt by Hamid Ali that the Istanbul conference was the first time that 'Asiatic Womanhood was fully represented' and that they had felt emboldened enough to challenge stereotypes and challenge imperialist policies.[104]

One of the resolutions put forward by the Indian delegation, and accepted unanimously, was on the question of women's suffrage in India. The resolution supported Indian women in their demand for the abolition of all sex disqualifications and their recommendations that 'a Committee with a strong representation of women should be appointed to consider their legal disabilities'. Suffrage was still an international concern in 1935, but there were discussions about amalgamating the IAWSEC with the ICW, as the 'suffrage and equal citizenship' element of the alliance was no longer an obvious focus. However, Hamid Ali noted that it was the countries still doing active work in the field of women's suffrage who were most strongly opposed to this amalgamation, and that the countries most in favour of amalgamation were those who had not worked on suffrage and mainly worked on social reform.[105]

There was no AAWC conference in 1935. With Indian women engaged in domestic nationalist agitations and burdened with a weak organizational structure, there was no impetus from other Asian women to continue with the conference. When it was announced that the Istanbul conference would take place in 1935, plans to hold the conference in Java or Japan were postponed and continued to be postponed thereafter. In 1934, with hopes to hold the next conference in Japan, Kaur, Hamid Ali, and Rajwade sent letters of contact respectively to Mr Miyaki, the Counsel General for Japan, Colonel Aihara, the Japanese trade officer who had visited Simla recently, and Professor Tan Yuan Shan of China who had been at Santiniketan.[106] Attention soon turned to Java. Letters were sent to women workers in Java, without reply, and Cousins tried to enlist the help of a Javanese

[104] 'Asiatic Women in International Conference', *Modern Review* (September 1935): 277–9.

[105] NMML, AIWC Papers, Microfilm 8, file 96, Shareefah Hamid Ali, *Report on the International Congress of Women, 12th Session.*

[106] NMML, AIWC Papers, Microfilm 7, file 89, Rajwade to AAWC Committee, 14 September 1934.

woman staying in Adyar. In December 1935, Cousins met two women, from China and Japan, in Travancore who certainly did not think that a conference could be held in their countries though the Japanese woman suggested that delegates might be willing to go to Java. These plans were not realized.[107] Indian women members of the permanent committee of the AAWC met annually until 1936, discussing among themselves their desire to broaden the representative nature of the conference. As no other host country was forthcoming, there was discussion about holding the second session in India, which many members were in favour of. However, there was opposition based on the concern that if an 'independent' nation were to host the conference, it might be taken more seriously and expand the international reach.[108] Hansa Mehta also explained that if India were to host the conference again it would look like no other country in Asia was actually interested in the conference (which was probably true!). However, it was also noted that it would be difficult to host a conference in India owing to the civil disobedience struggles that were escalating at that time.[109]

In January 1936, the ICW held a joint conference with the NCWI in Calcutta. This was another opportunity for Indian women to demonstrate organizational and leadership abilities though this time the focus was not solely on Asia. There were 24 overseas delegates from Britain and Ireland, Belgium, Romania, Switzerland, France, Denmark, Greece, Holland, Australia, and New Zealand. Representing Asia, there was only one visitor from China in addition to the Indian delegates. Burmese delegates were included as part of the Indian contingent according to the programme. Professor Tomiko Wada Kora's letter of regret that she and other Japanese women could not attend was reproduced in the programme, where she congratulated the conference as the first international conference for women in the 'Orient'. Lady Aberdeen, president of the ICW, was also unable to attend but in her letter of address noted that this was

---

[107] NMML, AIWC Papers, Microfilm 7, file 89, Minutes of AAWC Permanent Committee, 2 January 1935; memo by Rajwade, 22 July 1936.

[108] NMML, AIWC Papers, Microfilm 7, file 89, AAWC notes, 1934–1936.

[109] NMML, AIWC Papers, Microfilm 9, file 113, Circular no. 5 of 1935, 12 May 1935.

the first time that European and Antipodean representatives would hear issues relating to women discussed in the space of Asia.[110] In the inaugural address by the maharani of Baroda, she was progressive enough to acknowledge that not all Indian women enjoyed political rights yet.[111] She discussed the franchise advancements made in the 1935 Government Act and expressed her hopes for eventual universal adult franchise in India. Aimed at facilitating better understanding, suffrage was not the key issue of concern at this meeting. One of the resolutions was related to the franchise, but solely Indian franchise, and was merely an appreciation of the 1935 reforms, urging enfranchised Indian women to use their right to vote.[112] There was no discussion of ongoing franchise concerns in other member countries, or neighbouring countries.

The IAWSEC met again in Zurich in 1937 for a study conference and in Copenhagen in 1939 for a full congress. Only one Indian delegate, Mrs J. Vakil from Bombay, attended the Zurich meeting, but there were three Indians at the Copenhagen Congress: Kunwarani Maharaj Singh, Kamaladevi Chattopadhyay, and Malini Sukhtankar.[113] Following the 1939 IAWSEC conference in Copenhagen, delegates Kamaladevi and Sukhtankar were extremely disappointed with the way they were treated, especially the focus on their clothing and the lack of opportunity to speak.[114] Rajwade forwarded these complaints to Corbett Ashby, mentioning that similar complaints had been raised after the 1935 Istanbul Conference. In 1935, the AIWC had received 'an assurance that the Alliance will cultivate a more equalitarian and truly world attitude in all matters'. However, concerned about the differential treatment to delegates from Eastern countries and the lack of

[110] *Joint Conference of the International Council of Women and the National Council of Women in India, January 30th to 4th February 1936* (Calcutta, 1936), 14, 16–17.

[111] Kamala Chatterjee, 'International Conference of Women', *Modern Review* (March 1936): 310–15.

[112] *Joint Conference Report 1936*, 70.

[113] 'Indian Women Visitors in Europe', *Bulletin of the Indian Women's Movement*, 22 (December 1939): 2.

[114] NMML, AIWC Papers, Microfilm 13, file 207, Sukhtankar and Chattopadhay to Rajwade, 16 July 1939.

inclusion, Rajwade suggested that the AIWC might disaffiliate from the IAWSEC or be forced to form some sort of coalition within: 'but we want to avoid any emphasis on such differences as Eastern and Western or Asian and European in a body which claims to be a world organization'.[115]

It was evident that stereotypical attitudes towards Indian and 'Eastern' women persisted. Kamaladevi and Sukhtankar suggested that the best means to get an effective Indian voice in international meetings was to link more closely with 'Eastern countries':

> [I]f India and the Eastern problems are to have a chance and India play any part in this organisation, then what she needs is not an effectual place on the Board, which is at present more a show than a reality, we feel, but a closer linking up with the Eastern countries, such as Burma, Ceylon, Malaya, China, Siam and even Australia and New Zealand who share much in common with us and thus be able to form a solid block to be able to make its impact felt on the Alliance. This would be an invaluable contribution to the Alliance itself and would radically alter its present composition and character which is so predominently [*sic*] European.[116]

Despite these recommendations to the AIWC committee, the AAWC had already proved ineffective. And, despite some efforts to forge Asian networks, Indian suffragettes still wanted to be part of international feminist bodies, while chafing at the prejudice against or stereotypical perceptions of 'Eastern' women's experiences. Without equal alliances, Indian suffragettes naturally became more insular.

Asian Relations Conference, 1947 and after

In 1947, a pan-Asian conference was held that brought many Asian women together once more. The Asian Relations Conference held in New Delhi in April was organized by the Indian Council of World Affairs and had a large number of female delegates. Inaugurated by

[115] NMML, AIWC Papers, Microfilm 13, file 207, Rajwade to Corbett Ashby, 21 September 1939.

[116] NMML, AIWC Papers, Microfilm 13, file 207, 'The International Women's Congress at Copenhagen: Our Impressions' (July 1939).

Jawaharlal Nehru, and presided over by Sarojini Naidu, while boycotted by the Muslim League, just a few months before Indian independence, the conference was convened to discuss five key issues: Nationalism; Migration; Economic Development; Cultural Problems; and Women Problems.[117] Female delegates were sent from India, Ceylon, Indonesia, Palestine, Egypt, Burma, Malaya, China, the Philippines, Iran, Korea, Cambodia, and Tajikistan. Observers from Siam and Bhutan were present. Once again there were obvious omissions from major 'Asian' countries. Among the 12 Indian women who attended, the majority were AIWC members and included Naidu, Rajwade, and Kaur.[118]

On 30 March, the group convened to discuss the status of women and women's movements in two sessions. The first was chaired by Princess Safiyeh Firouze of Iran, the second by Professor Paz Policarpio-Mendez of the Philippines. Kamaladevi Chattopadhyay initiated the discussions with a sketch of the historical background and then current status of women's movements. It was generally accepted that feminist movements had not developed along the Western model in Asia, and that the main women's movements in the East were inspired or vitalized by political and economic upheavals. For example, it was asserted that Asian women had been particularly useful in violent and non-violent revolutions.[119] The subject of franchise was discussed as a distinct issue where it was noted that women in Persia, Egypt, and Malaya did not have the vote, that in Palestine it was extremely limited, and there were also 'undesirable features' in India, China, Burma, Philippines, Bhutan, and Indonesia where some measure of female franchise had been won. It was agreed that the principle of universal adult franchise should be recognized in all Asian countries to ensure full democratization.[120] However, as Avabai

---

[117] 'The Inter-Asian Relations Conference', *The Round Table: The Commonwealth Journal of International Affairs* 37, 147 (1947): 237–43.

[118] 'Asian Relations Conference', *International Women's News* 41, 9 (1947): 123–5; Avabai Wadia, 'The Asian Relations Conference', *Roshni* 2, 5 (June 1947): 45.

[119] 'The Asian Relations Conference: New Delhi 1947', *Roshni* 2, 5 (June 1947): 11.

[120] 'The Asian Relations Conference', *Roshni* (June 1947): 16.

Wadia put it later, the discussions had all been couched in terms where it was made clear that the women were not taking an 'anti-masculine stance' and that the issue of women's rights were part of a wider concern about the rights of citizenship and part of a broader progressive movement taking part in the region.[121] At the conference, the women proposed to form an Association of Asian Women and revive the AAWC. Yet again, these plans were not realized.

Regional associations for women continued to flourish, and the connections between the AIWC and PPWA continued. In 1939, the Australian president of the PPWA invited Kaur, Rajwade, and Hamid Ali to attend their next conference in New Zealand in 1940. No Indian woman was able to attend due to the ongoing war and other commitments.[122] However, clearly Australian feminists wanted to include India into their 'Pacific' identity, replacing earlier Commonwealth and colonial networks. Eleanor Moore, honorary secretary of the Australian WILPF, sent a letter to 'Friends in India' in 1938 on these connections. She explained that though India did not border the Pacific Ocean geographically, it had been decided that India should be 'included among "Pacific countries", being so closely connected with the issues that concern us all on this side of the world'. She also hoped that Indian women would attend the 1940 PPWA in New Zealand.[123] The PPWA was renamed the Pan-Pacific and South-East Asia Women's Association after the Second World War.[124]

There were other pan-Asian women's conferences after Indian independence. In 1949, the Conference of the Women of Asia

---

[121] Wadia, 'The Asian Relations Conference', 46.

[122] NMML, AIWC Papers, Microfilm 13, file 207, Sweet to Sukhtankar, 24 October 1939; Sukhtankar to E. E. Andress, 4 October 1939.

[123] NMML, AIWC Papers, Microfilm 13, file 207, Eleanor M. Moore to 'Friends in India', 30 November 1938; *Bulletin of Indian Women's Movement* (January 1939).

[124] Bessie M. Rischbieth, *March of Australian Women: A Record of Fifty Years' Struggle for Equal Citizenship* (Perth: Paterson Brokensha, 1964), 124.

was held in Beijing.[125] The 1957 United Nations seminar on civic responsibilities of Asian women in public life was held in Bangkok. The UN invited 21 member governments to send delegates. Fifteen countries did so: Burma, Cambodia, China, Hong Kong, India, Indonesia, Japan, Korea, Malaya, Nepal, Pakistan, Philippines, Sarawak, Singapore, and Thailand.[126] However, as a UN-sponsored initiative, pan-Asianism remained in the shadows of international organizing. Nevertheless, there was also an increase of Asian representation in international women's bodies. The president of the IAW from 1964 was the Pakistani Begum Anwar Ahmed (following the Sri Lankan Ezlynn Deraniyagala's term from 1958 to 1964).[127]

* * *

Indian women were getting involved in Asian networks to further their own thinking and campaigns on suffrage. These included broader conceptions of 'Asia' than used in the modern day, to include the 'Middle East' and also to look to the Pacific. These Eastern networks provided counterpoints to the Western-dominated international feminist networks, which Indians had engaged with since the end of the First World War. Though Asian feminist networks emphasized different conceptions of the family, spirituality, and domesticity as particular to 'Asia', the principle of desiring and demanding equal suffrage was universal. Female suffrage was also seen as a marker of modernity. Ultimately, these new Asian feminist networks were not successful as longstanding collaborations. Indian suffragettes had dominated these initiatives to create new regional associations in Asia, but faced too much competition from alternative forms of association. Their attempts to find unity with Asian women were also based on Orientalist stereotypes about Asian women, though the impetus

---

[125] See Armstrong, 'Before Bandung'.

[126] TWL, LSE, Marjorie Chave Collisson Papers, 7CHC, United Nations, 1957 Seminar on the Civic Responsibilities and Increased Participation of Asian Women in Public Life, Bangkok, 5 to 16 August 1957.

[127] Rischbieth, *March of Australian Women*, sec. appendix A.

behind these networks had been to challenge such stereotypes. It is clear that Indian women had long-standing networks through imperial ties with Britain and other British colonies which were deeper than those with countries that were merely geographically proximate. In the ultimate fight to challenge suffrage laws in India, Indian women had to return to those imperial connections, but also look inwards to nationalist organizing in their final campaign to introduce full adult suffrage in India. The next chapter looks more closely as to how Indian women increasingly allied their suffrage campaigns with nationalist aims and rhetoric in the 1930s and 1940s.

5

Indian Suffragettes and Nationalism
Rejection of British Networks

The women's movement in India is very closely related to our movement in Britain—and so far as their demand for their political enfranchisement is concerned is the direct outcome of it.

—Emmeline Pethick-Lawrence, 1938[1]

Though the Indian suffrage movement remained connected to the British women's movement, the methods and demands for suffrage, particularly by the 1930s, had diverged in many ways. By 1930 women were enfranchised in British India along the same terms as men, but there was a clear disparity in numbers owing to the lack of women who owned property. In the elections of 1925 and 1926 women electors constituted less than 5 per cent of the total electorate.[2] Indian suffragettes began to remobilize to urge for the franchise to

[1] Emmeline Pethick-Lawrence, *My Part in a Changing World* (London: Victor Gollancz, 1938), 337.

[2] There were 52,157 women out of a total electorate of 1,128,778 constituting 4.62 per cent (Letter from Joint Secretary to Government of India to India Office, London, 28 March 1929 in IOR: L/P&J/6/1878, file 1913).

be widened for women, offering a range of solutions from literacy qualifications, further property qualifications, group voting, or full adult franchise. The 1919 Government of India Act may have left the responsibility to provincial politicians to enfranchise women, and Indian women had actively campaigned on this issue in the Indian subcontinent, but in order to expand the franchise, and discuss the best method to do so, Indian suffragettes once again looked to the British government for assistance and returned to campaign in the imperial metropolis.

The Indian women's movement had developed greatly during the 1920s; they were engaging with international women's networks, and their transnational identities were shifting considerably away from uncritical imperial loyalty. At the same time, nationalism and self-determination was becoming increasingly important to the Indian suffragette. Their concerns about expanding the franchise reflected domestic nationalist concerns about the nature of political represen-tation in India, specifically relating to 'communal' divisions. It was with the rise of nationalist perspectives, and disillusionment with some Western interference, epitomized by the Mayo controversy, that Indian suffragettes began to simultaneously reject British female interventions while exhorting imperial leaders to finally ensure that female enfranchisement was enshrined in the constitution. As Mrinalini Sinha has explained, many of these tensions were inher-ent in the fight for suffrage within an imperial state.[3] Thus, in this chapter I will interrogate some of these tensions as they manifested themselves back in the imperial metropolis during the 1930s, before shifting the focus finally to the nationalist question in India and fran-chise struggles up until the enactment of the 1950 constitution.

A major shift in nationalist politics and determination for repre-sentation was evident in reaction to the 1927 Indian Statutory Commission. Known as the Simon Commission and designed to con-sider further political reform, it drew fierce criticism from Indian natio-nalists because no Indians were included at all in the committee. Even though the NUSEC had campaigned for British female representation,

---

[3] Sinha, 'Suffragism and Internationalism: The Enfranchisement of British and Indian Women under an Imperial State', *Indian Economic and Social History Review* 36, 4 (1999): 461–84.

they had not asked for Indian women to be included either.[4] However, the commission did consider female franchise. Although Indian nationalists boycotted the Simon Commission, a deputation of women led by dowager rani of Mandi from UP presented a memorandum in December 1928. They pointed out that women only had 50,000 votes out of one and half million in the province (that is, 3.33 per cent). They argued that this disparity was largely because women did not ordinarily possess property and so demanded new franchise qualifications for women. They also asked for some reserved seats for women in the legislative council, which were not based on nomination but on election. However, this was to be a temporary measure only.[5]

Not only was the low number of women eligible to vote an issue, but so was the low turnout of those who were eligible to vote. Sir John Simon noted in the Punjab in 1928 that though 21,000 women were able to vote, only 1,190 did so in the 1926 election. This was in contrast to the turnout of male voters, which was over 50 per cent. Meanwhile, in UP there was only 10 per cent turnout for women and not a single woman had voted in Allahabad. Nawab Muzaffar Khan, director of public information for the Punjab government, told Simon that special arrangements had not yet been made for separate polling booths for women, which particularly deterred Muslim women in purdah from voting.[6] With a phrase, echoing John Stuart Mill and suggested by the British campaigner Eleanor Rathbone, that was to resonate within the Indian women's movement, the Simon Commission concluded that the women's movement in India 'holds the key to progress' and recommended that female franchise be increased by enfranchising wives and widows aged over 25 of existing voters, raising the ratio to 1:2.[7]

4 Sinha, 'Suffragism and Internationalism', 467–8.

5 Mss Eur F77/326, 'Petticoats and Politics', *Indian Daily Telegraph*, 6 December 1928.

6 Mss Eur F77/325, Sir John Simon Papers, India Newscuttings, No. 6: 'Unwieldy Constituencies in the Punjab', *Civil & Military Gazette*, 5 November 1928; 'Elastic Electoral System for U.P.', *Pioneer*, 7 December 1928.

7 Cmd 3569, Indian Statutory Commission, *Report of the Indian Statutory Commission*, vol. II, *Recommendations* (London: His Majesty's Stationery Office, 1930), 93–4.

Following the Simon Commission, the British government held three consecutive RTCs in London, between 1930 and 1932, to discuss the constitutional future of India. They centred on the nature of political representation and the potential for dominion status for India. It is the second one, attended by Mohandas Gandhi, Congress figurehead, which often receives the most attention.[8] What has particularly escaped attention is that Indian women attended all three conferences as delegates and that female franchise was discussed. Begum Jahanara Shahnawaz attended all three, Radhabai Subbarayan the first two, and Sarojini Naidu attended the second only. It was at these conferences women were recognized as a separate political constituency—a fact that was reflected not only in government attitudes but also in the responses of the three main official women's organizations, namely the AIWC, the NCWI, and the WIA.

The 1930s were also a decade of growing nationalist activity in India, with which many Indian suffragettes were involved. In 1930, Gandhi led his well-publicized salt march to Dandi to protest against unjust taxes (including those on salt). He was accompanied by many women, including Naidu. The salt march kicked off the civil disobedience movement, which was characterized by no-tax campaigns and boycotts of British goods and institutions, as well as more violent tactics. As a result, between January 1932 and March 1933 alone, 120,000 Indians (men and women) were arrested. The Indian National Congress suspended these campaigns when in negotiation with the government over constitutional reform, but nationalist fervour (and communal tensions) continued to deepen. It was this backdrop of growing anti-colonialism, with nationalist women being imprisoned and subject to police brutality, which explains why the suffrage fight could not be disentangled from domestic and nationalist ties and identities.

In this chapter I will discuss the various constitutional negotiations over female franchise from 1930 to 1935, both in Britain and

---

[8] Famous images of Gandhi standing on the steps of 10 Downing Street, and visiting Lancashire mills in 1932, are associated with this delegation of Indians in London. See James D. Hunt, *Gandhi in London* (New Delhi: Promilla & Co., 1978), chapter 7 for more on the contemporary interest in Gandhi on his 1931 visit to the UK.

India, that is, the three RTCs, the 1932 Lothian Franchise Committee, and the JPC held in London in 1933. I will discuss the continuing activities of Indian women residing in Britain and mobile Indian campaigners leading up to the 1935 Government of India Act. This chapter ends with an overview of negotiations after 1935, including those in the Constituent Assembly in the lead up to Partition and Independence in 1947 and a new constitution that enshrined full adult franchise in India in 1949. The activities of the three main women's organizations dominate the narrative of female franchise, as they were intimately entwined with the dominant nationalist narratives about political representation and communalism. Tensions emerge both between Indian suffragettes and British allies in this period, and also within the Indian women's movement; thus it will become evident that ongoing transnational networking affected the imperial identities of Indian suffragettes and also influenced their understanding of national identities and national citizenship in a colonial and postcolonial world.

The First Round Table Conference

When the initial list of delegates was prepared for the inaugural 1930 RTC in London female delegates were not included. Congress boycotted the conference because many leaders were imprisoned at the time. The three official women's organizations in India, the AIWC, NCWI, and WIA, also withdrew any initial demands for female participation.[9] However, Indian women were very interested in ongoing franchise debates related to potential self-government. Mrinalini Sen, on behalf of the London branch of the WIA, made various representations to British MPs in the spring of 1930 to ask that the RTC should formulate a scheme for self-government and that it should be fully representative. She met with Wedgwood Benn, the secretary of state for India, and with the Labour MP Edith Picton-Tubervill alongside other female MPs in a committee room at the House of Commons. At a Women's International League meeting

---

9 Pearson, 'Reserved Seats—Women and the Vote in Bombay', *Indian Economic and Social History Review* 20, 47 (1983): 53.

in honour of Indian women resident in Britain, Sen raised the issue again. She discussed 'what Indian women are looking for from British women at this juncture' and asked for their support in their demands for self-government and recognition of the status of women in any new constitution.[10]

The British independent MP Eleanor Rathbone petitioned for both British and Indian women to be included in the RTC delegation. She was to take up the issue of Indian women's franchise vociferously over the next few years, having been president of the NUSEC and having attended IWSA conferences in Geneva, Rome, Paris, and Berlin. Rathbone told NUSEC members in 1928 that as long as 'imperialism is an unescapable fact, its responsibilities are also an unescapable fact', and these responsibilities included those towards Indian women.[11] As Sinha argues, British women, especially Rathbone, heavily influenced the terms of the debate on Indian female suffrage into the 1930s. It was because of British women, Sinha argues, that Indian suffrage was based both on nationalism and a new inter-war internationalism.[12] British women's organizations, such as the WFL and St Joan's Social and Political Alliance, also sent letters to the India Office specifically asking for British women to be involved in the RTC, aggrieved that equal participation in British politics had not extended to these imperial negotiations.[13] These demands for British women continued into November 1930 even after the Indian women had been appointed.[14]

No British women were invited to any of the conferences, but two Indian women were eventually appointed to the first.

---

[10] 'Women's Indian Association', *Indian Ladies Magazine* (June 1930): 555–6.

[11] *Women's Leader*, 13 July 1928, quoted in Ramusack, 'Catalysts or Helpers?', 113.

[12] Sinha, 'Suffragism and Internationalism', 472–3.

[13] TWL, St Joan's Social and Political Alliance Minute Book, 7 November 1930, 2SJA/A1/6; 'Women and the Round Table Conference', *The Vote*, 19 September 1930, 300.

[14] Margery Corbett Ashby, for example, was 'bitterly disappointed', hoping at least that a British woman could be included as 'technical adviser' ('Woman to Date', *The Scotsman*, 17 November 1930, 14).

Radhabai Subbarayan's nomination was made mainly through family connections. Her husband was chief minister of Madras, her father was a prominent social reformer, and she had been educated at Somerville College, Oxford.[15] Begum Jahanara Shahnawaz was appointed partly out of convenience. Her father, Muhammad Shafi, was a trained barrister and leading Muslim official in British India. She was already in London, having served as her father's private secretary during the earlier Imperial Conference, but was invited to serve on the RTC independently of her father (as a representative of Indian women).[16] The WIA used its journal, *Stri Dharma*, to express its displeasure with these appointments. In October 1930, one of the editors decried the existing system of nomination of women to political posts which implied that only women with official connections and those who were loyal to the imperial system could get seats.

> Such have been the appointment of Mrs Subbarayan and Mrs Shah Nawaz to the RTC. They have absolutely no credentials from the organised women of India to say that they represent the opinions of Indian womanhood. They represent only themselves and as such women will wish them good luck, but they will mis-represent the thirty thousand prisoners, including many of Indian's best women.[17]

As a correspondent would later complain in the AIWC journal *Roshni*, Shahnawaz was appointed by the British government because of her family connections and because they wanted '"safe" men and women to represent India at such gatherings'.[18] Neither woman was involved in the executive committees of the main women's organizations in India, though Shahnawaz had been a member of the AIWC since its inception in 1927.

The other Indian delegates were divided by interest groups: Muslims, Hindus, Sikhs, Christians, Parsees, Depressed Classes, Europeans, Anglo-Indians, Landlords, Labour, and Universities. Princes,

[15] 'Women and the Round Table Conference', *The Vote*, 19 September 1933, 300.

[16] Jahan Ara Shahnawaz, *Father and Daughter: A Political Autobiography* (Lahore: Nigarishat, 1971), 100–3.

[17] 'Women and the Elections', *Stri Dharma* 13, 12 (October 1930): 532.

[18] 'Correspondence', *Roshni* 2, 7 (October 1941): 108.

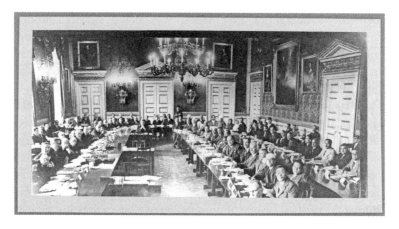

IMAGE 5.1   Round Table Conference, London, November 1930
© The British Library Board, Photo 784/1 (81)

representatives of provinces, liberals, and members of the Justice Party also attended. These different interests were exploited in discussions at the conferences, where much of the disagreement over constitutional reform centred on the nature of political quotas. It was with this so-called quota system in mind that the women delegates ventured to discuss female representation, as well as the franchise, implicitly querying whether women constituted a separate interest that required factional representation too.

The first conference was inaugurated on Wednesday, 12 November 1930 (see Image 5.1). On the following Thursday, Shahnawaz made her first speech to remark on the nature of the conference and the involvement of women delegates. She had prepared the speech beforehand and consulted Subbarayan. Subbarayan told her the speech was too emotional for British tastes, but Shahnawaz did not alter her speech, which, in her estimation, received a very positive reaction not only from the men at the conference but also from the public.[19] The *Manchester Guardian* described it as the 'greatest personal triumph' and *The Scotsman* as a 'remarkable triumph', recounting the 'storm of applause' at the end of the speech as well as notes of congratulations

---

[19] Shahnawaz, *Father and Daughter*, 106.

that were passed round the table from the other delegates including the prime minister.[20]

Shahnawaz recounted that on her return to the hotel, members of the public held up placards with her photograph and sentences from her speech including 'We are trying to combine Western freedom of thought and action with Eastern restraint.'[21] In an interview with the *Daily Herald* in October 1930, Shahnawaz evoked Kipling: 'East is still East, and West is West.'[22] At the conference, she played to stereotypes about 'Eastern restraint' although she was keen to disabuse Orientalist notions about the 'so-called unchanging East' pointing out:

> Ten years ago who could have thought of Indian women coming to London and taking part in the deliberations of such a Conference? To-day, not only a Hindu, but a Muslim woman, belonging to a family the women of which have always observed strict purdah, are actually sitting with their brethren around one Table in order to evolve a suitable constitution for their country.[23]

The *Daily Mail* argued that her address typified the 'revolution' that had taken place in recent years in terms of women's rights around the world. In an interview the following day Shahnawaz was keen to stress that, despite the continued incidence of purdah, women in India enjoyed many freedoms and advances and she was uneasy with the existing misunderstandings that British people, including British women, had about Indian women.[24]

Shahnawaz appealed to sentiment then, as criticized by Subbarayan but lauded by the British press, in evoking recent improvements for Indian women. She also expressed her public gratitude to the secretary of state and Lord Irwin not only for inviting women but

---

[20] *Manchester Guardian*, 21 November 1930, 8; 'Indian Womanhood', *The Scotsman*, 21 November 1930, 11.

[21] Shahnawaz, *Father and Daughter*, 107.

[22] 'Mrs Shah Nawaz, a Prominent Delegate to the Imperial Conference, Tells "How We Women Are Changing India"', *Daily Herald*, 7 October 1930, 8.

[23] Indian Round Table Conference, 12 November 1930–19 January 1931 Proceedings (Cmd. 3778), 5th Plenary Meeting, 20 November 1930, 113.

[24] 'The Women of India' and 'Begum Shah Nawaz', *Daily Mail*, 22 November 1930, 10, 11.

for making the conference politically representative. However, she had no intention of being a wallflower. She articulated her desire for the conference to agree on dominion status for India and this appeared to take priority over women's issues. She explained that once India had control over legislation Indians would be able to enact social change, but she mentioned that social reform 'depends mostly upon its women'. She argued that reform was being stifled by the foreign government.

> Almost as soon as our men got the franchise, they did not hesitate in giving us our share; and now that the women of India are coming forward and taking an active part in the political life of the country, the solution of all these problems will not be difficult to find. With women to guide in social matters, the men of a country can achieve greater success in social reform.[25]

Subbarayan and Shahnawaz met with various British women in London during 1930, seeking their advice and discussing the franchise question in Shahnawaz's hotel room. As an article for the *The Vote* put it, although female franchise was ultimately the concern of Indian women, 'indirectly, however these questions are also of great concern to the women of this country, for we know by experience that the inferior status of women in any one country has a damaging effect on the status of women in every other country'.[26] Nancy Astor, the American-born Conservative MP for Plymouth, organized a dinner meeting of 50 women who were leading figures in various professions for Shahnawaz to meet; another meeting with female MPs was organized at the Ladies' Carlton Club. As part of the Indian delegation and along with her parents, Shahnawaz was invited to a number of society events in the last two months of 1930 including those organized by the British–American Dance Club, the Royal Empire Society, the British Federation of University Women, and a meeting with the editors of the *Spectator*.[27] Shahnawaz also became good friends with Ishbel MacDonald, daughter of Ramsay, with whom she discussed

---

[25] Shahnawaz, *Father and Daughter*, 115.

[26] 'British Women for India?', *The Vote*, 6 March 1931, 76.

[27] *The Times*, 4 November 1930, 17; 15 November 1930, 15; 27 November 1930, 17; 6 December 1930, 15; 11 December 1930, 19; *Morning Post*, 11 December 1930, 9.

issues related to women.[28] Shahnawaz and Subbarayan consulted with Indian women who lived in London too, specifically Rameshwari Nehru and Dhanvanthi Rama Rau.[29]

Interest in these women extended beyond London and indeed beyond Britain. Much of the attention was on their appearance. The *Irish Times*, for example, was keen to remark that both women wore 'native dress' and also that Subbarayan wore a big diamond on the side of the nose while pointing out that Shahnawaz did not.[30] The Associated Press had used similar descriptions of Subbarayan's 'flowing Eastern gown' and diamond nose ring, which were picked up by the *Washington Post*.[31] The *New Zealand Herald* was filled with admiration for Shahnawaz's speeches at the conference and described her as an 'astonishingly advanced woman of the East', but was also quick to describe her 'beautiful hair' and the 'golden embroideries' on her sari. The paper reported on an interview in which Shahnawaz had wished to point out some of the ignorance she had encountered about Indian women. She explained that purdah was not a cage and

'Do you know', she went on, 'I was asked quite seriously the other day whether we had bathrooms in India? That question showed to me very plainly that most of the women of England can know very little about India.'[32]

A correspondent for the *Auckland Star* reported on the 'remarkable women' at the first conference, explaining that Kipling's teachings on the 'unchanging East' were no longer appropriate. Particularly entranced by Shahnawaz, with her 'short stature' but 'forceful character', the reporter quoted her remark, 'I have always believed in co-operation

---

[28] Ishbel was a Labour Party member for London County Council but also acted as hostess for her father at 10 Downing Street including at a luncheon that Shahnawaz attended on 16 October 1930 (*The Times*, 17 October 1930, 17); Shahnawaz, *Father and Daughter*, 115–16.

[29] NMML, AIWC Papers, Roll 2, File 14, Shahnawaz to Rajwade, 14 April 1931.

[30] 'London Letter: The Round Table Conference', *Irish Times*, 23 December 1930, 6.

[31] 'Rights for Women in India Demanded', *Washington Post*, 23 December 1930, 3.

[32] 'Begum Shah Nawaz', *New Zealand Herald*, 16 January 1931, 5.

with England.'[33] In the final session of the first conference, on 19 January 1931, Shahnawaz rose to speak again. She concluded her contribution to the conference with heartfelt thanks for the friendship between 'England' and India, for allowing Indians to sit around the table on an equal platform, and with thanks to the 'British nation for their kind hospitality, help and sympathy'.[34] It is no surprise that Shahnawaz was seen as a British loyalist by many Indian women.

Female franchise and representation dominated Subbarayan's and Shahnawaz's activities though. The first RTC convened a franchise subcommittee on all questions relating to voting in India, and both Shahnawaz and Subbarayan sat on this subcommittee. On 20 December 1930, Shahnawaz and Subbarayan submitted a memorandum to the subcommittee. They decided to ask for full adult franchise, in line with the policy of the national Indian women's organizations, seeing fit to broaden the debate about female franchise to include all other disenfranchised groups. Subbarayan was particularly critical of the property qualification, arguing that civic spirit was not peculiar to those with more wealth and argued that the electorate needed to be broadened to reflect the views of all sections of people. However, in subsequent discussion, both women conceded that adult franchise would not be practical immediately and discussed a number of concessions that would at least increase the female franchise a little. It is this timidity that played into imperial hands, allowing arguments about the illiteracy of Indians and the logistics of voting (especially with the custom of purdah), to stand and prevent further franchise advances.

On 22 December 1930, Shahnawaz told the committee that her focus was on full adult franchise; she was hoping to increase the franchise to 25 per cent of the adult population and to broaden the rural vote, but mentioned that in the first instance every man and woman who could read and write should be given the vote immediately.[35] At the next meeting, on 30 December, Shahnawaz asserted: 'there is no such thing as a feminist movement in my country', explaining that men and women worked together in India. Women were not the only

---

[33] 'Oriental Women', *Auckland Star*, 15 January 1931, 12.

[34] Cmd. 3778, final session, 19 January 1931, 511–12.

[35] BL, Q/RTC/23: 2nd meeting of franchise subcommittee, 22 December 1930.

disenfranchised group in India. However, describing women as born administrators and rulers of the home, of domestic finances, and as 'custodian of the future generation'—'[i]n many instances you will find that a woman can far more intelligently exercise her vote than a man in the same position will be able to do'—Shahnawaz did not wish to challenge the idea that women occupied separate, domestic spheres.[36]

The franchise subcommittee presented their report to the rest of the delegates on 16 January 1931. Unable to comment on the question of the composition of the legislature and while 'generally' agreeing that adult suffrage was the ultimate goal, the main recommendation of the committee was that an expert Franchise Commission should be appointed in order to find a solution to increase the electorate to between 10 and 25 per cent of the total population. The committee acknowledged that there was 'great disparity' between the voting ability of men and women and that special qualifications would be needed to reduce this difference, but felt that they were not qualified, and had not seen enough evidence, to provide recommendations other than that the Franchise Commission find a solution to this and that in the first instance the age limit should be reduced from 25 to 21 for women.[37] The women did gain broad support for their demands though. Numerous letters of support were sent to them or to various MPs by British women.[38] A report in the *Guardian* commended the originality of Subbarayan and Shahnawaz's demands that the female vote should be enshrined in the constitution and not just left to the discretion of Indian legislatures.[39]

Subbarayan and Shahnawaz also decided to ask for reserved seats for women in all the legislatures for the next three elections as a way

[36] For more on the application of the separate sphere ideology in India, see Tanika Sarkar, *Hindu Wife, Hindu Nation* (Delhi: Permanent Black, 2001) and Partha Chatterjee, *The Nation and Its Fragments: Colonial and Postcolonial Histories* (Princeton: Princeton University Press, 1993).

[37] Q/RTC/23. Indian Round Table Conference Franchise Committee 1930–1: 'Draft Report of subcommittee' (January 1931); Cmd. 3778, subcommittee no.VI (Franchise), 385–7.

[38] BL, Mss Eur F341/163. Begum Shahnawaz, 'Women's Movement in India', December 1942.

[39] 'Parliament of all India', *Manchester Guardian*, 23 December 1930, 4.

to jump-start the number of female MPs and give them experience in political office.[40] Referring to the experience of Britain where it had taken 12 years to only elect 15 female MPs, as well as to the slow progress in Canada and Australia, Shahnawaz asserted that the 'theory that women need only a fair field and no favour does not yet apply in this world—certainly not in India'.[41] They had the support of British female MPs who sent in a memorandum advocating that wives or widows of existing Indian male voters be given the vote, when aged over 21. Shahnawaz discussed this on 30 December, also restating the demand for reserved seats for women in legislatures for the next 11 years after which 'we are quite prepared to take our chance in a fair field and no favour'.[42] The *Guardian*'s special correspondent supported the policy, citing the experience of other countries where women were finding it hard to get elected when their entry into public political life was new.[43]

However, official Indian women's organizations (such as the AIWC, NCWI, and WIA) opposed political quotas for women, especially concerned that not only would communal divisions enter the women's movement, but sex divisions in society would also be created. Geraldine Forbes has argued that the desire of Indian women to dissociate from reserved seats derived from the dominant ideology of the 'new women' which advocated that women reject gender competition and emphasize the special interests of their sex.[44] This perspective can be exemplified by Shahnawaz's speech to the minorities subcommittee on 22 December 1930 in which she urged the men to settle their differences and work for Hindu–Muslim unity on 'behalf

[40] Q/RTC/23. Indian Round Table Conference 1930–1, Franchise Committee.

[41] Charles A. Seldon, 'Indian Women Ask Equality as Voters', *New York Times*, 23 December 1930, 7.

[42] Q/RTC/23, 3rd meeting of franchise subcommittee, 30 December 1930.

[43] 'Parliament of all India', *Manchester Guardian*, 23 December 1930, 4.

[44] Geraldine Forbes, 'Women of Character, Grit and Courage: The Reservation Debate in Historical Perspective', in *Between Tradition, Counter-Tradition and Heresy: Contributions in Honour of Vina Mazumdar*, ed. Lotika Sarkar, Kumud Sharma, and Leela Kasturi (Delhi: Rainbow Publishers, 2002), 234.

of the women of India': 'As sisters we expect of you, as daughters we beg of you, as mothers we demand of you to come to a settlement.'[45] Although Shahnawaz would later support the communal award for separate Muslim electorates, which was seen as tacit support for separate seats for Muslim women as well, the narrative of united womanhood prevailed. This narrative of a united *Indian* womanhood was allied to nationalist sentiment as the idea of 'global sisterhood' was not invoked. Undoubtedly, the women at the conferences and the official women organizations were elite and privileged women whose demands were couched in self-interest. However, this was the case for all the delegates at the conferences and so the women were not unique in this regard.

Although organized women in India had previously been in favour of nominated seats for women to political posts, by the time of the RTCs they had decided to make a unified stand against separate seats for women. There were multiple reasons for this, including the question of merit, which often raises its head when quotas are discussed. Forbes argues that Gandhi's example was very influential, especially after his fast in 1932, as women felt more included in his version of nationalism.[46] As separate electorates had already been enshrined in the Morley–Minto reforms of 1909, the women's organizations may have been fighting against political inevitability but they were particularly concerned that agreeing to a separate electorate would allow for these reserved seats to be divided into further allocations for women by 'community'. Although the Muslim League had a women's arm which was generally in favour of seats for Muslim women and despite the fact that there were multiple women's societies based on religious and community lines, the WIA, AIWC, and NCWI had always been decidedly non-communal. Therefore, they were willing to accept a small proportion of elected female politicians, idealistically believing that if a full adult franchise was introduced then it would only be a matter of time before a fair share of women were elected.

[45] BL, Q/RTC/24. Indian Round Table Conference 1930–31, Minorities Committee.

[46] Forbes, 'Votes for Women: The Demand for Women's Franchise in India 1917–1937', in *Symbols of Power: Studies on the Political Status of Women in India*, ed. Vina Mazumdar (Bombay: Allied Publishers, 1979), 14–15.

Alongside reserved seats the Indian legislature already had nominated seats to which women could be selected (as Muthulakshmi Reddi had been nominated in Madras in 1927).[47]

In the aftermath of the first conference, the leaders of the WIA continued to express their concern about the lack of female representation on the conference, their disgust that it had gone ahead despite the political situation, and their concern that Subbarayan, in particular, was too loyal to the imperial government, as she had made recommendations that did not reflect Indian nationalist thought.[48] Acting independently at the first RTC, and with only Shahnawaz as ally and sounding board, Subbarayan was keen to defend her belief in the validity of asking for special voting privileges for Indian women in a pamphlet published in 1933.

> As the Committee was not prepared to recommend immediate introduction of adult franchise, my colleague Begum Shah Nawaz and I jointly put forward certain proposals on the question of the political status of women and *we did so only after making a careful study of the subject and after consulting as far as possible the views of such Indian women in India and in England as we could approach in the short space of time at our disposal and we clearly understood that we had their support.*[49]

Subbarayan pointed out in the pamphlet that in September 1930, prior to sailing to Britain for the RTC, she had asked Indian women for their views but the WIA refused to recognize the conference. She also questioned the percentage of women who opposed special privileges, asserting that there was no doubt that the opposition was not representative of the unanimous decision of either the national women's organizations, let alone all of Indian womanhood. However, Subbarayan claimed that she did speak informally

---

[47] D. Graham Pole, 'The Report of the Joint Select Committee', *Modern Review*, 7, 1 (January 1935): 54. A total of 40 out of 145 members of the Central Legislative Assembly were nominated by the Government of India to their post, and there were nominated positions at provincial level too.

[48] 'Mrs Subbarayan's Commonsense', *Stri Dharma* 14, 5 (March 1931): 180.

[49] Radhabai Subbarayan, *A Statement on the Political Status of Women under the New Indian Constitution* (Madras: Madras Publishing House, 1933), 25. Emphasis in original.

with some members of the WIA and believed that they were in favour of special qualifications as a minimum: 'It was only in May 1931 that I learnt that there was a divergence of views among women in India.'[50]

In the April 1931 edition of *Stri Dharma* the WIA put forward its demands for adult suffrage, preferable to the 'anomalies and inequalities which will come about by fancy franchises for numerical reasons'.[51] It was with these concerns that, by May 1931, the WIA had called a meeting alongside the AIWC and NCWI to draft a memorandum condemning the recommendations of the conference and demanding that only full adult franchise would be accepted. This had followed the 1931 Karachi Indian National Congress meeting which had resolved in favour of adult franchise, and a promise that Gandhi had given south Indian women that he would secure adult franchise for women.[52] Subbarayan was not the only female leader concerned about these demands; Muthulakshmi Reddi had hesitations but the three women's organizations were determined to present a united front on this issue.[53] Forbes, however, has been critical of the ways in which the main Indian women's organizations suppressed dissenting views, presenting an ideal vision of 'sisters under the sari', and thus quashed democratic impulses or meaningful discussion about female representation and political desires.[54] Anupama Roy has also argued that the demand for universal franchise masked social tensions and the 'complex interlocking of ideological, colonialist, nationalist, masculinist and suffragist formulations' over women's rights and women's 'place'.[55]

After the first conference, Subbarayan consulted Rathbone regularly for her advice on the female franchise question and how to deal with the often vociferous criticism from the main Indian women's

---

[50] Subbarayan, *A Statement on the Political Status*, 27.

[51] 'Notes and Comments', *Stri Dharma* 14, 6 (April 1931): 230.

[52] 'Women and the New Constitution', *Stri Dharma* 14, 7 (May 1931): 286.

[53] Mrinalini Sinha, *Specters of Mother India: The Global Restructuring of an Empire* (Durham: Duke University Press, 2006), 212–13.

[54] Forbes, 'Women of Character', 235.

[55] Anupama Roy, *Gendered Citizenship: Historical and Conceptual Explorations* (New Delhi: Orient Longman, 2005), 147.

organizations.[56] For example, on 19 March 1931, Subbarayan worried that 'sentiment' was influencing women who had got too excited by the 'appreciation and applause' of Congress during the civil disobedience movement:

> [They] think the interest of women are quite safe and need no special attention. They believe in a 'fair field and no favour'. They will not discuss but keep saying 'our men are very good to us and we need not worry about our interests in the future'.[57]

In May 1931, Subbarayan explained to Rathbone that the prominent women's organizations had declared that they wanted 'equality and no privileges', and used the phrase 'a fair field and no favour' again. She argued that because Sarojini Naidu, a leading female member of Congress and the WIA and an ally of Gandhi, was opposed to reservation of seats, those who were in favour of reservation were too intimidated to speak out. She asked Rathbone to take on the cause of reservation with her own networks. Subbarayan specifically asked Rathbone to ask Sir Philip and Mabel Hartog to write to the WIA; the ICW in London to write to the Bombay Council of Women; and the Women's International League to write to the AIWC.[58] She evidently felt that Western female intervention would be needed by Indian women.

The Second Round Table Conference

The AIWC and WIA had expressed their disappointment with the appointments of Subbarayan and Shahnawaz to the first RTC, but when a second was being put together and it was evident that Gandhi would attend in 1931, attitudes softened. In correspondence, members of the AIWC agreed that though Subbarayan and Shahnawaz were both perfectly able women, it was imperative that they send their

[56] Criticism came not only from the WIA, AIWC, and NCWI, but also other women's organizations such as the Bombay Congress group Rashtriya Stree Sabha and the RSS group Desh Sevika Sangh (see Pearson, 'Reserved Seats', 53).

[57] TWL, Rathbone Papers, 7ELR/07, Subbarayan to Rathbone, 19 March 1931.

[58] 7ELR/07, Subbarayan to Rathbone, 1 May 1931.

own representatives this time. Meanwhile, British women's organizations made renewed attempts to pressure for British women to
be involved.[59] Concurrently, as discussed in the previous chapter, a
Burma RTC was called for in November 1931 and British women's
organizations became involved in heavy petitioning for British and
Burmese women delegates.[60] The London branch of the WIA also
made efforts to liaise with British women's organizations for the
Indian RTC; while in India, a deputation of 15 women visited the
viceroy and suggested the names of 11 women who could be included
in the next delegation. Subbarayan and Shahnawaz were not included
in that list.[61] The March 1931 WIA memorandum explained that 2 or
3 women out of 100 members was not an adequate number, and that
at least a dozen were needed to bring forward the views of women.[62]
Subbarayan, now back in India, urged Rathbone to speak to the prime
minister and secretary of state to explain that it was not enough to
increase the number of women at the second conference, but that
they had to be allowed a voice on key subcommittees, especially the
Federal Structures Committee.[63] Ultimately Subbarayan was called
back to attend the conference, as was Shahnawaz. Only one more
woman delegate was added: Sarojini Naidu, close political ally of
Gandhi.

At the second conference Naidu positioned herself as representative of the official women's organizations, perhaps more so than
her Congress affiliation. She presented the memorandum that the
three women's organizations had put forward on franchise, which
explained that the 'accredited leaders of the Nation' had made a declaration on the equal rights and obligations of all citizens that had
stated that sex would not be a barrier. The memorandum emphasized
their disapproval of the recommendations to allow the wives and
widows of enfranchised men to vote, stating that women should earn

---

59 'British Women for India?', *The Vote*, 6 March 1931, 76.
60 BL, L/PO/9/3, Burma Round Table Conference.
61 'Women at the Round Table Conference', *Stri Dharma* 14, 9 (July 1931):
387–8.
62 Women's Indian Association, *Memorandum on the Status of Women in
the Future Constitution of India* (Madras: Lodhra Press, March 1931), 8.
63 7ELR/07, Subbarayan to Rathbone, 30 March 1931.

citizenship rights of their own individual accord.[64] In an interview with the *Manchester Guardian*, Naidu explained that the demand for full adult franchise was the only demand fitting for a 'civilised country' as women did not want to see any discrimination either in their favour or against others. Having been brought up as a Hindu in the predominately Muslim state of Hyderabad, she also saw her role at the conference as that of bringing harmony between the communities, but her main focus was on strengthening India as a nation.[65]

Subbarayan's speech to the Federal Structures Committee on 18 September 1931 reveals how defensive she felt about her position and her actions in the previous conference. She admitted that in the previous year, with Shahnawaz, they had asked for open elections and also some reserved seats, but for 'everything we did last year we consulted as far as possible the views of such Indian ladies in India and in England as we could approach in the short space of time at our disposal, and clearly understood that we had their support'.[66] Having been criticized following the first conference, Shahnawaz was keen to ally with the most prominent Indian women's organizations and Naidu at the second conference. Together they submitted a joint memorandum, presenting the manifesto on full adult franchise issued by the WIA, AIWC, and NCWI, isolating Subbarayan who stuck to her individual suggestions. They claimed that the manifesto was 'an authoritative statement of representative opinion, duly considered and widely endorsed, on the case and claim of Indian women', warning the committee to resist any pleas 'advanced by small individual groups of people, either in India or in this country, for any kind of temporary concessions'.[67] These official associations did not acknowledge, of course, that they represented only a small proportion of Indian women themselves. In 1931, for example, the

[64] Q/RTC/2. Indian Round Table Conference (Second Session) 1931. Appendix IV, Memorandum Representing the Views of a Number of Indian Women's Organisations: Presented by Mrs Naidu.

[65] 'The Women of India', *Manchester Guardian*, 14 September 1931, 4.

[66] RUSC, Lady Astor Papers, MS1416/1/1012, Speech made by Mrs Subbarayan at the Federal Structures Committee, 18 September 1931.

[67] Q/RTC/2. Indian Round Table Conference (Second Session) 1931, 'Memorandum by Mrs Naidu and Begum Shah Nawaz with reference to Appendix XIV'.

WIA had nearly 72 branches and just over 4,000 members. Though women could speak in vernacular languages at annual conferences, they were generally English-speaking.[68]

Avabai Mehta, a member of the London WIA, described how all three women were much in demand by women's organizations during the second RTC, noting that Naidu was the 'undisputed leader and an orator', Subbarayan was 'quiet and efficient', and Shahnawaz was 'accomplished' and aware of her role as representative of Muslim women.[69] The Equal Rights Committee, the Actresses' Franchise League, the National Union of Women Teachers, the Open Door Council, St Joan's Social and Political Alliance, the Six Point Group, and the WFL submitted a joint memorandum early in 1932 to the members of the RTC and Lothian Committee in support of Indian women's organizations. They dismissed the need for 'privileges or special rights' and expressed the need to enfranchise as many women as possible.[70] The three women delegates were honoured at the Lyceum Club by the London committee of the WIA; a number of other Indian women, who resided in Britain, attended alongside British colleagues. Subbarayan spoke about the bond between the women of East and West, while Shahnawaz protested that Naidu had not been able to 'twist her round her finger' to change her recommendations from the first conference but had been persuaded by the strong feelings of young women in India. Naidu told the meeting that the ideal of Indian womanhood was equal partnership with men.[71]

As Renuka Ray was to put it in 1973, Indian women spokespeople strongly objected to separate elections because they resisted applications of 'divide and rule'.[72] Thus, political representation and the citizenship issue were intimately tied to Indian women's antagonism towards the imperial state. This antagonism soon became directed

---

[68] 'Women at the Round Table Conference', *Stri Dharma* (July 1931): 387.

[69] Avabai B. Wadia, *The Light Is Ours: Memoirs and Movements* (London: International Planned Parenthood Federation, 2001), 71.

[70] 'Equal Rights for Women', *Indian Ladies Magazine* (March–April 1932), 392–3; see also Q/IFC/39.

[71] 'Social Work in India', *The Times*, 30 September 1931, 14.

[72] BL, Mss Eur F341/19, Mithan J. Lam, *Women in India: A General Survey of Their Condition Status and Advancement* (New Delhi: The All India Women's Conference, 1973), 2.

against British women, too, relations with whom had already been strained after the publication of *Mother India* in 1927. These relations had not been helped when internationalist ally Margery Corbett Ashby appeared to support Mayo's publication, as Rathbone had done initially.[73] Indian women were keen to assert authority, which is why they were unwilling to show any weakness by conceding over seats or franchise, as British women had advised them to do. Despite her own loyalties, Subbarayan soon also became afraid of 'Englishwomen' 'butting in' and tried to tread a fine line between using British contacts and asserting Indian women's independence on these matters. In a letter of 8 January 1932, Rathbone responded:

> By the by, if when you or others are pressing for reservation of seats you are again criticised (as you told me you had been) on the ground that you are being too much influenced by Englishwomen, you can tell your critics that the English women's societies which have interested themselves in India are just as much divided as Indian women themselves.... Another point I should like to put to you is this: that it is really inconsistent of Indian women to say that they want perfect equality between the sexes and yet that they resent Englishwomen expressing any views about Indian affairs. So long as this country is concerned with India at all and is appointing Committees and placing projects before Parliament, it cannot be right that British men should be able and expected to express views and exercise influence, while British women are asked to keep their hands off.[74]

A year later, on 6 February 1933, Subbarayan wrote to Rathbone:

> I hope you will not mind if I request you to keep this matter strictly confidential. It is not because I do not wish to acknowledge my appreciation of your help but because the suspicion that I am 'a tool in the hands of the Br. women' will do harm to our cause.[75]

These tensions and a turn away from British assistance became more apparent over the decade. Though Indian suffragettes continued to

---

[73] Christine Bolt, *Sisterhood Questioned? Race, Class and Internationalism in the American and British Women's Movements, c. 1880s–1970s* (Abingdon: Routledge, 2005), 61.

[74] 7ELR/07, Rathbone to Subbarayan, 8 January 1932.

[75] 7ELR/07, Subbarayan to Rathbone, 6 February 1933.

value British friendship and support, they were increasingly keen to assert leadership and direction over Indian franchise demands.

The Lothian Committee 1932 and the Immediate Aftermath: Campaigning Back in India

Following recommendations at the first RTC, a Franchise Commission was set up to look into the multiple issues relating to franchise that needed to be decided for the new constitution. This commission was chaired by Lord Lothian (Philip Henry Kerr), former under-secretary of state for India, and also included two women: Radhabai Subbarayan and the Conservative MP Mary Pickford. Prime Minister Ramsay MacDonald had urged Lothian to attach special importance to the question of increasing the female franchise, as well as to improve the representation of labour. Before leaving for India, Lothian and Pickford met with Corbett Ashby, Lady Layton, Lady Hartog, and a couple of other women representatives from British women's groups to informally discuss women's enfranchisement in India.[76] The committee toured India in early 1932, and also liaised with provincial subcommittees. Both the main committee and subcommittees met with 311 witnesses and received at least 1,307 written statements. In their final report they concluded that adult suffrage was impracticable, that each province had offered different recommendations because their electoral rolls were already so different, and that though most representatives of women's organizations desired equality with men this was not practical either.[77]

Eleanor Rathbone did not get a seat on the Lothian Committee (even though she offered to pay for a second British woman to be on the committee) and decided to follow them out to India, in an unofficial capacity, from January to March 1932.[78] She was not allowed to engage with the committee but met with various British and Indian women residing in India and sent back circulars to Britain on her activities. Rathbone was unable to convince AIWC members, such as Shareefah Hamid Ali, to change their mind on reservations

---

[76] Q/IFC/92, 'Women's Franchise', memorandum 7 January 1932.
[77] L/PJ/9/63, Indian Franchise Committee, 'English Summary'.
[78] Q/IFC/39, Rathbone to Lothian, 23 December 1931.

of seats. At a meeting at Bombay, she faced criticism from a group of women who told her that they 'were determined to take nothing from Englishwomen', telling her to mind her own business and that she was a spy and an 'English K. Mayo'. However, she did meet some Indian women who were keen on reservations of seats and limited franchise advancements. Rathbone was convinced that only a minority, swayed by Congress, actually wanted full adult suffrage.

Rathbone stayed at Subbarayan's house when she visited Madras, maintaining that friendship though Subbarayan was busy with the committee.[79] Subbarayan's appointment to the Indian Franchise Committee (IFC) was probably inevitable given her connections and her experience at the first RTC, but women leaders in India continued to deride her involvement. Following her work on the committee, Subbarayan was coldly dismissed by the joint secretary to the IFC. In private correspondence in November 1932, he expressed the feeling that the delegates at the RTCs had been pursuing personal ends and hoped never to meet Subbarayan again.[80]

The AIWC and WIA met on 17 February 1932 to decide on a strategy of response to the IFC. Concerned that the committee was unrepresentative, they suggested that Shahnawaz should be appointed as an additional member, and reiterated the demands of the memorandum they had sent to the second RTC in favour of full adult suffrage and no reservation of seats.[81] The IFC did not appoint Shahnawaz but did meet with various female witnesses at both national and provincial levels. For example, the UP committee, which included Mrs J.P. Srivastava, had received 11 responses from women to their questionnaire and had interviewed seven women. Miss S.I. Vincent and Begum Habibullah met the committee on 10 March 1932 in Lucknow on behalf of the Oudh branch of the AIWC. They toed the AIWC line and demanded full adult suffrage, suggesting that a group system of voting might work if direct, individual voting was impracticable in the

---

[79] Mss Eur F341/156, Rathbone Circulars, 7 February 1932, 9 February 1932, 6 March 1932; Q/IFC/39, Rathbone to Lothian, 9 April 1932.

[80] BL, Mss Eur F138/15. Sir John Gilbert Laithwaite Papers, T. C. S. Jayaratnam to Laithwaite, 25 November 1932.

[81] L/PJ/9/63, Indian Franchise Committee, Lakshmibai Rajwade to Prime Minister, 19 February 1932.

first instance. In the questionnaire responses, women varied between agreeing with the AIWC, opposing the wifehood qualification, and suggesting only wives, not widows, should be enfranchised. They also varied in their agreement on the degree of literacy needed, and whether 5 or 10 per cent seats should be reserved for women.[82]

When Mrs Rustomji Faridoonji, vice president of the AIWC, met the IFC in Delhi on 23 March, she was questioned by Sir Mohammed Yakub who pointed out that women in England had only got the franchise five years ago after a long campaign. Faridoonji retorted that the comparison was not valid:

> No doubt England struggled to get this right and other countries also struggle; but that is no reason why we should also undergo the same ordeal. We feel that we have come in at a critical period and that we can go faster than the other countries. We are moving with the times.

Then, when B. R. Ambedkar asked her whether she was certain that the majority of women in India were progressive, Faridoonji affirmed this was the case from what she had seen.[83] As the Bombay AIWC put it in a memorandum, the AIWC did not support reserved seats because imposing a minimum would limit the number of women who might be elected through open elections and they also had no concerns about electing male politicians who could speak on behalf of a fully representative electorate. They pointed out that in the German Reichstag women only occupied about 10 per cent of seats despite their superior education, and that the number of women MPs in Britain had declined in the last election, but they used these examples to prove that they wanted equal civic rights and not the 'special glorification of their sex'.[84] The IFC was unable to find any precedents from other countries where women had reserved seats, apart from the precedent of communally reserved seats that had been introduced in India.[85] It was clear that these recommendations regarding female quotas were only being imposed in India, not globally, and this created discontent.

[82] Q/IFC/73, UP Papers.
[83] Q/IFC/36, Delhi and All-India Evidence.
[84] Q/IFC/23, Bombay Evidence File.
[85] L/PJ/9/82, Indian Franchise Committee.

Rajkumari Amrit Kaur gave evidence before the IFC in Lahore in April 1932, as chair of the AIWC, along with Lakshmibai Rajwade, Lady Adbul Qadir, Mrs Miles Irving, and Mrs Bhola Nauth (who, it appears, had returned to India then but was still engaging with the vital question of suffrage). When the chair suggested that not all women wanted the vote, Kaur pointed out that the AIWC had held several public meetings for years where representatives of all 'classes of women from the highest to the lowest' attended. She argued that there was a live consciousness among women and a desire to use their vote and take an active part in elections. Subbarayan took the opportunity to get Kaur to acknowledge that the AIWC had been in favour of reservation of seats in 1929, to which Kaur responded that the outlook had changed since then. Kaur also pointed out that the British House of Commons did not have reserved seats for women, even though they only had 15 female MPs, as their electorate was fully representative.[86]

Afterwards, Hilda Gray presented an address on the suffrage issue and the IFC to the East India Association at Caxton Hall, Westminster, in July 1932. A friend of Rathbone, she had previously lived in India and been a member of the NCWI, and had recently returned from accompanying Rathbone on her Indian tour. Gray explained that the great contrast between suffrage movements in Britain and India was that while in Britain suffrage had been awarded with great difficulty, Indians had received votes 'almost before women had realized that votes were worth having'.[87] Dismissive of the demands for full adult franchise, Gray wondered how the women's organizations could hope for the electorate to be raised from around a quarter of a million to 60 million women 'by a stroke of a pen'. She could neither understand why they would not accept any concessions nor why they were unwilling to 'descend from the heights of idealism' which could stagnate social reform. Gray explained that the Lothian Committee proposed to increase the female franchise through property or literacy

[86] SSC, Suffrage Collection, International, India, 'Report of the Evidence given by Rajkumari Amrit Kaur Chairwoman of the AIWC on the 4th April 1932 before the Indian Franchise Committee at Lahore'.

[87] Mrs R. M. Gray, 'The Advance of Indian Women', *Asiatic Review* (October 1932): 560.

qualifications and praised the work of Subbarayan for converting Indian women to these 'practical' proposals.[88] Lady Pentland, in the Chair, also expressed her admiration for the work of Subbarayan, known as she was for her activities in London during the RTCs. The Indian civil servant Sir Henry Lawrence, however, insisted that Indian women should demand full adult suffrage and mentioned his discussions on this matter with Gandhi, who supported this view.[89] Meanwhile, Mrs Evelyn Bell campaigned hard, in long back and forth correspondence with the India Office, to enfranchise the wives, widows, or mothers of Indian soldiers, but these suggestions were not taken on.[90]

Gray (and Rathbone) epitomized some of the concerns and divisions about the full adult suffrage demand being put forward by Indian women and the way in which this was linked to projection of a national identity. Rather than accepting concessions, which would allow for greater female representation in the short term, and thus potentially give women more influence over social reform matters, it was clear that full adult franchise was a political issue about citizenship rights and independence that female nationalists were not going to budge on. Though they continued to argue that women's voices in political spaces were distinct, and that women had different priorities in the public sphere which meant their voices needed to be heard, the official line clearly also took inspiration from broader social justice campaigns and Indian nationalists on the need to take a hard-line stance.

Throughout this time, local women's bodies were discussing and passing resolutions on franchise. Led by members of the AIWC and WIA, and thus generally by urban, middle class women, the franchise issue was nevertheless being discussed across major centres in India. Saraladevi Chaudhurani, for example, gave a presidential address at the Tamil Nad Women's Conference in October 1931 in which she lamented the inadequate number of women delegates at the RTC but

---

[88] Gray, 'The Advance of Indian Women', 564–5; 'The Women's Movement in India', *The Times*, 13 July 1932, 12.

[89] 'Discussion on the Foregoing Paper', *Asiatic Review* (October 1932): 573, 576.

[90] L/PJ/9/94, Evidence and Papers of Franchise Committee (1930–3).

insisted that Indian women had to convince the government and their men folk that they needed equal rights to 'make ourselves the best Indian women'. However, she also insisted that the women's field was in the home, seeing no contradiction in the desire to be leaders in the home and public sphere.[91] In July 1932 the WIA, the AIWC, and NCWI met again to produce further memoranda in which they continued to regret the recommendations of the IFC and demand that the views of organized women be listened to: 'It would seem that India's women had per force ... to be treated as an appendage rather than as a vitally integral part of the body politic.'[92]

The report of the IFC was published in May 1932. The committee had been unable to deliver more than recommendations that the female franchise in India be increased along various lines, including literacy, that the wives and widows of male voters be enfranchised, and that a number of seats be reserved specifically for female candidates. It was on the basis of these recommendations that discussion of female franchise was discussed at the third RTC.[93] Congress once again refused to attend, and the effectiveness of these conference negotiations was called into question; there was less organized pressure relating to female participation and so only Shahnawaz was recalled to the RTC in London. As the sole female at the third conference, Shahnawaz put forward a new suggestion on franchise, aware of some of the impracticalities of introducing full adult franchise. She suggested that a group system of voting might be introduced whereby, for example, 10 people would share a vote, but the conference rejected this view and accepted the proposals of the Lothian Report which would enfranchise wives and widows (aged over 21) of male property owners and also introduced a new literacy qualification as an alternative for women.[94]

Meanwhile, the government introduced the Communal Award in August 1932 which allocated seats along 'community' lines in each

[91] Mss Eur F341/161, Forbes Collection, Saraladevi Chaudhurani, 'Tamil Nad Women's Conference, Erode', *Stri Dharma* (October 1931): 561–5.

[92] L/PJ/9/83, Rajwade to Lothian, 19 July 1932.

[93] 'Threefold Difficulty', *The Scotsman*, 23 November 1932, 16.

[94] J. A. Shahnawaz, 'Women Voters in India', *The Times*, 27 January 1933, 8. Shahnawaz also arranged meetings with women MPs and representatives of the leading women's organizations, towards the end of 1932.

province, as well as reserved separate seats for women, some of which were along communal lines. Gandhi infamously refused to accept separate electorates for 'Untouchables', threatening to fast until death, which led to the Poona Pact compromise, but reserved seats were still written into the 1935 Government of India Act.[95] Subbarayan had written to Rathbone in despair about the Communal Award, as the most prominent women's organizations considered boycotting seats. Rathbone reassured Subbarayan that women should take up these reserved positions and then work together to demonstrate that they did not believe in communal divisions.[96]

The British government's White Paper on Indian constitutional reforms was published in March 1933. It took on board the Lothian recommendations but introduced amendments that anyone eligible to vote through educational qualifications or wifehood would have to apply to be put on the electoral rolls, rather than be automatically added. This was likely to reduce the number of potential female voters.[97] Within a span of 12 months, the government position had been clarified and cemented further. Not only was full adult franchise not on the immediate agenda, but communally reserved seats were also enshrined for women. In response, the AIWC, WIA, and NCWI put forward new proposals reiterating their opposition to the Communal Award, reserved seats, and the wifehood qualification and suggested that a new way to increase the electorate might be to enfranchise all women over 21 in urban areas. Subbarayan was quick to criticize these proposals, explaining that the urban qualification was not practicable or reasonable and a 'fair distribution of voting power is as important a question as that of having an adequate number of women voters'.[98] The demands by the main women's organizations had changed once again. Aware that full adult franchise was not possible, their suggestions showed that they were now moving closer to Subbarayan's demands, of whom they had recently been so critical.

---

[95] Judith Brown, *Modern India: The Origins of an Asian Democracy* (Delhi: Oxford University Press, 1984), 279–82. The Poona Pact increased representation for 'Untouchables' but not separate electorates.

[96] 7ELR/07, Rathbone to Subbarayan, 2 September 1932.

[97] Everett, *Women and Social Change in India*, 124.

[98] 'Topics of the Day', *Indian Ladies Magazine* (May–June 1933), 132–3.

Following the publication of the White Paper, the British govern-ment planned a Joint Select Committee to consider the proposals before the new Government of India Act was passed by parliament. The WFL believed it was vital for British women to be appointed to this committee. 'We also think it is essential that women in India should be consulted about the Proposals which especially concern them, and that Indian women should come to this country to attend for consultation with the Joint Committee of the House of Lords and Commons when it is chosen.'[99] The AIWC, WIA, and NCWI also realized that it was essential to send female representatives to London to meet with the committee.

The Joint Parliamentary Committee 1933: Return to London

In the summer of 1933, the JPC for Indian reform met in London to finalize the recommendations of various meetings, committees, and the White Paper to work towards the final version of the 1935 Government of India Act. The official women's organizations in India, as before, were extremely eager that their representatives should attend. Shahnawaz was the first Indian woman associated with the JPC; she was keen to give evidence and argue for the necessity of increasing the provisions made in the White Paper.[100] She sat on the committee and also submitted a memorandum in August 1933. She noted that both British and Indian women's organizations felt that the recommendations of the White Paper were inadequate in regard to female enfranchisement and noted that the Simon Commission had recommended a ratio of one female voter to two male voters. However, Shahnawaz differed from the official women's organiza-tions in her support of the Communal Award.[101] The AIWC, however, urged Shahnawaz to use her connections, especially with Rathbone and Lady Hartog, to come over to the official point of view especially in regard to rejecting the wives and widows qualification. The AIWC

[99] 'Indian Women's Franchise', *The Vote*, 24 March 1933, 92.

[100] 'Indian Women's Claims', *The Vote*, 14 July 1933, 220.

[101] L/PJ/9/141, Begum Shahnawaz, Memorandum submitted to the Joint Select Committee on Indian Constitutional Reform (August 1933), 3–4.

asked Shahnawaz to work with the women's organizations in England to press for votes for women 'on their own rights'.[102]

By June 1933, representatives of the AIWC, NCWI, and WIA, Muthulakshmi Reddi, Rajkumari Amrit Kaur, and Shareefah Hamid Ali respectively, had arrived in Britain keen to arrange a meeting with the JPC to present their evidence on female franchise questions. Reddi planned the trip to coincide with her visit to the ICW in Chicago, and it was not until August that the three women were able to meet the committee. In fact, they were only able to meet a subcommittee, rather than the whole JPC as they had hoped, much to Kaur's dismay. However, the subcommittee did include the secretary of state and the chairman of the JPC, and Kaur was reassured that this was not a reflection on the lack of importance of the women's question but a matter of timing and logistics.[103]

Fifty years later though, Kamaladevi was acerbic about the JPC's attitude towards the female representatives. She criticized the 'continued obstruction, dilatory tactics' and indeed opposition from some sections to their appearance before the committee even though 'reactionary, sectarian, anti-national and communal bodies were readily called'. Despite her distrust of British officials, Kamaladevi warmly pointed out that the 'one bright spot in this deepening gloom was the sincere and continued support given to the Indian women's cause by a section of the British women'. For example, Grace Lankester from the London branch of the WIA got together 22 women's groups to provide written support for the Indian women's delegation. Kamaladevi also recalled one of the three female delegates (though she did not say which one) praising the support from British sympathizers, who were not only courteous and willing to help, but did not mind the expense or inconveniences as they were compelled to help the Indian women's delegation through their inborn 'spirit of helpfulness and friendliness towards others of their own sex'.[104]

---

[102] AIWC Papers, Roll 3, File 34, Mukerjee to Shahnawaz, 1 June 1933.

[103] See various letters in NMML, Rajkumari Amrit Kaur Papers, Subject File 2, Correspondence re Evidence before Joint Select Committee on Indian Constitutional Reforms.

[104] Kamaladevi Chattopadhyaya, *Indian Women's Battle for Freedom* (New Delhi: Abhinav Publications, 1983), 101–3.

The JPC was a major political get-together, which would determine much of Britain's relationship with India, so press coverage continued to deal with not only the larger questions of India's sovereignty but also issues of franchise. The WFL organ the *The Vote* expressed concern in September 1933 after the secretary of state, Samuel Hoare, suggested that the Act should contain a clause with the condition that franchise could not be amended for a number of years, and then after that left to Indian legislators. *The Vote* was concerned that the franchise legislation for women would merely replicate the White Paper proposals. The WFL, therefore, asked their readers to petition any organizations (women's or mixed) to pass resolutions urging the JPC to give the 'most generous measure of franchise possible to Indian women' and not less than a proportion of one woman to four-and-a-half men, as proposed by the Lothian Committee. The paper acknowledged that though British and Indian women's organizations disagreed on method, they agreed on the necessity to increase the franchise and to petition the JPC.[105]

The demand for female suffrage, though, was now more visibly associated with domestic politics in India and with 'national' identity. This is exemplified by Kaur's article for the *Modern Review*, published in April 1933. She not only acknowledged the influence the emancipation of women in Europe and America during the war had on the Indian women's movement, but was also keen to discuss the specifics of the Indian suffrage fight. As we have seen, Indian suffragettes presented themselves as being above communal divisions in India. She described women as 'being by nature imbued' with a deeper love for their country and mentioned how Indian women had realized that 'country must come before community'. Kaur also emphasized that this was a struggle for equality for *all* Indian women and that her colleagues would refuse to 'accept any safety in any sphere for one class at the cost of any of our sisters'.[106] These were the demands and assertions that clearly marked the movement as a nationalist struggle, as much as a gendered fight.

Kaur also addressed a public meeting, presided over by Corbett Ashby, with the following remarks: 'We have come to tell you what

---

[105] 'The Indian Women's Franchise', *The Vote*, 22 September 1933, 301.

[106] Rajkumari Amrit Kaur, 'The Woman's Movement in India', *Modern Review* (April 1933): 400–3.

we want and not hear from a committee or even from friendly Englishwomen what they want.'[107] Kaur found a great deal of support from British women's organizations during this visit, including the London committee of the WIA. Upon her return to India, she proposed to the AIWC that they set up a permanent link with the British women's organizations which had shown their support through a liaison group. Grace Lankester was to head the British side, while Kaur initially acted as liaison officer for the AIWC.[108] The five British societies were the BCL, the WFL, the Women's International League, the Six Point Group, and St Joan's Social and Political Alliance. From May 1934 the group in Britain began to publish a *Bulletin of the Indian Women's Movement*, edited by Lankester, which included information about Indian women's activities in India and abroad. It was printed every few months until 1939 when the Second World War limited communications.

During her visit Kaur attended the BCL Conference and a BCL afternoon party too. The AIWC also wanted her to get in touch with the Women's Institute to see if their village institutes could be replicated in Indian villages. Emmeline Pethick-Lawrence also renewed her interest in the Indian suffrage question. She met Kaur in July 1933 and was very pleased to support the delegation's opposition to communal quotas for women. Pethick-Lawrence praised this 'united group representing the whole of the progressive womanhood of India' for 'actually putting into practical expression a spirit that would solve most of the world's problems'.[109] At a meeting of the London branch of the WIA in the same month, Kaur also proclaimed that 'Indian women are greater Nationalists than men', when discussing female demands for enfranchisement.[110] Kaur is said to have described

---

[107] Chattopadhyaya, *Indian Women's Battle for Freedom*, 103–4.

[108] Ruth Woodsmall, 'Pen Portrait of Rajkumari Amrit Kaur', in Mss Eur F341/146, Rajkumari Amrit Kaur.

[109] NMML, Rajkumari Amrit Kaur Correspondence Files: Daisy Solomon to Kaur, 23 June 1933; H. Todhunter to Kaur, 2 August 1933; A. L. Hindekoper to Kaur, 3 August 1933; Emmeline Pethick-Lawrence to Kaur, 22 July 1933.

[110] S. Muthulakshmi Reddi, *Mrs Margaret Cousins and Her Work in India* (Adyar: Women's Indian Association, 1956). The Indian women representatives were invited to tea at the Indian Students' Hostel in London too (NMML, AIWC Papers, Roll 4, File 38, Kaur and Hamid Ali circular, 9 August 1933).

British women's groups as 'progressive'. While she was thankful for their support, she was disappointed with the 'cavalier treatment accorded to us in official quarters'.[111] Despite nationalist rhetoric, Kaur was cognizant that this did not mean rejection of British friendship networks.

Kaur also corresponded with Isabel Ross of the Women's International League who offered advice on the wording of the resolutions the women's organizations were putting forward. In addition, she wrote to give her thanks to the St Joan's Social and Political Alliance and WFL for their resolutions of support.[112] Betty Archdale of the Six Point Group was keen to help, too, and ensured that the group sent letters of support to the JPC. As their Chair, Monica Whately, put it to the committee, the Six Point Group abhorred the proposal to enfranchise women on their husband's qualification, describing it as 'entirely repugnant to the social and spiritual ideas of the East', which has received 'united opposition of Indian women', 'with which the Six Point Group identifies with'. The Six Point Group also urged, in separate correspondence, that the JPC meet with representatives from the BCL. Rathbone had set up a British Committee for Indian Women's Franchise in April 1933 consisting of cross-party MPs, leaders of British women's organizations, and others who had Indian connections. It was noted that 'Miss Rathbone does not represent the opinion of a large section of British women or of Indian women', and the JPC did not agree to meet with any BCL women.[113] The JPC did meet with Rathbone's British Committee for Indian Women's Franchise though, who favoured enfranchising wives of existing male voters and introducing a simple literacy test. Opposition to women's franchise

---

[111] 'In the Realm of Women', *Indian Ladies Magazine* (September–October 1933), 233.

[112] Rajkumari Amrit Kaur Correspondence Files: Isabel Ross to Kaur, 14 July 1933; Florence Barry to Kaur, 19 August 1933; Florence A. Underwood to Kaur, 19 August 1933.

[113] Rajkumari Amrit Kaur Correspondence Files: Betty Archdale to Kaur, 28 June 1933, 16 July 1933; Six Point Group to JPC, 17 July 1933; Monica Whately to JPC (no date).

proposals came from Muslim League spokespersons and Winston Churchill.[114]

When Kaur, Reddi, and Hamid Ali did meet the JPC, Kaur read out a statement on behalf of the three women's organizations in India, adhering to the opinion that adult suffrage was the only logical and fair method to enfranchise Indians. They reiterated their opposition to communal divisions within the female franchise and to reserved seats for women, but did approve of joint electorates: 'We strongly urge the necessity of the specific recognition of woman's inherent right to full citizenship and equal opportunities with men for public service to the country.' The memorandum, read out by Kaur, noted the full support of the BCL, the Women's International League, the St Joan's Social and Political Alliance, the Six Point Group, the London branch of the WIA, Dr Maude Royden's Congregation of the Guild House, and Monica Whately's 'group of women'. It also noted associations who had invited the Indian representatives to tea and who had sympathized with the demands, but differed slightly on some of the points. These associations were: Friend's House, Lyceum Club, the National Council of Women, and the National Union. They further noted the help extended by Dhanvanthi Rama Rau in addressing many meetings and putting forward the main points of the memorandum in many places in Britain.[115]

Sushama Sen and Lalita Mukerji also presented evidence to the JPC on behalf of the Mahila Samiti's Ladies' Association. They met the committee immediately after Kaur, Reddi, and Hamid Ali. Sen, who had met Pankhurst in 1910, had returned to London in April 1933 with her family and had been persuaded by Rathbone and Pickford to give evidence. Sen was a member of the AIWC, but did not feel that the AIWC had a mandate in their views on the franchise question at this time. As representatives of women of Bengal, Sen and Mukerji noted their protest at the reduction of female voting strength put forward in the White Paper compared to Lothian's recommendations. Sen also published a memorandum that noted

[114] Jana Matson Everett, *Women and Social Change in India* (New Delhi: Heritage, 1981), 131.

[115] Reddi, *Margaret Cousins*, Appendix.

concern about literacy qualifications unfairly favouring urban women over rural women. If adult franchise was not possible, she suggested that at least female enfranchisement equal one third of the total electorate.[116] Sen was now allied with Rathbone and agreed that wives could be enfranchised as an interim measure.[117] In her distancing from the official women's stance, and alliance with Rathbone, Sen found a natural supporter in Subbarayan, who commended her for being practical on the issue. Pickford also wrote to Sen after she met the JPC, congratulating her on her 'clear and dignified statement' 'without any tint of political or feminist bitterness'.[118] It was clear that the JPC was eager to take on Sen's recommendations rather than those of Kaur, Reddi, and Hamid Ali.

The London branch of the WIA had continued to be active on the issue of suffrage throughout the decade, led by members such as Dhanvanthi Rama Rau, Rameshwari Nehru, and Avabai Mehta, who arranged meetings and activities seeking to educate British women about Indian demands.[119] They had held a meeting in September 1932 in London to pass their own resolution regretting the recommendations of the Lothian Committee and endorse demands for full adult suffrage.[120] Upon her return to India in 1933, Reddi praised the London branch of the WIA for all their work and also the British women's liaisons group. 'We were very much struck with the sincerity, with the earnestness and with the enthusiasm of the British women of all shades of opinion for the Indian women's cause,' remarked Reddi; 'We found them extraordinarily energetic, ever courteous,

---

[116] *Joint Committee on Indian Constitutional Reform [session 1932–33]. Volume I. Report*, (112), 2324–31. See also Everett, *Women and Social Change in India*, 128–30.

[117] Barbara N. Ramusack, 'Catalysts or Helpers? British Feminists, Indian Women's Rights, and Indian Independence', in *The Extended Family: Women and Political Participation in India and Pakistan*, ed. Gail Minault, 109–50 (Delhi: Chanakya Publications, 1981), 136.

[118] Sushama Sen, *Memoirs of an Octogenarian* (Delhi: Chatterjee and Sen, 1971), 356, 363, 607–8.

[119] Santha Rama Rau, *Gifts of Passage* (London: Victor Gollancz, 1961), 24. See also AIWC Papers, Roll 2, File 25. Other known members include Hannah Sen and Achamma Matthai.

[120] Q/IFC/92, Avabai Mehta to Lothian, 9 September 1932.

willing, nay, eager on their part to hear our point of view.' Although she acknowledged that there were misunderstandings about Indian women, evident in British women's responses to *Mother India*, Reddi believed that the work of allies in Britain had done much to dispel these myths.[121] It was clear then that, despite increasing nationalist sentiment, Indian suffragettes enjoyed the friendship of British women and that they could be relied on in their suffrage fights. However, Reddi also felt extremely disappointed that her meeting with the JPC had not been more effective. She was consoled by Rajwade: 'It is not an individual defeat.... You went to England at a sacrifice and tried to render service to your sisters. That should be sufficient satisfaction for anybody.'[122]

Shahnawaz, too, remained a familiar figure among liberal political circles in Britain. She was invited to address the East India Association with a paper 'Indian Women and the New Constitution' on 13 June 1933.[123] Lady Astor had been unable to take up her scheduled chair position, and so the meeting was chaired by Lady Procter. Several members of the Indian delegation and Indian politicians were present including Mancherjee Bhownaggree, Chuni Lal Katial, and Yusuf Ali, Indian women such as Rama Rau and Lady Abbas Ali Baig, and a number of British Knights and Ladies. Pickford and Rathbone both were also present and involved in the discussions afterwards. Shahnawaz's paper set out the present situation for Indian women in terms of the franchise, the recommendations of the IFC, and the demands of the three main women's organizations at this stage. As mentioned earlier, they were now keen to accept literacy as an educational qualification for women but also suggested that all women in urban areas, above a certain age, should be given the vote. Although keen to stress that women were not communal, they now accepted that some reserved seats for women were inevitable since the principle had been accepted under the Communal Award, and also suggested that women should have reserved seats in the upper legislatures.

---

[121] 'Editor's Notes', *Indian Ladies Magazine* (November–December 1933), 265–6.

[122] AIWC Papers, Roll 4, File 38, Rajwade to Reddi, 11 September 1933.

[123] Begum Shahnawaz, 'Indian Women and the New Constitution', *Asiatic Review* 29, 99 (July 1933): 435–45.

In the ensuing discussion, Rama Rau recommended the urban qualification too. While Pickford and Rathbone both acknowledged that the
White Paper had not done justice to the claims of Indian women, they
reiterated the need for reserved seats for women precisely because
they did not have a full electorate.[124]

In adding some closing remarks to the East India Association
event, Shahnawaz thanked all the participants for their support. She
especially thanked certain members, making allusions to the help of
people in England.

> I would like to take this opportunity of thanking all my friends here,
> especially Miss Rathbone and Miss Pickford, for the wonderful help
> which they have given me at almost every step in this country. I need
> not say that if our efforts are crowned with success, I shall not feel but
> I shall consider it my duty to tell my people that it has been mostly due
> to the very great help which has been given to me by almost all the
> women's organizations and many of the women M. P.'s in England.[125]

Conscious of her audience but also the need for British political
support for the female cause, she went on to later reiterate: 'I have
every hope that, with the kind help and support of all our friends in
England, we will succeed in getting at least the very moderate figure of
women voters recommended by the Lothian Committee, accepted by
both Houses of Parliament.' She ended with these remarks, likening
India to a child, conscious therefore of the paternalistic (and maternalistic) attitudes of Britain to her empire:

> India's expectations today from this country are similar to those
> of a child which is growing up and claims a home with peace and
> prosperity. Satisfy those aspirations like a loving parent. Guard against
> emergencies by all means, but give ungrudgingly, remembering always
> that a happy and contented child will be a greater jewel than a discon-
> tented and unhappy one.[126]

The 1935 Government of India Act and After

It was clear that pressure was mounting on the British and Indian
governments to implement a satisfactory proposal that would expand

[124] 'In Woman's Realm', *Indian Ladies Magazine* (July–August 1933), 174–5.
[125] Shahnawaz, 'Indian Women and the New Constitution', 457.
[126] Shahnawaz, 'Indian Women and the New Constitution', 458.

the female electorate. The demands for full adult franchise were not being taken seriously, but there were multiple other options on the table. In August 1933, R. H. A. Carter from the India Office wrote to the reforms commissioner in India, W. H. Lewis, alerting him that the proposals in the White Paper affecting women's franchise had attracted great attention and considerable criticism, noting the 'active campaign' by women's societies. In February 1934 the India Office official Butler wrote to his colleague Laithwaite about the ongoing decisions to be made about female enfranchisement. Butler suggested that Rathbone's recommendation to make application uniform for men and women was impossible. He also acknowledged that the moderate proposals were unlikely to meet either her demands or those of the women's parliamentary committee she chaired. Butler knew that it was essential to implement a system of voting that women would wholeheartedly support, 'since we have hitherto not satisfied them, and social reform is a vital feature of India's future'.[127]

The 1935 Government of India Bill was the government's major intervention in the Indian constitution, hoping to stave off self-government for the immediate future while placating the demands of Indian nationalists. It would give even more representative powers to Indian people and was seen as the last intervention that would be made by the government on franchise matters. Although there had been evident sympathy for demands to increase the female electorate, as in 1919, the government was reluctant to take on further responsibility on this matter. However, as one MP put it, there were many who still felt that it was their imperial responsibility to intervene: 'Before England relinquishes her responsibility for the franchise in India, I hope action will be taken to improve the political position of Indian women.' They went on to remark (as quoted in the *Hindu*): 'Until the women of India are as free as their sisters in the West, all the people of India will suffer from a heavy handicap.'[128]

As Rama Rau observed, Rathbone continued to be active on the Indian woman suffrage question in 1934, often obscuring the

[127] L/PJ/9/141, R. A. Butler to Laithwaite, 13 February 1934.
[128] 'From the Editor's Table', *Indian Ladies Magazine* (September–October 1934): 189.

continuing official women's organizations' demands for full adult suffrage.[129] In April 1934 Rathbone and other members of her committee met the secretary of state. They expressed no objection to require application to prove literacy qualification. However, a month later, Rathbone wrote to Samuel Hoare, having consulted with Subbarayan and Sushama Sen, suggesting that joint electorates might be introduced to fulfil women's reserved seats as joint electorates already elected women in municipal elections. During readings of the Government of India Bill, Rathbone put forward a proposal that if the election ratio was less than 1:4.5 at the next election then the regulations might be amended again before the following Indian election. This was seen as likely to create more unrest among women in India, who were already opposed to differential qualifications, and Rathbone withdrew the amendment.[130]

Rathbone continued to maintain a lively correspondence with Indian campaigners during these years. Reddi wrote to Rathbone in July 1934, thanking her for a copy of Sylvia Pankhurst's *Suffragette Movement in England*, telling Rathbone that it had given her a better idea of the British suffrage movement and that she would pass it on to others as it 'cannot but inspire us Indian women'.[131] According to Kamala Satthianadhan, it was Labour women in Britain who were continuing to make demands for full suffrage for Indian women. Agatha Harrison was one such ally to Indian women. Hamid Ali was in London in 1935 and continued to publicize the concerns of Indian suffragettes to British audiences:

> We do not know what full citizenship means. As women, we are not going to be put off by certain concessions, the securing of which seems to give particular pleasure to English women who really mean well but scarcely understand, I am afraid, our broader outlook on what is desirable for all India. We appreciate just as much as the men what nationhood means and what citizenship of a free country really is.

[129] AIWC Papers, Roll 6, File 59, Rama Rau to Kaur, 9 February 1934.

[130] L/PJ/9/141, Laithwaite to Sir F. Stewart, 21 April 1934; Rathbone to Samuel Hoare, 15 May 1934; Rathbone to Sir Archibald Carter, 20 May 1935; Telegram, 22 May 1935.

[131] 7ELR/01, Reddi to Rathbone, 12 July 1934.

She went on to argue that concessions granted to women did not give them any political advantages and were just an admission of the way in which the British government regarded the status of women. Thus, it was clear to Hamid Ali that women had to push for full independence of India as it was only then that they felt Indian women would receive complete equality in citizenship, trusting Indian men much more than British men.[132]

The conception of citizenship was important to female nationalists as well. Kaur wrote a piece for the *Modern Review*, published in November 1934, in which she spoke of the female demand for their 'inherent right to citizenship'. She described this as gaining equal political rights to men but explained that citizenship was also something larger than mere political freedom or privileges; civic rights also inferred duties to the nation.[133] Thus, the right to vote was intimately related to the nationalist mission of social reform and progress, and women were conceived to have an important part to play in this new nation though their roles were portrayed as separate and different to men. Therefore, while in their fight for political equality women faced no obstacles from male nationalist leaders, other issues about women's position in society were not addressed by male politicians. These issues included challenging inheritance rights or gendered employment, which were not seen as related to nationalist ideology.

The different educational qualifications required for voting eligibility, on a province by province basis, created discontent among Indian suffragettes, and it was an issue raised at the 1935 AIWC. Margery Corbett Ashby and Maude Royden attended the conference in Karachi and told Indian women that the JPC reforms had fallen far short of the 'deserved expectations of Indian women', promising to continue to campaign on this issue.[134] In the meantime, women's organizations started gearing up for the first general elections to take place after the 1935 Government of India Act—over 1936 and 1937.

---

[132] 'News about Indian Women', *Indian Ladies Magazine* (July–August 1935): 131.

[133] Rajkumari Amrit Kaur, 'The Responsibility of Women as Citizens in the India of Today', *Modern Review* (November 1934): 524.

[134] K. Alamelumangathayaramma, 'Women's Franchise', *Indian Ladies Magazine* (March–April 1935): 40–1.

As women newly qualified to vote now had to apply to be enrolled, unlike property owners, it was imperative that eligible women do so. Margaret Cousins addressed various women's groups in south India urging women to enrol. Reddi also prepared a memorandum on this issue and members of the AIWC distributed leaflets and went from house to house explaining to women the necessity of taking advantage of the vote.[135] Upon her return to India, Shahnawaz had become more closely involved with the Muslim League and urged Muslim women to register and also ensure that Muslim women were returned to seats in the new legislatures.[136]

During the 1936–7 elections, roughly 5 million women voted, and they voted overwhelmingly for Congress. There had been 72 female candidates contesting unreserved seats and only 8 were elected. Nine women took up seats in uncontested seats, and 40 women filled in reserved seats.[137] Vijayalakshmi Pandit, the sister of Jawaharlal Nehru, contested a rural constituency against another woman in the United Provinces. She, naturally, stood on the Congress ticket and was successful and became minister for local self-government and public health. In February 1939 Pandit addressed an audience at a high school in Allahabad in which she discussed her recent visit to Britain, where 'many eminent English women' had expressed surprise at her ministerial appointment. Explaining that India had a tradition of equality, Pandit argued that women in the 'East' did not compete with men to get ahead but that both sexes helped each other in the work of building a progressive nation.[138] Following the election, the British MP Ellen Wilkinson congratulated Indian women for returning more

[135] NMML, Muthulakshmi Reddi Papers, Bound Speeches and Writings & TWL, PC/06/047, *AIWC 11th Session, Ahmedabad, December 23 to 27, 1936*.

[136] Sahodari, 'News about women in India', *Indian Ladies Magazine* (March–April 1936): 68; 'Current Comments', *Indian Ladies Magazine* (July–August 1936): 149; 'Current Comments', *Indian Ladies Magazine* (November–December 1936): 236.

[137] Note these figures are according to Kamaladevi in Chattopadhyaya, *Indian Women's Battle for Freedom*, 112. See also J. K. Chopra, *Women in the Indian Parliament (A Critical Study of their Role)* (New Delhi: Mittal Publications, 1993), 18–19.

[138] Vijayalakshmi Pandit, *So I Became a Minister* (Allahabad: Kitabistan, 1939), 120–1.

women to the legislatures than any other legislatures that she knew of, despite their limited franchise.[139] And, the BCL met in 1937 in London for their 13th annual conference with the theme of 'Duties and Rights of Women under Democracy'. Begum Sultan Mir Amiruddin spoke of the great turnout of women in the recent Indian elections and also reiterated that they had more women representatives than in any other country of the empire.[140] With such perceived successes, although women continued to agitate for full franchise, the impetus was no longer as pressing as it had once been and attention shifted towards working towards independence and the guarantee promised of full adult suffrage then.

The Constituent Assembly, Indian Independence, and the 1950 Constitution

Female suffrage was not a major issue between 1936 and 1949 as many Indian suffragettes believed they had won victory in 1935. In 1941, Begum Sultan Mir Amiruddin wrote a piece for *Roshni* in which she detailed the great strides Indian women had made in politics. In 1941, the ratio of men to women voters was 5:1 and the number of women elected to legislatures put India at the third position, after the USA and Russia. She remarked that she had forecast the appointment of women ministers in India at a meeting of the BCL in London in 1937, but the British women there had found it hard to believe that India would surpass Britain. Amiruddin explained that 'feminist leaders' in India had not been obstructed by men to the same degree as women in the West.[141] And so, taking on such arguments, Indian women such as Amiruddin continued to argue that the Indian women's movement was fundamentally different from Western examples, and despite all the challenges of the previous decades assumed that political gender equality was inevitable. Thus, the question and definition of feminism continued to engage Indian women, as did the peculiarities of their colonial predicament. In 1942, again in *Roshni*,

[139] 'Current Comments', *Indian Ladies Magazine* (May–June 1937): 118.
[140] 'Current Comments', *Indian Ladies Magazine* (July–August 1937): 161
[141] Begum Sultan Mir Amiruddin, 'The Women's Movement and its Implications', *Roshni* (July 1941): 38–49.

Kamaladevi Chattopadhyay claimed that 'feminism' had not found a place in India or any colony, as the 'supreme question' was that of national freedom. She explained that even in 1935 the AIWC was too enthralled by London and Geneva, but in the last few years Indian women were moving away from the 'borrowed world' of the West and looking Eastwards.[142]

In 1942 many Indian suffragettes were engaged with the Quit India movement—a more radical civil disobedience movement demanding that the British leave India immediately, in the wake of discontent over Indian involvement in the Second World War. Violence was met with repression. Naidu was imprisoned again, alongside many other Indian women (in total some 100,000 Indian men and women had been arrested by 1943, although colonial officials were reluctant to put women into jail).[143] The Muslim League officially opposed the Quit India movement and over the 1940s the relationship between Congress and Muslim League members began to break down further, including that between women's activists such as Shahnawaz and other members of the AIWC.[144] The Second World War was a period of great uncertainty in Indian domestic politics, and so demands for full adult franchise were put on hold as the future was unknown, with the exact nature and political constitution of an independent India (and Pakistan) still under negotiation.

However, female engagement in politics continued to be an important area for intervention. In 1946 women demanded to be involved in the constituent assembly, which was set up to look into drafting a new constitution that would come into effect after independence. The AIWC prepared a women's rights charter for the assembly, in which they demanded equality for women in the franchise and public

---

[142] Kamala Devi, 'Behind the Programme–and Forward', *Roshni* (October 1942): 6–12.

[143] See Kamala Visweswaran, 'Small Speeches, Subaltern Gender: Nationalist Ideology and Its Historiography', in *Subaltern Studies IX: Writings on South Asian History and Society*, ed. Shahid Amin and Dipesh Chakrabarty (New Delhi: Oxford University Press, 1996), 83–125.

[144] Shahnawaz was arrested in 1946 for her Muslim League activities in the Punjab; see Azra Asghar Ali and Shahnaz Tariq, 'Begum Jahanara Shahnawaz and the Socio-Cultural Uplift of Muslim Women in British India', *Journal of the Research Society of Pakistan* 45, 2 (2008): 128.

life and demanded that marriage should not prejudice the inherent rights of women.[145] The All-India Congress Committee responded by instructing the provinces to elect a required number of women to the assembly, and the AIWC put forward suggestions. Pandit, Naidu, Mehta, and Kaur were among the women elected. In practice this meant that only women who were both members of Congress and the AIWC were elected to the constituent assembly, and the elite nature of women's representation was solidified.[146]

The AIWC remained keen to ensure Indian women were represented internationally too. Pandit and Hamid Ali had both been part of Indian delegations for the new United Nations in 1947 and Kaur had worked with the United Nations Educational, Scientific and Cultural Organization (UNESCO).[147] As noted in Chapter 3, Hamid Ali had been vocal regarding the need for equal franchise to be included in the new UN charter despite British and American attempts to 'dilute' franchise rights. Hansa Mehta was president of the AIWC in 1946 and she continued to maintain international contacts and stress that the wifehood qualification for female franchise had to be removed as soon as possible and replaced with adult franchise.

General elections in India took place at the end of 1945 and the beginning of 1946. Congress won a majority of the seats, although the Muslim League won all Muslim seats. Despite a still limited 'democracy', the electorate had expanded to 40 million voters (male and female) by 1946, which was the second largest electorate in the non-communist world.[148] After independence, it was generally accepted among the Indian political elite that women in India would be enfranchised. The 1931 Karachi resolutions where Gandhi had insisted upon full adult suffrage were to become embodied in the 1949 constitution.[149] There were also attempts to appoint women

[145] Mithan Lam, *Women in India: A General Survey of their Condition Status and Advancement* (New Delhi: AIWC, 1973), Appendix.

[146] Vijay Agnew, *Elite Women in Indian Politics* (New Delhi: Vikas Publishing House, 1979), 129–31.

[147] 'Presidential Address', *Roshni* (February 1947): 4–18.

[148] James Chiriyankandath, '"Democracy" under the Raj: Elections and Separate Representations in British India', in *Democracy in India*, ed. Niraja Gopal Jayal (New Delhi: Oxford University Press, 2001), 78.

[149] Chattopadhyaya, *Indian Women's Battle for Freedom*, 108–9.

in leading political roles. However, out of the 299 seats on the constituent assembly to which members were elected in 1946, only 15 were held by women.[150] As ever, there were some high-profile female appointments. Immediately after independence, for example, Kaur was appointed minister of health in the first new government of India. The new constitution was adopted from 26 November 1949 and enforced formally on Republic Day, 26 January 1950, when Indian people were no longer British subjects but citizens of the Republic of India. The first elections to the new Lok Sabha took place over 1951–2; roughly 173 million Indian men and women voted, but out of 489 seats only 22 went to women.[151]

* * *

In 1932 the Indian National Congress invited members of the India League (in London) to visit India to investigate charges of police brutality against imprisoned Indian nationalists. The delegation of two British women (the former Labour MP Ellen Wilkinson and Monica Whatley), a British man (Leonard W. Matters, also a former Labour MP), and an Indian man (Krishna Menon) found reliable information that women had been sexually threatened, abused, beaten, and raped in prisons. British officials, before the delegation had produced its report, dismissed the group as being dominated by 'suffragettes'.[152] Not only was 'suffragette' an insult, but the report also showed that Indian women had many concerns other than equal suffrage. The partition of India and Pakistan in August 1947 was not only to take thousands and thousands of lives, but women involved were subject to horrific brutality, sexual violence, and mental torture. The suffrage fight needs to be put within this context.

Kamaladevi Chattopadhyay argued in her memoirs that Indian women became particularly disillusioned with British authorities

[150] See Priya Ravinchandran, 'Women Architects of the Indian Republic' blog, https://15fortherepublic.wordpress.com/, accessed 7 August 2017.

[151] http://www.elections.in/parliamentary-constituencies/1951-election-results.html, accessed 7 August 2017; Sushama Sen was one of the MPs elected in 1952.

[152] Government of India, Home Department, Political, file no 40/XII, 1932, quoted in Forbes, *Women in Modern India*, 153.

after the successive decisions that hurt their interests such as the Communal Award, Lothian Franchise Committee, and White Paper of the 1930s. She argued that women realized that they needed to achieve their independence through Indian channels, and thus became more involved in Gandhi's civil disobedience campaigns.[153] As Sanjam Ahluwalia has argued, the struggles of Indian women leaders in the 1930s and 1940s were intermeshed with the middle-class politics of building a nation state. Though they disagreed with Gandhian politics at times, they were careful never to advocate a break from mainstream nationalist politics, relying upon their political legitimacy through this association. These female leaders did not wish to be judged as socially disruptive, anti-family, or anti-male, as has been evident in their suffrage rhetoric.[154] This is especially evident after 1935, when the major women's organizations no longer vociferously demanded full adult suffrage or laboured the point about reservation, as these arguments became subsumed into broader nationalist demands for independence and the right to create India's own constitution. However, they continued to insist upon representation.

Although Indian suffragettes were concerned about their franchise and citizenship rights within an imperial state and became increasingly aware that their political emancipation could only be achieved through national independence, they also knew they would have to build pressure and support through the various international networks they had built up over the decades. The colonial relationship still existed and thus Indian women were still compelled to visit Britain to lobby parliament and politicians in their favour; they continued to rely on British women's organizations and individuals for their support in influencing opinion. Yet, in their fight for independence, many suffrage campaigners chafed under the paternalistic and maternalistic direction from non-Indian women. Having previously embraced imperial, colonial, international, and Asian identities, by the late 1930s they were working out what it meant to be an *Indian* woman and an *Indian* citizen that demanded most attention.

[153] Chattopadhyaya, *Indian Women's Battle for Freedom*, 105.

[154] Sanjam Ahluwalia, *Reproductive Restraints: Birth Control in India, 1877–1947* (Urbana: University of Illinois Press, 2008), 99, 101.

Indian women were not the only politically marginalized group in India. As Lakshmi Menon put it, their political representation was on a par with Scheduled Castes though women constituted a much larger percentage of the population.[155] Though Indian suffragettes envisaged a utopia of adult franchise, these negotiations and the communal lines that had already been drawn into Indian politics compelled them to think along factional lines too. Despite the pressure that British politicians including Eleanor Rathbone put on Indian women, the majority were keen to press for utopian ideals rather than embark on creating new constitutions that disadvantaged women, and other groups, from the outset. Ultimately though, we cannot commend these Indian suffragettes for listening to or developing a truly national movement or campaign for female votes in India, even when they professed to be campaigning for *all* Indian women. The franchise campaign remained dominated by elite, urban women, with very little discussion of the intersectional political constraints on women from the lower castes or classes in urban or rural areas. However, the rhetorical push for universal franchise in the 1930s was valuable. Independence brought in full adult franchise easily for India, enfranchising in a sweep millions of women who have since taken an active role in one of the largest 'democracies' in the world.

[155] Lakshmi N. Menon in *Twentieth Century* quoted in 'Women's Franchise and the New Constitution', *Modern Review* 66, 1 (January 1936): 101.

Epilogue

Women, Votes, and Seats in the Indian Subcontinent after 1947

The process of independence and partition for India and Pakistan was fraught. Within two years of independence, the Nehru government's plans to follow through on the Congress commitment to full adult suffrage were a logistical and bureaucratic challenge. India was not only dealing with the integration of princely states and the relocation of refugees, but also needed to expand the electoral roll more than fivefold, to enrol over 173 million people. As Ornit Shani has described, there were many difficulties in enrolling such a large number of people, of whom 85 per cent had never voted to elect representatives to a legislative assembly before. The process of preparing the electoral roll that would be used in the first elections between October 1951 and February 1952 had to begin in September 1947. This formed the basis for the rolls that continue to be used today.[1]

---

[1] See Ornit Shani, 'Making India's Democracy: Rewriting the Bureaucratic Colonial Imagination in the Preparation of the First Elections', *Comparative Studies in Society and History* 36, 1 (2006): 83–101.

Voting in general elections in India today lasts over a month. With such a huge country and a massive population, the elections are a logistical nightmare that cannot, yet, take place on one day. In 1988 the franchise age was lowered from 21 to 18. With a large illiterate population, many voters rely on the symbols of political parties to cast their votes (although remarkably in the 1984 elections 3,696 candidates stood as independents). Men and women can visit separate polling booths. The principle of the secret ballot is maintained, but all voters leave with a mark: an ink mark on their left forefinger from which the fingerprint taken in order to ensure that people do not cast their vote twice. Elections, therefore, are like a ritual, ingrained into regular community life, and thus turnout is relatively high, compared to that in other democracies, in most rural and urban areas.[2]

The issue of female representation at local and national levels in India continues to exercise domestic and international activists. In the last election, in 2014, only 11 per cent of parliamentary seats were occupied by women. Despite early advances in representation, India lags behind most other countries, including neighbours Pakistan and Nepal.[3] To counter these concerns, a Women's Reservation Bill was proposed in 1996, to introduce a quota to ensure that at least 33 per cent of parliamentary seats were taken up by women. This bill has been languishing in parliament, awaiting approval, since 2010. During the 2014 elections, Indian women's groups produced a 'womanifesto', demanding that all major political parties demonstrate commitment to ensure that this bill is passed. Despite support from all major parties, as of 2017, the bill has still not been enacted. The demands for separate seats and enshrined representation for women show how far the women's movements have changed since the 1930s, when campaigners insisted on a 'fair field and no favour', optimistically assuming that national independence would lead

---

[2] Walter Hauser and Wendy Singer, 'The Democratic Rite: Celebration and Participation in the Indian Elections', in *Democracy in India*, ed. Niraja Gopal Jayal (New Delhi: Oxford University Press, 2001), 292.

[3] Sabarathinam Selvaraj, 'Even India's Neighbours Have More Women in Parliament', *Scroll.in*, May 2014, available at www.scroll.in/article/664775/ Even-India's-neighbours-have-more-women-in-parliament, accessed 7 August 2017.

to natural equality without the need for the kinds of interventions feminists in the twenty-first century now demand.

The Indian Women's Movement after 1947

The generation of Indian suffragettes discussed in this book is long gone. Many were involved in politics and social campaigning after 1947, as indeed suffrage was never their sole concern. Although they generally came from privileged backgrounds and had the advantages of well-connected political networks and access to resources, the Indian women who had campaigned for the female vote were not a homogenous group. Closely allied with women's organizations which sympathized with the Indian nationalist movement and the Indian National Congress, the political sympathies of Indian suffragettes varied, as did their recommendations on the best ways to obtain the vote and to achieve parity in political representation. As we have seen, though the question of gaining the franchise was allied to an acceptance of a democratic assembly (based on the imperially imposed British model), Indian women did not merely look to the British suffrage movement for inspiration. Their relations with other campaigners were often fraught and their subjective position often created tensions. They were internationally engaged and outward looking, and yet they were also acutely aware of the peculiarities of an Indian political system characterized by imperial rule and autonomous princely states. In November 1929, for example, Muthulakshmi Reddi explained that the position of India was very different from Ireland (or other British colonies). Thinking internationally, drawing upon the examples of Japan and Turkey, who were combining social and political advancements, Reddi also held up the model states of Mysore and Baroda, as they all pointed the way towards full responsible government. She argued that constitutional advancement and extension of the franchise was an inevitable necessity of national progress and efficiency, evident already in the tremendous activity and awakening of Indian women.[4]

---

4 NMML, S. Muthulakshmi Reddi Papers, Bound Speeches and Writings, Speech at Bezwada Women's Conference, November 1929.

By 1947, the work of the NCWI and WIA had already largely been subsumed by the AIWC. By 1945, the AIWC had 25,000 members.[5] This organization continues its work towards the uplift of women in India today. Its main headquarters are in New Delhi, where they maintain a hostel and library, and continue to publish the journal *Roshni*. The AIWC's main focus today relates to issues of education and health provisions, harking back to its apolitical nature when it had been set up. Yet, after 1947, former suffragettes remained intimately connected to the work of AIWC. Lakshmi Menon, for example, was president from 1955 to 1958, as was Mithan Lam (née Tata) from 1961 to 1962.

Indian women continued to look and work internationally after 1947. We have seen how notable Indian women were involved in the early years of the United Nations, and this international body continues to be one of the main focal points for international activism. The IAW, ICW, and WILPF all continue to flourish. Since the Second World War, combined with the growing strength of the UN, such international women's organizations have embraced more global forms of communication and activism, taking on issues of human rights and social welfare. As former colonies around the world gained independence from European empires, the dynamics of international feminism changed but tensions have remained. In the 1970s and 1980s, at conferences sponsored by the UN during the Decade for Women, tensions emerged between women from the 'First World' and the 'Third World' (note how the terminology of East and West had changed by then) about what was or was not a 'feminist' issue, echoing some of the debates about terminology and concerns regarding the Euro-American dominance of such organizations in the 1920s and 1930s.[6]

Female Political Representation after 1947

Despite certain stereotypes about South Asian women, India, Pakistan, and Bangladesh have had female prime ministers in the

---

[5] Jana Everett, '"All the Women Were Hindu and All the Muslims Were Men": State, Identity Politics and Gender, 1917–1951', *Economic and Political Weekly* 36, 23 (9 June 2001): 2072.

[6] Leila J. Rupp, 'Challenging Imperialism in International Women's Organizations, 1888–1945', *NWSA Journal* 8, 1 (1996): 19.

twentieth century: Indira Gandhi (1966–1984), Benazir Bhutto (1988–90; 1993–6), Khaleda Zia (1991–6; 2001–6), and Sheikh Hasina (1996–2001; 2009–). However, there have been continuing concerns about the prevalence of nepotism. Moreover, the number of women in the Lok Sabha has fluctuated over the twentieth century. In 1957, 22 women were elected to the Lok Sabha (out of a total of 403 representatives). In 2014, the percentage of women in parliament was 11.2 per cent (61 women in a Lok Sabha of 543 seats).[7] Both Pakistan and Bangladesh have reserved seats for women in their parliaments, unlike India. Following Bangladesh's independence in 1971, women occupied 15 seats in its first parliament, and 50 in the 2008 parliament.[8]

Although women in the interwar period had opposed reserved seats, the presence of quotas continue to dominate and characterize Indian politics. Although quotas for religious groups were removed with independence, special provisions were made to address caste inequalities. The 1950 constitution enshrined the use of reserved seats for 'socially and educationally backward classes of citizens and scheduled classes and scheduled tribes'. These provisions continue until today. It is within this context that the question of reserved seats for women remains alive in the twenty-first century.

During the 1950s and 1960s, the women's movement remained largely silent on the issue of representation. However, in 1973, the All India Panchayat Parishad (concerned with village governments) passed a resolution recognizing the need for more female representation and recommended that at least one-third of seats be reserved for women. They recognized that women had been neglected in rural development programmes and urged political parties to look at their process of putting forward candidates. Following various debates, an amendment to the constitution was passed in December 1992, and

---

[7] David Lal, Abhiruchi Ojha, and Nidhi Sadana Sabharwal, 'Women's Political Representation in the 16th Lok Sabha: Continuity, Contestation or Change?', *Women's Link* 20, 3 (2014): 8.

[8] Nusrat Jahan Chowdhury, 'Gender Quotas and Women's Representation in Parliament: Lessons from Bangladesh', in *Public Policy and Governance in Bangladesh: Forty Years of Experience*, ed. Nizam Ahmed (Abingdon: Routledge, 2016), 140.

ratified in April 1993, which ensured that one-third of all seats in panchayats were reserved for women.[9]

With these ongoing debates, and with the entry of nearly one million women into Panchayati Raj institutions, the women's movement was energized to make similar demands for the central and state governments in 1996. All major political parties also supported this demand. In 1996 the United Front government introduced an amendment bill proposing that one-third of seats be reserved for women. The bill faced considerable opposition within parliament. The women's movement was divided, too, on the question of whether or not there should be quotas within these seats that incorporated the reservations for Scheduled Castes and Tribes. One may remember that Indian suffragettes often expressed discontent that the government appeared to give more attention to 'outcastes' than women. These tensions have still not been resolved. However, these amendment bills have highlighted how Indian women still face issues of political representation, and that the question of how women should be considered as a political constituency has not been resolved a century on from the first demands for the female vote.[10]

Of the 543 MPs elected in 2014, only 61 were female. This was only an increase of three female MPs from the 2009 election. Women constitute only 11 per cent of the current Lok Sabha. Only 12 per cent of the Aam Aadmi Party (AAP) and Congress candidates were women, and only 9 per cent of Bharatiya Janata Party (BJP) candidates were female. There was one transgender candidate who contested as an independent. It was with this gender discrepancy in mind that on 8 March 2014, International Women's Day, a number of women's activist groups in India launched a 'womanifesto' through the online petition site avaaz.org, which they urged all parties to adopt as part of their election manifestos. The womanifesto had a six-point plan, calling for action on education, justice, and equal opportunities for women. The womanifesto also asked parties to commit themselves to the Women's Reservation

---

[9] Kumud Sharma, 'Power and Representation: Reservation for Women in India', *Asian Journal of Women's Studies* 6, 1 (31 March 2000): 47–87.

[10] Sharma, 'Power and Representation'; Mary E. John, 'Alternate Modernities? Reservations and Women's Movement in 20th Century India', *Economic and Political Weekly* 35, 43/44 (28 October 2000): 3822–9.

Bill. The three major national parties (Congress, AAP, and BJP) all agreed to this at the time. The medium may have changed, now with the use of online tools such as online petitions and social media, to gain attention, nationally and internationally, but the reasoning and indeed many of the concerns about female representation persists. However, as Malavika Vyawahare succinctly summarized on the issue of female representation for the *New York Times*, there remains no guarantee that more women in the Lok Sabha would bring pressing female issues to the fore.[11]

The suffrage movement had primarily been concerned with getting women the vote, but what has happened to turnout since Independence? The number of men registered to vote has always been higher than women in independent India. In 1952, 29.73 million women cast votes (a turnout of 38.1 per cent), while 50.97 million men voted.[12] In the general elections from 1962 to 2014, the average size of the female electorate has been 47.7 per cent compared to men, who have made up 52.2 per cent of the electorate. Meanwhile, turnout for women has steadily increased from just 38.8 per cent in the 1957 election (compared to 56 per cent for men) to 65.7 per cent turnout in 2014 (compared very favourably to 67.1 per cent male turnout).[13] The record turnout of 66.4 per cent for the 2014 Indian general elections constituted 553,801,801 people, of which 260,565,022 were female.[14] According to the 2011 census, women comprise 48.37 per cent of the total population but only 65.46 per cent of women in India are literate and so the ease of using the electronic voting system, despite concerns about tampering, is seen as a crucial reason for such a high turnout.

Meanwhile, Pakistan adopted universal adult suffrage soon after independence in 1947 as well. This right was reaffirmed in 1956,

[11] Malavika Vyawahare, 'Rhetoric about Women's Issues Outpaces Political Progress', *New York Times*, 9 May 2014, available at <http://india.blogs.nytimes.com/2014/05/09/rhetoric-about-womens-issues-outpaces-political-progress/?_r=0>, accessed 7 August 2017.

[12] BL, Mss Eur F341/15, *In the Service of the Nation* (New Delhi: All India Women's Committee, 1980), 81.

[13] Lal, Ojha, and Sabharwal, 'Women's Political Representation', 4–5.

[14] Electoral Commission of India, available at http://eci.nic.in/eci_main1/GE2014/STATE_WISE_TURNOUT.htm, accessed 7 August 2017.

following Pakistan's first constitution, although it was not until 1970 that Pakistan held its first direct general elections (previously constituent assemblies were formed through indirect elections of provincial assemblies). Pakistan's 1973 constitution reaffirmed women's right to vote again and also provided reserved seats for women in both houses of parliament.[15] Although some women's rights were suspended under General Zia-ul-Haq's military regime (1977 to 1986), in 1988 Benazir Bhutto became Pakistan's first female prime minister.

* * *

The focus in this book has not solely, or particularly, been on the suffrage movement and activities within the Indian subcontinent. In my focus on transnational networks and identities, I have not discussed the everyday campaigning that took place on the ground in India and have glossed over the varied political developments in Indian provinces. Despite the criticisms of the universalizing, homogenizing tendencies of some of the international women's associations that Indian suffragettes engaged with in the interwar period, they too were often guilty of these same tendencies in their attitudes towards Indian women (and Asian women more broadly). These women were operating at a time when the national imagery was being shaped. Often invoking notions of Indian women and history that relied on Hindu role models and ideas of Vedic age, they frequently alienated other women. Their desire to present Indian women as one political category, while being dismissive of rights and reservations of Muslims and in turn Scheduled Castes, revealed their inability to acknowledge the intersectional experiences of and class or religious issues for Indian women.

I have not discussed this religious imagery in much detail, only briefly alluding to how this came through in the rhetoric of campaigners such as Sarojini Naidu or Herabai Tata, as my focus has been on the ways in which these women projected and considered their political identity through spatial terms. The postcolonial position of

---

[15] Tariq Ahmed, 'Pakistan', Library of Congress blog, available at https://blogs.loc.gov/law/2015/03/women-in-history-voting-rights/, accessed 7 August 2017.

India continues to create tensions though. Western women such as Dorothy Jinarajadasa and Margaret Cousins were instrumental in the development of women's associations and the suffrage movement in India. The English language was the dominant mode of communication for transnational networking. Feminism has still been seen by many Indian women as a Western ideology. In 1991, Madhu Kishwar wrote a piece, 'Why I Do Not Call Myself a Feminist', for India's leading women's journal *Manushi*, explaining that the term was still associated with the rhetoric of India's colonial oppressors. This invoked debate, as in the interwar period, as to whether there was something distinctly South Asian about Indian feminism or whether it was a Western import.[16] Indian women were writing, conversing, and imagining feminist citizenship in vernacular languages. How were terms such as 'suffrage' and 'feminism' translated and understood? Aspects of these questions remain to be answered.

Indian women continue to desire that they lead and define their movement, rather than have its definitions imposed upon them. The 2014 womanifesto is an example of the ways in which Indian women asserted their own method of demanding political change. Recent reactions and responses to publicized rape cases, and Western interventions, reveal ongoing tensions. In the wake of the release of the film *India's Daughter* by British filmmaker Leslee Udwin in 2015, relating to the rape case of Jyoti Singh in Delhi in 2012, Kavita Krishnan, secretary of the All India Progressive Women's Association, voiced her concern about the ongoing colonial mentality that depicts Indian women who need to be saved and men who need to be civilized by Western interventions.[17] When American and other women in major world cities were involved in a Women's March on 21 January 2017, in part to protest against the inauguration of US President Trump, women in India organized an 'I Will Go Out' march in an attempt to make public spaces safer for women.

---

[16] Vijay Agnew, 'The West in Indian Feminist Discourse and Practice', *Women's Studies International Forum* 20, 1 (1997): 7–8.

[17] Kavita Krishnan, 'Nirbhaya Film: Solidarity Is What We Want, Not a Civilising Mission', *Daily O*, 3 March 2015, available at http://www.dailyo.in/politics/kavita-krishnan-nirbhaya-december-16-indias-daughter-leslee-udwin-mukesh-singh-bbc/story/1/2347.html, accessed 7 August 2017.

In the early twentieth century, Indian women engaged in multiple networks, working and thinking internationally, carving out their own spaces within global dialogues about women's rights. These connections and identities were not confined to India or the imperial motherland. Indian women were able to find a voice and show how common suffrage issues were for women around the world. They may have shared some common affinity with women from the 'East', but they did not always gravitate along racial lines. These women were not saints, but exhibited huge bravery in times of fierce imperial repression. These transnational discussions about suffrage and political representation continued after India won equal suffrage rights following Independence. It was only in 2015 that women in Saudi Arabia were able to vote for the first time, albeit only in municipal elections, as the country is run nationally by an absolute monarchy.

The Indian women's movement still faces challenges, as does the global women's movement. It is remarkable then that Indian women engaged so directly and forcefully with the suffrage movement at a time of colonial subjection. And it is also remarkable that they did so on the international stage, recognizing the benefits of transnational networks to further their campaigns and to promote the position of Indian women as well as women around the world. It is through their travel, correspondence, petitioning, marching, and publishing that a range of Indian suffragettes were able to ensure that Indian women's rights were not overlooked either in India or in other parts of the world. They were able to empathize with women in other colonies, other parts of Asia, and in the Western world. Despite various limitations, Indian suffragettes used their experiences and networks abroad to shape the political future of India, with long-lasting legacies for the way we understand and study political identities, activism, and representation in the Indian subcontinent today.

Appendix 1
Brief Timeline

18 November 1910	Black Friday suffrage march in London
1910	Public auctions of Sophia Duleep Singh's belongings because of her refusal to pay taxes
1911	London WFL fair with Ramdulari Dubé
17 June 1911	Coronation Procession in London
1912/13	Mussoorie Suffrage Society established
9 July 1914	British Dominions Overseas Woman Suffrage Union established
1917	System of Indian indenture emigration abolished
1917	Foundation of WIA
December 1917	Indian ladies' deputation to Montagu
Summer 1919	Southborough Committee meetings held in London
Autumn 1919	Herabai and Mithan Tata tour UK
1919	Government of India Bill passed
1919–20	Dorothy Jinarajadasa tours Australia and other parts of world
June 1920	IWSA Geneva Conference

1920	Travancore enfranchises women
1921	Imperial Conference discusses Indians living overseas
May 1921	Madras enfranchises women
1921	Bombay enfranchises women
1922	Burma enfranchises women
May 1923	IWSA Congress in Rome
1924	Indians and Arabs in Kenya given vote
4 March 1925	Australian Cabinet Bill enfranchising Indians passed
1925	Bengal enfranchises women
1925	BCL set up
1926	General Elections in India
May–June 1926	IAWSEC conference in Paris
1926	Punjab and Assam enfranchise women
1927	Central Provinces enfranchise women
1927	Foundation of the All-India Women's Educational Conference
1927	Publication of Katherine Mayo's *Mother India*
1928/9	Sarojini Naidu visits the USA
June 1929	IAWSEC conference in Berlin
1929	Eleanor Rathbone's conference in London
1929	Indians in Fiji win franchise on the basis of a communal electoral roll
1929	Bihar and Orissa enfranchise women
August 1930	Pan-Pacific Women's Conference, Honolulu
December 1930	First RTC in London
1931	Universal adult suffrage introduced in Ceylon
January 1931	All-Asian Women's Conference, Lahore
May 1931	Joint memorandum from the AIWC, NCWI, and WIA on franchise sent to parliament
November 1931	Burma RTC
December 1931	Second RTC
1932	Lothian Committee (IFC) tours India

August 1932	Communal Award in India
December 1932	Third RTC
1933	British Committee for Indian Women's Franchise set up
1933	ICW in Chicago
Summer 1933	Joint Parliamentary Committee meets in London
1933	Government's White Paper on constitutional reforms in India
1935	Government of India Bill passed
April 1935	IAWSEC conference in Istanbul
January 1936	Joint ICW/NCWI conference in Calcutta
1936/7	General Elections in India
1937	IAWSEC conference in Zurich
1939	IAW in Copenhagen
1944	Universal adult suffrage introduced in Jamaica
1945/6	General Elections in India
1946	Cabinet Mission in India
10 to 24 February 1947	First session of the Status of Women Commission, UNO, in New York (attended by Begum Shareefah Hamid Ali)
14/15 August 1947	Partition and independence for India and Pakistan
26 January 1950	Constitution of India enacted
1953	Universal adult suffrage introduced in Guyana

Appendix 2
Brief Biographies

Kamaladevi Chattopadhyay

Kamaladevi was born in 1903, in Mangalore. She was widowed at the age of 12. In 1919, she married Harindranath Chattopadhyay, brother of Sarojini Naidu. In 1921 Kamaladevi joined her husband in the UK and enrolled on a social work diploma course at Bedford College, London. She returned to India, with her husband, in 1922. After her return to India, Kamaladevi became actively involved with the AIWC and became friends with Margaret Cousins. She contested the 1926 elections, the first Indian woman to do so, but was unsuccessful. She became involved in Gandhi's Salt Satyagraha in 1930 and was arrested for entering the Bombay Stock Exchange to sell packets of salt. In the meantime, she had divorced Harindranath. After 1947, Kamaladevi was an active promoter of handicrafts, theatre, and dance. She died in 1988.

Margaret Cousins

Margaret Cousins was born in 1878 in Ireland. She married James Cousins in 1903. She was the co-founder of the Irish Women's

Franchise League with Hanna Sheehy-Skeffington in 1908, and was arrested in London in 1910 for suffrage activities. The Cousins became Theosophists and moved to south India in 1915. She co-founded the WIA in 1917 and the All-India Women's Conference in 1926. She was editor of *Stri Dharma*, the WIA's journal, and contributed regular pieces to *New India*, a newspaper founded by Annie Besant. In 1923, she was appointed as honorary magistrate in Madras. She was an active campaigner for Indian women's suffrage and was arrested in 1932 for her support for the Indian nationalist movement. A stroke left her paralysed in 1944 and she died in Adyar, Madras, in 1954.

Shareefah Hamid Ali (née Tyabji)

Shareefah Tyabji was born in 1883 in Baroda, Gujarat. Her father, Abbas Tyabji, was a chief justice and a vocal supporter of Gandhi. In 1910 she married her cousin Hamid Ali. She was actively involved with the AIWC and attended the 1935 IAWSEC Conference in Istanbul. She died in Mumbai in 1971.

Dorothy Jinarajadasa (née Graham)

Born Dorothy M. Graham, Jinarajadasa was married to the Sri Lankan Theosophist Curuppumullage Jinarajadasa, who was president of the Theosophical Society from 1945 to 1953. She was one of the founder members of the WIA in Adyar, Madras, in 1917. She died in 1963.

Rajkumari Amrit Kaur

Amrit Kaur was born in Kapurthala Palace at Lucknow in either 1887 or 1889 (accounts vary). She was the daughter of the Raja Harnam Singh, a member of the princely family of Kapurthala State, and was raised a Christian. She studied at Sherbone School for Girls in Dorset from 1902 to 1905. Kaur was head girl in her final year as well as captain of the school hockey and cricket teams, and then went on to study at the University of Oxford. A member of the AIWC from inception, she gave evidence to the Lothian Franchise Committee in 1932 and the JPC in London in 1933. She served as one of Gandhi's private secretaries for 16 years and was an active member of the non-cooperation movement. Kaur was the first female member of the first cabinet of independent India as minister of health. She died in 1964.

Sarojini Naidu (née Chattopadhyay)

Sarojini Naidu was born Sarojini Chattopadhyay in Hyderabad in 1879. She studied at Girton College, Cambridge, from 1895 to 1898. She was married to Dr Govindarajalu Naidu in 1898, who had studied medicine at Edinburgh, and they had three children. Relatively well known within literary circles for her poetry collections *Golden Threshold* (1905) and *Bird of Time* (1912), by 1913 she was becoming a well-known political orator, and close political ally of Mohandas K. Gandhi (whom she met in London in 1914). She was an active member of the Indian women's movement and Indian nationalist movement. In 1925 Naidu was president of the Indian National Congress. She was arrested in 1930 for her involvement in the civil disobedience movement. Naidu was appointed governor of the United Provinces in 1947. She died in Lucknow in 1949.

Rani Lakshmibai Rajwade (née Joshi)

Dr Rani Lakshmibai Rajwade was born in 1887. She was the daughter of Sir Moropant Joshi, who was a nationalist, social reformer, and a promoter of woman's emancipation and education. She studied at the Grant Medical College in Bombay and then went to England to further her training, accompanying Gopal Krishna Gokhale. There she met Emmeline Pankhurst. Lakshmibai married Major General Raja C. R. Rajwade of Gwalior State who was a widower with four sons and two daughters. She practised medicine in Bombay and was actively involved with the AIWC. Jawaharlal Nehru appointed her as the head of the section of women's welfare, education, and advancement under the National Planning Committee. She died in 1984.

Eleanor Florence Rathbone

Eleanor Rathbone was born in London in 1872. Her family was from Liverpool, and they had hosted the well-known Hindu reformer Rammohun Roy in 1831. Rathbone attended Somerville College, Oxford, from 1893 to 1896. She was on the executive committee of the NUWSS and was president of NUSEC from 1919 to 1929. She was elected Independent MP for the Combined Universities seat in 1929 and was MP until her death in 1946. She was involved in a number of political campaigns during her time in parliament including those relating to family allowances, refugees, and Indian female suffrage.

Muthulakshmi Reddi (née Ammal)

Muthulakshmi Ammal was born in Madras in 1886. She studied at Madras Medical College and in 1912 became one of the first female doctors in India. In 1914 she married Dr Sundara Reddi. In 1925–6, she went to the United Kingdom to pursue postgraduate training in women's and children's diseases. Reddi was also actively involved with the WIA and AIWC. In 1926 she was nominated to a seat in the Madras Legislative Council and unanimously elected as deputy president. In 1930 she resigned her seat in protest at the imprisonment of M. K. Gandhi. She was an active and vocal social reformer, particularly concerned about the issues of child marriage, female infanticide, and the devadasi system. She died in 1968.

Lolita Roy and Leilavati Mukerjea

Lolita Roy, born in 1864, from Calcutta, was the wife of an Indian barrister, Piera Lal Roy. The Roy family moved to London and are recorded in the 1901 UK census in the Brentford district of Middlesex. Roy had six children. Her son, Indra Lal Roy, born in 1898 and educated at St Paul's School, served in the Royal Air Force during the First World War. She was president of the London Indian Union from 1908, a society that brought Indian students in London together. In 1910, she became a committee member of the National Indian Association (founded in 1870), a group of British and Indian men and women living in England who were interested in Indian affairs and reform.

Leilavati Mukerjea (née Roy), born in 1888, was the daughter of Lolita. She was a keen violinist who often played at social gatherings for the National Indian Association. In 1911 Mukerjea was president of the London Indian Union.

Mrinalini Sen (née Luddhi)

Mrinalini Sen was born Mrinalini Luddhi in 1879 and was from Bengal. She was married to Nirmal Chandra Sen, the son of Brahmo Samaj reformer Keshub Chunder Sen. Nirmal was appointed education advisor for Indian students in London in 1913. They had one son and three daughters. She was involved in suffrage agitation in London in 1919, and attended conferences including the 1920 IWSA conference in Geneva. Her lectures and writings were published in 1954. She died in 1972.

Sushama Sen

Sushama Sen was married to the barrister Prosanto Kumar Sen. She was born in 1887 in Calcutta. She lived in London in 1911 and returned to London in 1933 for the JPC on Indian Reforms. She was an active member of the AIWC, including her role as treasurer in 1930. She published her autobiography in 1971.

Begum Shahnawaz

Jahanara Shahnawaz was born in 1896 in Baghbanpura, near Lahore. Her father, Muhammad Shafi, was a trained barrister and the leading Muslim official in British India, and her mother had presided over the All India Muslim Ladies' Conference in 1921. Her husband was a lawyer. Shahnawaz had been a member of the AIWC since its inception in 1927. She was in London in 1930 having served as her father's private secretary during the Imperial Conference, and was invited to serve on the RTC. She attended both subsequent RTCs. She was a member of the Muslim League, and in 1937 was elected to the Punjab Legislative Council. She was arrested in 1947 for her role in civil disobedience. She died in Pakistan in 1979.

Sophia Duleep Singh

Sophia Duleep Singh, born in 1876 in Norfolk, was fifth of the six children of Maharaja Duleep Singh and the German–Abyssinian Bamba Muller. He had become the Maharaja of Punjab in 1843 when he was just five years old, but the Punjab was annexed in 1849 and he was exiled from India. Maharaja Duleep Singh converted to Christianity and eventually settled in England, becoming a naturalized British citizen and a favourite of Queen Victoria. In 1896, Queen Victoria gave Sophia, her god-daughter, 'Faraday House' in Hampton Court as a 'grace and favour' home. She was a member of the WSPU and the WTRL. She was a member of the Black Friday suffrage deputation of 1910. Duleep Singh also worked as a VADS nurse for sixteen months at Percy House Auxiliary Hospital in Isleworth, Middlesex. She died in 1948.

Radhabai Subbarayan

Born in 1892 in Mangalore, Radhabhai Subbarayan's husband was the chief minister of Madras and her father was a prominent social reformer. She had been educated at Presidency College, Madras, and Somerville College, Oxford. Subbarayan was involved in various small-scale women's and reform groups in India including the Ladies' Recreation Club in Madras, the Niligari Ladies' Club at Ooctamund, and the Girl Guides Executive Committee. She was the first woman to be elected to the senate of Madras University by the graduates and had then been elected to the syndicate of the university by the senate. In 1938, Subbarayan was elected to the council of state from a general constituency—the first woman member of the council. And, in February 1939, she was involved in the debates about the Dissolution of Muslim Marriages Act, which permitted Muslim women to divorce their husbands. Subbarayan also worked to enforce monogamy in Hindu Law through the council of state. She died in 1960.

Herabai Tata and Mithan Lam

Herabai Tata was born in Bombay in 1879. At 16 she married into the Tata family of industrialists and gave birth to her daughter, Mithan (also known as Mithibai), a year later. In 1909, Herabai became a Theosophist and met Annie Besant at a Theosophical convention in Benares in 1912. Herabai and Mithan travelled to London in 1919 to give evidence to the Southborough Committee on constitutional reforms. The Tatas remained in London until 1923 as Mithan pursued a postgraduate degree at the LSE and trained as a barrister at Lincoln's Inn (one of the first ten women to be called to the Bar in the UK). Upon her return to Bombay in December 1923, Mithan enrolled in the Bombay High Court. She married Jamshed Shorab Lam in 1933. She became active with the AIWC, and served as its president from 1961 to 1962. After 1947, Mithan was involved in a number of social and political reform activities. She died in 1981.

Avabai Wadia (née Mehta)

Born in Colombo in 1913, Avabai Mehta lived in Britain from 1928 to 1938, with her mother, to pursue her school and university education (she was called to the Bar in 1934). The Mehtas, originally from Bombay, had been posted in Colombo and had strong links with the Theosophical Society. Both mother and daughter soon became involved with British women's organizations and their final fight for female franchise in the UK as well as broader equal rights for women in Britain and internationally. At around the age of 16, Wadia joined the London Committee of the WIA through the invitation of the Theosophist Dorothy Jinarajadasa. Wadia and other members would address a variety of groups about adult franchise, education, and political rights. In June 1932 she attended the BCL conference and presented a paper on 'Women's Suffrage in India'. The Mehtas met prominent suffragettes such as Charlotte Despard, Florence Underwood, Monica Whately, and Margery Corbett Ashby among many others; Wadia also visited the League of Nations twice on behalf of the AAWC. She was later heavily involved in family planning initiatives. She died in 2005.

Bibliography

Periodicals

Argus (Australia), The
Asiatic Review
Auckland Star
Bath Chronicle
British Australasian
British Commonwealth League: Report of Annual Conference
Bulletin of Indian Women's Movement
Common Cause, The
Daily Herald (Australia)
Daily News and Leader
Dominion (New Zealand), The
Equal Rights
Evening Post (New Zealand)
Herald (New Zealand)
Independent Hindustan, The
Indian Annual Register, The
Indian Ladies' Magazine, The
Indian Magazine and Review
Indian Review
Indian Social Reformer
The International Woman Suffrage News: Jus Suffragii

Irish Citizen
Irish Press
Irish Times
Literary Digest
Madras Mail
Modern Review
New India
New York Times, The
Observer, The
Otago Daily Times
Pax International
Press (New Zealand), The
Queen, The (The Lady's Newspaper)
Queenslander, The
Roshni
Scotsman, The
Statesman, The
Stri Dharma: Official Organ of the Women's Indian Association
Suffragette, The
Thames Star, The
Times, The
Times of India, The
Tribune, The
United India
Vote, The
Votes for Women
West Australian, The
Women's Leader and Common Cause, The
Young India

Archival Sources

All-India Women's Conference Margaret Cousins Memorial Library, New Delhi, India

File no. 1-II (1920–27), Papers and Correspondence Regarding Women Franchise in India and Revision of Electoral Roll of the Madras Legislative Council.

File no. 34-I (1933), Rani Laxmibai Rajwade's Correspondence as Hony. Organizing Secretary, AIWC Relating to the Franchise Committee and Other Matters.

Bodleian Library, Oxford, Special Collections

Irene Ward Papers.
Southborough Papers.

British Library, St Pancras, Asia and Africa Reading Rooms, India Office Records (IOR) Files

L/I/1/171, Indian States: Enfranchisement of Women.
L/I/1/549, Franchise in India.
L/PO/1/6, East Africa. Kenya.
L/PO/1/10, Indians Overseas.
L/PO/3/9, Burma Round Table Conference.
L/P&J/6/1323, Ordinance of the Provincial Council of Natal extending the Municipal franchise to women, 1914.
L/P&J/6/1642, Sex Disqualification (Removal) Act, 1919.
L/P&J/6/1878, Women Suffrage and Eligibility of Women for Membership of Legislative Bodies (1924–1930).
L/P&J/7/8345, Greasby Cooperative Women's Guild 1945.
L/P&J/9/8, Representations etc. Relating to Franchise for Women in India under the Reforms Scheme.
L/P&J/9/31, Franchise for Women (1921–3).
L/P&J/9/63, Franchise Committee.
L/P&J/9/82, Indian Franchise Committee Report.
L/P&J/9/83, Franchise Committee Report.
L/P&J/9/94, Franchise.
L/P&J/9/141, Franchise Women (1933–5).
M/1/181, Status of Women under New Constitution (1933).

British Library, St Pancras, Asia and Africa Reading Rooms, IOR, L/R/5 files, Native Newspaper Reports

L/R/5/99, United Provinces of Agra and Oudh 1928–31.
L/R/5/100, United Provinces 1932–3.
L/R/5/125, Madras 1918.
L/R/5/126, Madras 1919 (Part 1).
L/R/5/127, Madras 1919 (Part 2).
L/R/5/129, Madras 1921.
L/R/5/175, Bombay 1919 (Part 1).
L/R/5/176, Bombay 1919 (Part 2).

L/R/5/179, Bombay 1921.
L/R/5/200, Punjab 1918.
L/R/5/202, Punjab 1920–1.

British Library, St Pancras, Asia and Africa Reading Rooms, IOR: MSS EUR D1230, Papers of Sybil Mary Dorothy Bulkeley

Mss Eur D1230/1. National Council of Women in Burma, 1927.
Mss Eur D1230/3. Annual Reports National Council of Women in Burma.

British Library, St Pancras, Asia and Africa Reading Rooms, IOR: MSS EUR D903, Atholl Collection

Mss Eur D903/1, On the Memorandum by Begum Shah Nawaz.

British Library, St Pancras, Asia and Africa Reading Rooms, IOR: MSS EUR D1013, Pickford Collection

Photograph of Indian Franchise Committee and Staff.
British Library, St Pancras. Asia and Africa Reading Rooms. IOR: MSS EUR F77, Sir John Simon Papers.
Mss Eur F77/86. Correspondence with Eleanor Rathbone.
Mss Eur F77/326. News Cuttings Bound Volume, India No. 6 (November–December 1928).

British Library, St Pancras, Asia and Africa Reading Rooms, IOR: MSS EUR F118/84, Reading Collection

Letter from K. Radhabai Subbarayan to Lord Reading.

British Library, St Pancras, Asia and Africa Reading Rooms, IOR: MSS EUR F138, Sir John Gilbert Laithwaite Papers

Mss Eur F138/11, Second Round Table Conference.
Mss Eur F138/12, Biographical Notes and Photographs of British and Indian Delegates, Indian Round Table Conference Second Session 1931.
Mss Eur F138/15, Indian Franchise Committee.

British Library, St Pancras, Asia and Africa Reading Rooms, IOR: MSS EUR F341, Forbes Collection

Mss Eur F341/14, *All India Women's Conference Souvenir: Annual Conference 1978*. (Calcutta).

Mss Eur F341/15, *In the Service of the Nation* (New Delhi: The All India Women's Conference, 1980).

Mss Eur F341/19, Mithan J. Lam, *Women in India: A General Survey of their Condition Status and Advancement* (New Delhi: The All India Women's Conference, 1973).

Mss Eur F341/31, Dr (Mrs) S. Muthulakshmi Reddi, *Mrs Margaret Cousins and Her Work in India: A Brief Life Sketch of Her Colleagues and Comrades* (Adyar, Madras: Women's Indian Association, 1956).

Mss Eur F341/33, *Women's Indian Association: Golden Jubilee Celebration 1917–1967* (Madras: WIA, 1967).

Mss Eur F341/107, Kamaladevi, *At the Cross-Roads*, ed. Yusuf Meherally (Bombay: The National Information and Publications Ltd., 1947).

Mss Eur F341/125, Indirabai M. Rau, *Smrutika: The Story of My Mother as Told by Herself* (Pune: Krishnabai Nimbkar, 1988).

Mss Eur F341/126, Vijaya Lakshmi Pandit, *So I Became a Minister* (Allahabad: Kitabistan, 1939).

Mss Eur F341/129, *Sarala Ray Centenary Volume* (Calcutta: Sarala Ray Centenary Committee, 1961).

Mss Eur F341/138, Durgabai Deshmukh.

Mss Eur F341/146, Rajkumari Amrit Kaur.

Mss Eur F341/147, Mithan J. Lam.

Mss Eur F341/150, Hansa Mehta.

Mss Eur F341/152, Sarojini Naidu.

Mss Eur F341/155. Begum Aizaz Rasul.

Mss Eur F341/156, Eleanor Rathbone.

Mss Eur F341/157, Muthulakshmi Reddy.

Mss Eur F341/159, Renuka Ray.

Mss Eur F341/161, Saraladevi Chaudhurani.

Mss Eur F341/163, Begum Shah Nawaz.

Mss Eur F341/171, Bombay Presidency Women's Council.

Mss Eur F341/182, 'Stri Dharma'.

Mss Eur F341/183, 'Suffrage for India'.

Mss Eur F341/186, Women's Indian Association.

Mss Eur F341/187, 'Women's Politics'.

British Library, St Pancras, Asia and Africa Reading Rooms, IOR/Q/IFC, Indian Franchise Committee Papers

Q/IFC/21, Evidence File—Bengal.
Q/IFC/23, Evidence File—Bombay.
Q/IFC/25, Evidence File—U.P.
Q/IFC/33, Evidence File—Assam.
Q/IFC/36, Delhi and All-India Evidence.
Q/IFC/39, Memoranda on Special Subjects—Women.
Q/IFC/49
Q/IFC/73, U.P. Papers.
Q/IFC/92, Lord Lothian Papers.
Q/IFC/103

British Library, St Pancras. Asia and Africa Reading Rooms, IOR/Q/RTC. Indian Round Table Conference

Q/RTC/2, Indian Round Table Conference (Second Session) 1931 Committee Reports.
Q/RTC/23, Franchise Committee, 1930–31.
Q/RTC/24, Minorities Committee, 1930–31.

London School of Economic and Political Sciences Archive, Women's International League for Peace and Freedom Collection

WILPF/2/1, Yearly Reports (1915–1928).
WILPF/4/2, India, Minutes, Resolutions (1917–1930).

National Library of Ireland, Dublin, Manuscripts Division, Sheehy Skeffington Papers

Nehru Memorial Museum and Library, New Delhi, India, Microfilm Collection

All-India Women's Conference Papers.
National Council of Women in India Papers.

Nehru Memorial Museum and Library, New Delhi, Oral History Transcripts

Kamaladevi Chattopadhyay, Acc. 338.
Hansa Mehta, Acc. 41.

Nehru Memorial Museum and Library, New Delhi, Private Papers Collection

Hansa Mehta Papers.
Kamaladevi Chattopadhyay Papers.
Rajkumari Amrit Kaur Papers.
Rameshwari Nehru Papers.
Renuka Ray Papers.
Rukmini Lakshmipathi Papers.
S. Muthulakshmi Reddi Papers.
Miscellaneous Items: Acc. 612, Herabai Tata and Jaiji Petit Correspondence.

Reading University Special Collections, Nancy Astor Papers, MS1416

1/1/356, India 2, Women 1930.
1/1/357, India 3, Round Table Conference 1930.
1/1/1012, India 2, Women 1931.
1/1/1013, Indian Women's Franchise.
1/1/1014, India 1933, 2, Women.
1/1/1256, India 1934, 2, Women.
1/1/1257, India 1935, 2, Women.

Sophia Smith Collection, Smith College, Northampton MA, USA

Countries Collection: India, Boxes 19–21.
Elmina R. Lucke Papers, Boxes 1, 2.
International Alliance of Women Papers, Boxes 1–3.
International Council of Women Records, Box 2.
Ruth Woodsmall Papers, Boxes 14, 15, 23, 33, 42, 73.
Suffrage Collection, Box 19, Folder 18: International—India, 1932–1935.

Swarthmore College Peace Collection, Swarthmore College, Pennsylvania

Women's International League for Peace and Freedom 1915–1978, India Section, Microfilm Reel 133.76.

Women's International League for Peace and Freedom, US Section, General Correspondence Box 11, Folder 6: India, 1926–1933, Microfilm Reel 130.50.

United Nations Archives at Geneva, League of Nations Archives

General and Miscellaneous, Series 568; Series 7025.

Health, Series 11346.

Legal, Codification of International Law, Series 25640.

Legal, General, Series 13900, Series 18243.

Political, Series 1226, Series 2216, Series 19516.

Social, General, Series 320, Series 9668.

Social, Traffic in Women and Children, Series 669, Series 729, Series 26725.

Women's Questions, Series 3554.

University of Manchester Library, John Rylands Library, Special Collections. International Woman Suffrage Alliance Papers

IWSA/2/3, Correspondence [B].

IWSA/2/9, Correspondence [Fawcett].

IWSA/2/12, Correspondence [G].

IWSA/2/13, Correspondence [H].

IWSA/2/14, Correspondence [I].

IWSA/2/21, Correspondence [N].

IWSA/2/22, Correspondence [Newcomb].

IWSA/2/25, Correspondence [P&Q].

IWSA/2/31, Correspondence [T].

IWSA/2/33, Correspondence [U–V].

IWSA/2/34, Correspondence [W].

IWSA/3/104, Cuttings [India].

IWSA/3/141, Cuttings [British Dominion Women's Suffrage Union].

IWSA/3/144, Cuttings [Women's Suffrage].

IWSA/3/168, Cuttings [Women's Movements].

University of Manchester Library, John Rylands Library, Special Collections

GB 133. MML5/22, Manchester Men's League for Women's Suffrage Papers.

The Women's Library, London School of Economic and Political Sciences Archive, Eleanor Rathbone Papers

7ELR/01, S. Muthulakshmi Reddi.
7ELR/07, R. Subbarayan.
7ELR/08, Lord Sankey.
7ELR/09, Ramsay Macdonald.
7ELR/13, Lord Lothian.
7ELR/17, Miscellaneous.
7ELR/18, Shareefah Hamid Ali.
7ELR/19, Begum Shah Nawaz.
7ELR/21, Sarala Ray.
7ELR/23a, British Committee for Indian Women's Franchise.
7ELR/23b, Correspondence.
7ELR/24, Rajkumari Amrit Kaur.
7ELR/28, Mona Hensman.
7ELR/38, Sushama Sen.
7ELR/43, Indian Women's Education Association.

The Women's Library, London School of Economic and Political Sciences Archive

7AMR/1/09, 7AMR/3/01, Agnes Maude Royden Papers.
7MCA/C10-11, 17, Corbett Ashby Papers.
5ERI/1/A, Equal Rights International Papers.
PC/11/A.02, Ephemera.
7MGF/A/1/152-174, Volume IV, Fawcett Papers.
2/IAW/1/C/3-4/6-7; 21AW/1/H/10; 2IAW/1/J/1, International Alliance of Women.
7CHC, Marjorie Chave Collisson Papers.
3AMS/C/05/08, /09, /16, Meliscent Shepherd Correspondence.
PC/09/57a, Press Cuttings.
PC/06/040-042; PC06/047-048, Printed Collections.
5ICW/D/10, Records of the International Council of Women. Affiliated Councils: National Council of Women in India.

2SJA/A1/6-7, St Joan's Social and Political Alliance Minute Books.
Suffrage Pamphlets.

Published Reports

'The All India Women's Deputation', *Indian Journal of Gender Studies* (1998): 131–3.
British Dominions Women Citizens' Union. Report of Work 1917–1918 and of the Third Biennial Conference, London 1918 (1918).
British Commonwealth League Conference Report (London: British Commonwealth League, 1925).
Hutton, J.H. *Census of India, 1931. Vol. 1, Part 1* (Delhi: Manager of Publications, 1933).
Indian Statutory Commission, *Report of the Indian Statutory Commission.* Vol II: *Recommendations* (London: His Majesty's Stationery Office, 1930) Cmd 3569.
Joint Select Committee on the Government of India Bill (1919).
Marten, J. T., *Census of India, 1921. Volume I, Part II—Tables* (Calcutta: Superintendent Government Printing, 1923).
Report of the Special Session of the Indian National Congress held at Bombay. On 29th, 30th, 31st August and 1st September, 1918 (Bombay: D. D. Sathaye, 1918).
Subbarayan, Radhabai, *A Statement on the Political Status of Women under the New Indian Constitution* (Madras: Madras Publishing House, 1933).
Women's Indian Association, *Memorandum on the Status of Women in the Future Constitution of India* (Madras: Lodhra Press, March 1931).

Secondary Material

Adams, Jad, *Women and the Vote: A World History* (Oxford: Oxford University Press, 2014).
Agnew, Vijay, *Elite Women in Indian Politics* (New Delhi: Vikas Publishing House, 1979).
———, 'The West in Indian Feminist Discourse and Practice', *Women's Studies International Forum* 20, 1 (1997): 3–19.
Ahluwalia, Sanjam, *Reproductive Restraints: Birth Control in India, 1877–1947* (Urbana: University of Illinois Press, 2008).
Aiyar, Sana, *Indians in Kenya: The Politics of Diaspora* (Cambridge, MA: Harvard University Press, 2015).

Armstrong, Elizabeth, 'Before Bandung: The Anti-Imperialist Women's Movement in Asia and the Women's International Democratic Federation', *Signs: Journal of Women in Culture and Society* 41, 2 (2016): 305–31.

Ali, Azra Asghar, 'Indian Muslim Women's Suffrage Campaign: Personal Dilemma and Communal Identity 1919–47', *Journal of the Pakistan Historical Survey* 47, 2 (June 1999): 33–46.

Ali, Azra Asghar and Shahnaz Tariq, 'Begum Jahanara Shahnawaz and the Socio-Cultural Uplift of Muslim Women in British India', *Journal of the Research Society of Pakistan* 45, 2 (2008): 115–33.

Allen, Margaret, '"A Fine Type of Hindoo" Meets "the Australian Type": British Indians in Australia and Diverse Masculinities', in *Transnational Ties: Australian Lives in the World*, ed. Desley Deacon, Penny Russell, and Angela Woollacott, 41–56 (Canberra: ANU E Press, 2008).

Amos, Valerie and Pratibha Parmar, 'Challenging Imperial Feminism', *Feminist Review* 17, 1 (1984): 3–19.

Anagol, Padma, *The Emergence of Feminism in India, 1850–1920* (Aldershot: Ashgate, 2005).

Anand, Anita, *Sophia: Princess, Suffragette, Revolutionary* (London: Bloomsbury, 2015).

Badran, Margot, *Feminists, Islam, and Nation: Gender and the Making of Modern Egypt* (Princeton: Princeton University Press, 1995).

Ballantyne, Tony, 'Mobility, Empire, Colonisation', *History Australia* 11, 2 (August 2014): 7–37.

Banerjee, Sukanya, *Becoming Imperial Citizens: Indians in the Late-Victorian Empire* (Durham: Duke University Press, 2010).

Basu, Aparna, *Mridula Sarabhai: Rebel with a Cause* (New Delhi: Oxford University Press, 1996).

———, *The Pathfinder: Dr Muthulakshmi Reddi* (New Delhi: AIWC, 1987).

Basu, Aparna and Bharati Ray, *Women's Struggle: A History of the All India Women's Conference 1927–2002*, 2nd ed. (New Delhi: Manohar, 2002).

Bayly, C. A., *The Birth of the Modern World 1780–1914: Global Connections and Comparisons* (Oxford: Blackwell, 2004).

Besant, Annie, *Women and Politics: The Way out of the Present Difficulty* (London: Theosophical Publishing Society, 1914).

Bier, Laura, *Revolutionary Womanhood: Feminisms, Modernity, and the State in Nasser's Egypt* (Stanford: Stanford University Press, 2011).

Bisnauth, Dale, *The Settlement of Indians in Guyana 1890–1930* (Leeds: Peepal Tree, 2000).

Boittin, Jennifer Anne, *Colonial Metropolis: The Urban Grounds of Anti-Imperialism and Feminism in Interwar Paris* (Lincoln: University of Nebraska Press, 2010).

Bolt, Christine, *Sisterhood Questioned? Race, Class and Internationalism in the American and British Women's Movements, c. 1880s–1970s* (Abingdon: Routledge, 2005).

Bosch, Mineke, ed., *Politics and Friendship: Letters from the International Woman Suffrage Alliance, 1902–1942* (Columbus: Ohio State University Press, 1990).

Bressey, Caroline, 'Geographies of Solidarity and the Black Political Diaspora in London before 1914', in *Indigenous Networks: Mobility, Connections and Exchange*, ed. Jane Carey and Jane Lydon, 241–61 (New York: Routledge, 2014).

Brown, Judith, *Modern India: The Origins of an Asian Democracy* (New Delhi: Oxford University Press, 1984).

Burton, Antoinette, *Burdens of History: British Feminists, Indian Women, and Imperial Culture, 1865–1915* (Chapel Hill: University of Carolina Press, 1994).

———, 'The Feminist Quest for Identity: British Imperial Suffragism and "Global Sisterhood", 1900–1915', *Journal of Women's History* 3, 2, (1991): 46–81.

Candy, Catherine, 'The Inscrutable Irish–Indian Feminist Management of Anglo-American Hegemony, 1917–1947', *Journal of Colonialism and Colonial History* 2, 1 (2001).

———, 'Mystical Internationalism in Margaret Cousins's Feminist World', *Women's Studies International Forum* 32 (2009): 29–34.

———, 'Relating Feminisms, Nationalisms and Imperialisms: Ireland, India and Margaret Cousin's Sexual Politics', *Women's History Review* 3, 4 (1994): 581–94.

Chatterjee, Partha, *The Nation and Its Fragments: Colonial and Postcolonial Histories* (Princeton: Princeton University Press, 1993).

Chattopadhyaya, Kamaladevi, *The Awakening of Indian Women* (Madras: Everyman's Press, 1939).

———, *Indian Women's Battle for Freedom* (New Delhi: Abhinav Publications, 1983).

Chaudhuri, Maitrayee, *Indian Women's Movement: Reform and Revival* (New Delhi: Radiant Publishers, 1993).

Chesterman, John and Brian Galligan, *Citizens without Rights: Aborigines and Australian Citizenship* (Cambridge: Cambridge University Press, 1997).

Chiriyankandath, James, '"Democracy" under the Raj: Elections and Separate Representations in British India', in *Democracy in India*, ed. Niraja Gopal Jayal (New Delhi: Oxford University Press, 2001).

Chopra, J. K., *Women in the Indian Parliament (A Critical Study of Their Role)* (New Delhi: Mittal Publications, 1993).

Chowdhury, Nusrat Jahan, 'Gender Quotas and Women's Representation in Parliament: Lessons from Bangladesh', in *Public Policy and Governance in Bangladesh: Forty Years of Experience*, ed. Nizam Ahmed, 135–49 (Abingdon: Routledge, 2016).

Cousins, James H., and Margaret E. Cousins, *We Two Together* (Madras: Ganesh and Co., 1950).

Cousins, Margaret E., *The Awakening of Asian Womanhood* (Madras: Ganesh and Co., 1922).

Crawford, Elizabeth, *The Women's Suffrage Movement: A Reference Guide 1866–1928* (London: UCL Press, 1999).

Dampier, Helen, '"Going on with Our Little Movement in the Hum Drum Way Which Alone Is Possible in a Land like This": Olive Schreiner and Suffrage Networks in Britain and South Africa, 1905–1913', *Women's History Review* 25, 4 (2016): 536–50.

Davies, Thomas, *NGOs: A New History of Transnational Civil Society* (London: Hurst and Co., 2013).

De, Rohit, 'Mumtaz Bibi's Broken Heart: The Many Lives of the Dissolution of Muslim Marriages Act', *Indian Economic and Social History Review* 46, 1 (2009): 105–30.

De Haan, Francisca, Margaret Allen, June Purvis, and Krassimira Daskalova, eds, *Women's Activism: Global Perspectives from the 1890s to the Present* (London: Routledge, 2013).

Delap, Lucy, 'Uneven Orientalisms: Burmese Women and the Feminist Imagination', *Gender & History* 24, 2 (August 2012): 389–410.

———, 'The "Woman Question" and the Origins of Feminism', in *The Cambridge History of Nineteenth-Century Political Thought*, ed. Gareth Stedman Jones and Gregory Claeys, 319–48 (Cambridge: Cambridge University Press, 2011).

Delap, Lucy, Maria DiCenzo, and Leila Ryan, eds, *Feminism and the Periodical Press, 1900–1918* (Abingdon: Routledge, 2006).

Deutsch, Regine, *The International Woman Suffrage Alliance: Its History from 1904 to 1929* (London: IWSA, 1929).

de Silva, Chandra, 'A Historical Overview of Women in Sri Lankan Politics', in *Women and Politics in Sri Lanka: A Comparative Perspective*, ed. Sirima Kiribamune, 19–69 (Kandy: International Centre for Ethnic Studies, 1999).

deVries, Jacqueline, 'Popular and Smart: Scholarship on the Women's Suffrage Movement in Britain Still Matters', *History Compass* 11, 3 (2013): 177–88.

DuBois, Ellen, 'Woman Suffrage: The View from the Pacific', *Pacific Historical Review* 69, 4 (2000): 539–51.

DuBois, Ellen Carol, 'Woman Suffrage around the World: Three Phases of Suffragist Internationalism', in *Suffrage and Beyond: International Feminist Perspectives*, ed. Caroline Daley and Melanie Nolan, 252–74 (Auckland: Auckland University Press, 1994).

DuBois, Ellen and Haleh Emrani, 'A Speech by Nour Hamada: Tehran, 1932', *Journal of Middle East Women's Studies* 4, 1 (2008): 107–24.

Edib, Halidé, *Inside India*, ed. Mushirul Hasan (New Delhi: Oxford University Press, 2002).

Edwards, Louise and Mina Roces, eds, *Women Suffrage in Asia: Gender, Nationalism and Democracy* (London: RoutledgeCurzon, 2004).

Everett, Jana, '"All the Women Were Hindu and All the Muslims Were Men": State, Identity Politics and Gender, 1917–1951', *Economic and Political Weekly* 36, 23 (9 June 2001): 2071–80.

Everett, Jana Matson, *Women and Social Change in India* (New Delhi: Heritage, 1981).

Featherstone, David, *Solidarity: Hidden Histories and Geographies of Internationalism* (London: Zed Books, 2012).

———, 'The Spatial Politics of the Past Unbound: Transnational Networks and the Making of Political Identities', *Global Networks* 7, 4 (2007): 430–52.

Fletcher, Ian Christopher, Laura E. Nym Mayhall, and Philippa Levine, eds, *Women's Suffrage in the British Empire: Citizenship, Nation and Race* (London: Routledge, 2000).

Forbes, Geraldine H. 'Caged Tigers: "First Wave" Feminists in India', *Women's Studies International Forum* 5, 6 (1982): 525–36.

———, 'Votes for Women: The Demand for Women's Franchise in India 1917–1937', in *Symbols of Power: Studies on the Political Status of Women in India*, ed. Vina Mazumdar, 3–23 (Bombay: Allied Publishers, 1979).

———, 'Women of Character, Grit and Courage: The Reservation Debate in Historical Perspective', in *Between Tradition, Counter-tradition and Heresy: Contributions in Honour of Vina Mazumdar*, ed. Lotika Sarkar, Kumud Sharma, and Leela Kasturi, 221–39 (Delhi: Rainbow Publishers, 2002).

———, *Women in Modern India* (Cambridge: Cambridge University Press, 1998).

Gandhi, Leela, *Affective Communities: Anticolonial Thought and the Politics of Friendship* (Delhi: Permanent Black, 2006).

Gorman, Daniel, *The Emergence of International Society in the 1920s* (Cambridge: Cambridge University Press, 2012).

———, 'Wider and Wider Still? Racial Politics, Intra-Imperial Immigration and the Absence of an Imperial Citizenship in the British Empire', *Journal of Colonialism and Colonial History* 3, 3 (2002).

Gould, Harold A. *Sikhs, Swamis, Students, and Spies: The India Lobby in the United States, 1900–1946* (New Delhi: Sage, 2006).

Grewal, Inderpal, *Home and Harem: Nation, Gender, Empire, and the Cultures of Travel* (London: Leicester University Press, 1996).

Grimshaw, Patricia, 'Reading the Silences: Suffrage Activists and Race in Nineteenth-Century Settler Societies', in *Women's Rights and Human Rights: International Historical Perspectives*, ed. Patricia Grimshaw, Katie Holmes, and Marilyn Lake, 31–48 (Basingstoke: Palgrave Macmillan, 2001).

———, 'Settler Anxieties, Indigenous Peoples, and Women's Suffrage in the Colonies of Australia, New Zealand, and Hawai'i, 1888–1902', *Pacific Historical Review* 69, 4 (November 2000): 553–72.

Gray, R. M. 'Women in Indian Politics', in *Political India 1832–1932: A Co-Operative Survey of a Century*, ed. John Cumming (London: Oxford University Press, 1932).

Hannam, June, 'International Dimensions of Women's Suffrage: "At the Crossroads of Several Interlocking Identities"', *Women's History Review* 14, 3–4 (2005): 543–60.

Hauser, Walter and Wendy Singer, 'The Democratic Rite: Celebration and Participation in the Indian Elections', in *Democracy in India*, ed. Niraja Gopal Jayal (New Delhi: Oxford University Press, 2001).

Hooper, Paul F. 'Feminism in the Pacific: The Pan-Pacific and Southeast Asia Women's Association', *The Pacific Historian* 20, 4 (Winter 1976): 367–78.

Hunt, James D., *Gandhi in London* (New Delhi: Promilla and Co., 1978).

Ikeya, Chie, *Refiguring Women, Colonialism, and Modernity in Burma* (Honolulu: University of Hawai'i Press, 2011).

Jayal, Niraja Gopal, ed., *Democracy in India* (New Delhi: Oxford University Press, 2001).

Jayawardena, Kumari, *Feminism and Nationalism in the Third World* (London: Zed Books, 1986).

Jensen, Joan M., *Passage from India: Asian Indian Immigrants in North America* (New Haven: Yale University Press, 1988).

Jinarajadasa, Dorothy, 'The Emancipation of Indian Women', *Transactions of the Eighth Congress of the Federation of European National Societies of the Theosophical Society held in Vienna July 21st to 26th 1923*, ed. C. W. Dijkgraaf, 82–8 (Amsterdam: Council of the Federations, 1923).

———, *Why Women Want the Vote* (Adyar: Women's Indian Association, 1921).

John, Mary E., 'Alternate Modernities? Reservations and Women's Movement in 20th Century India', *Economic and Political Weekly* 35, 43/44 (28 October 2000): 3822–9.

————, 'Women and Feminisms in Contemporary Asia: New Comparisons, New Connections?', *Interventions* 9, 2 (2007): 165–73.

Khan, Noor-Aiman I., *Egyptian–Indian Nationalist Collaboration and the British Empire* (New York: Palgrave Macmillan, 2011).

Kishwar, Madhu, 'Gandhi on Women', *Economic and Political Weekly* 20, 41 (12 October 1985): 1753–8.

Kumar, Radha, *The History of Doing: An Illustrated Account of Movements for Women's Rights and Feminism in India 1800–1990* (London: Verso, 1993).

Lal, David, Abhiruchi Ojha, and Nidhi Sadana Sabharwal, 'Women's Political Representation in the 16th Lok Sabha: Continuity, Contestation or Change?', *Women's Link* 20, 3 (2014): 3–10.

Lam, Mithan, *Women in India: A General Survey of their Condition Status and Advancement* (New Delhi: AIWC, 1973).

Lambert-Hurley, Siobhan, *Muslim Women, Reform and Princely Patronage: Nawab Sultan Jahan Begam of Bhopal* (London: Routledge, 2007).

Legg, Stephen, 'An Intimate and Imperial Feminism: Meliscent Shephard and the Regulation of Prostitution in Colonial India', *Environment and Planning D: Society and Space* 28 (2010): 68–94.

Lester, Alan, 'Imperial Circuits and Networks: Geographies of the British Empire', *History Compass* 4, 1 (2006): 124–41.

Liddle, Joanna and Rama Joshi, 'Gender and Imperialism in British India', *Economic and Political Weekly* 20, 43 (26 October 1985): WS72–WS78.

Minault, Gail, ed., *The Extended Family: Women and Political Participation in India and Pakistan* (Delhi: Chanakya Publications, 1981).

Mohanty, Chandra Talpade, 'Introduction: Cartographies of Struggle: Third World Women and the Politics of Feminism', in *Third World Women and the Politics of Feminism*, ed. Mohanty, Chandra Talpade, Ann Russo, and Lourdes Torres (Bloomington: Indiana University Press, 1991), 1–47.

Montagu, Edwin S., *An Indian Diary* (London: William Heinemann, 1930).

Mukherjee, Sumita, 'The All-Asian Women's Conference 1931: Indian Women and Their Leadership of a Pan-Asian Feminist Organisation', *Women's History Review* 26, 3 (2017): 363–81.

————, 'Herabai Tata and Sophia Duleep Singh: Suffragette Resistances for India and Britain, 1910–1920', in *South Asian Resistances in Britain 1858–1947*, ed. Rehana Ahmed and Sumita Mukherjee, 106–21 (London: Continuum, 2012).

————, *Nationalism, Education and Migrant Identities: The England-Returned* (Abingdon: Routledge, 2010).

Newbigin, Eleanor, *The Hindu Family and the Emergence of Modern India: Law, Citizenship and Community* (Cambridge: Cambridge University Press, 2013).

Nijhawan, Shobna, 'Fallen through the Nationalist and Feminist Grids of Analysis: Political Campaigning of Indian Women against Indentured Labour Emigration', *Indian Journal of Gender Studies* 21, 1 (2014): 111–33.

———, 'At the Margins of Empire: Feminist–nationalist Configurations of Burmese Society in the Hindi Public (1917–1920)', *The Journal of Asian Studies* 71, 4 (2012): 1013–33.

Paisley, Fiona, 'Citizens of Their World: Australian Feminism and Indigenous Rights in the International Context, 1920s and 1930s', *Feminist Review* 58 (Spring 1998): 66–84.

———, *Glamour in the Pacific: Cultural Internationalism and Race Politics in the Women's Pan-Pacific* (Honolulu: University of Hawai'i Press, 2009).

———, 'White Women in the Field: Feminism, Cultural Relativism and Aboriginal Rights, 1920–1937', *Journal of Australian Studies* 21, 52 (1997): 113–25.

Pandit, Vijayalakshmi, *So I Became a Minister* (Allahabad: Kitabistan, 1939).

Paranjape, Makarand, ed., *Sarojini Naidu: Selected Letters 1890s to 1940s* (New Delhi: Kali for Women, 1996).

Pedersen, Susan, *Eleanor Rathbone and the Politics of Conscience* (New Haven: Yale University Press, 2004).

Pethick-Lawrence, Emmeline, *My Part in a Changing World* (London: Victor Gollancz, 1938).

Pearson, Gail, 'Reserved Seats—Women and the Vote in Bombay', *Indian Economic and Social History Review* 20, 47 (1983): 47–65.

Prasad, Birendra, *Indian Nationalism and Asia (1900–1947)* (Delhi: B. R. Publishing Corporation, 1979).

Rama Rau, Dhanvanthi, *An Inheritance: The Memoirs of Dhanvanthi Rama Rau* (London: Heinemann, 1978).

Rama Rau, Santha, *Gifts of Passage* (London: Victor Gollancz, 1961).

Ramusack, Barbara N., 'Cultural Missionaries, Maternal Imperialists, Feminist Allies: British Women Activists in India, 1865–1945', in *Western Women and Imperialism: Complicity and Resistance*, ed. Nupur Chaudhuri and Margaret Strobel, 119–36 (Bloomington: Indiana University Press, 1992).

Ray, Bharati, 'The Freedom Movement and Feminist Consciousness in Bengal, 1905–1929', in *From the Seams of History: Essays on Indian Women* (New Delhi: Oxford University Press, 1995), 174–218.

Rischbieth, Bessie M., *March of Australian Women: A Record of Fifty Years' Struggle for Equal Citizenship* (Perth: Paterson Brokensha, 1964).

Reddi, S. Muthulakshmi, ed., *Mrs Margaret Cousins and Her Work in India* (Adyar: Women's Indian Association, 1956).

Roces, Mina and Louise Edwards, eds, *Women's Movements in Asia: Feminisms and Transnational Activism* (Abingdon: Routledge, 2010).

Ross, Susan Deller, *Women's Human Rights: The International and Comparative Law Casebook* (Philadelphia: University of Pennsylvania Press, 2013).

Roy, Anupama, *Gendered Citizenship: Historical and Conceptual Explorations* (New Delhi: Orient Longman, 2005).

Rupp, Leila J., 'Challenging Imperialism in International Women's Organizations, 1888–1945', *NWSA Journal* 8, 1 (1996): 8–27.

———, 'Constructing Internationalism: The Case of Transnational Women's Organizations, 1888–1945', *The American Historical Review* 99, 5 (1994): 1571–600.

———, *Worlds of Women: The Making of an International Women's Movement* (Princeton: Princeton University Press, 1997).

Sandell, Marie, '"A Real Meeting of the Women of the East and the West": Women and Internationalism in the Interwar Period', in *Internationalism Reconfigured: Transnational Ideas and Movements between the World Wars*, ed. Daniel Laqua, 161–85 (London: I. B. Tauris, 2011).

———, *The Rise of Women's Transnational Activism: Identity and Sisterhood between the World Wars* (London: I. B. Tauris, 2015).

Sarkar, Tanika, *Hindu Wife, Hindu Nation* (Delhi: Permanent Black, 2001).

———, 'Politics and Women in Bengal: The Conditions and Meaning of Participation', *Indian Economic and Social History Review* 21, 1 (1984): 91–101.

Sharma, Kumud, 'Power and Representation: Reservation for Women in India', *Asian Journal of Women's Studies* 6, 1 (31 March 2000).

Scott, Joan W., 'Gender: A Useful Category of Historical Analysis', *The American Historical Review* 91, 5 (1986): 1053–75.

Sen Gupta, Padmini, *Pioneer Women of India* (Bombay: Thacker and Co., 1944).

Sein, Daw Mya, 'Towards Independence in Burma: The Role of Women', *Asian Affairs* 3, 3 (October 1972): 288–99.

Sen, Mrinalini, *Knocking at the Door (Lectures and Other Writings)* (Calcutta: Living Age Press, 1954).

Sen, Satadru, *Migrant Races: Empire, Identity and K. S. Ranjitsinhji* (Manchester: Manchester University Press, 2004).

Sen, Sushama, *Memoirs of an Octogenarian* (Delhi: Chatterjee and Sen, 1971).

Shahnawaz, Jahan Ara, *Father and Daughter: A Political Autobiography* (Lahore: Nigarishat, 1971).

Shani, Ornit, 'Making India's Democracy: Rewriting the Bureaucratic Colonial Imagination in the Preparation of the First Elections', *Comparative Studies in Society and History* 36, 1 (2006): 83–101.

Shepherd, Verene, *Transients to Settlers: The Experience of Indians in Jamaica 1845–1950* (Leeds: Peepal Tree, 1993).

Siddiq, Muhammad, 'Hasrat Mohani', *Journal of the Pakistan Historical Society* 32, 1 (January 1984): 31–70.

Sinha, Mrinalini, 'Nations in an Imperial Crucible', in *Gender and Empire*, ed. Philippa Levine (Oxford: Oxford University Press, 2004), 181–202.

———, *Specters of Mother India: The Global Restructuring of an Empire* (Durham: Duke University Press, 2006).

———, 'Suffragism and Internationalism: The Enfranchisement of British and Indian Women under an Imperial State', *Indian Economic and Social History Review* 36, 4 (1999): 461–84.

Sinha, Mrinalini, Donna J. Guy, and Angela Woollacott, 'Introduction: Why Feminisms and Internationalism?', *Gender & History* 10, 3 (1998): 345–57.

Slate, Nico, *Colored Cosmopolitanism: The Shared Struggle for Freedom in the United States and India* (Cambridge, MA: Harvard University Press, 2012).

Smitley, Megan, '"Inebriates", "Heathens", Templars and Suffragists: Scotland and Imperial Feminism c.1870–1914', *Women's History Review* 11, 3 (2002): 455–80.

Snaith, Anna, *Modernist Voyages: Colonial Women Writers in London, 1890–1945* (Cambridge: Cambridge University Press, 2014).

Southard, Barbara, 'Colonial Politics and Women's Rights: Woman Suffrage Campaigns in Bengal, British India in the 1920s', *Modern Asian Studies* 27, 2 (1993): 397–439.

———, *The Women's Movement and Colonial Politics in Bengal: The Quest for Political Rights, Education and Social Reform Legislation, 1921–1936* (Delhi: Manohar, 1995).

Stolte, Carolien, 'Bringing Asia to the World: Indian Trade Unionism and the Long Road towards the Asiatic Labour Congress, 1919–37', *Journal of Global History* 7, 2 (July 2012): 257–78.

———, '"Enough of the Great Napoleons!" Raja Mahendra Pratap's Pan-Asian Projects (1929–1939)', *Modern Asian Studies* 46, 2 (March 2012): 403–23.

Stolte, Carolien and Harald Fischer-Tiné, 'Imagining Asia in India: Nationalism and Internationalism (ca. 1905–1940)', *Comparative Studies in Society and History* 54, 1 (January 2012): 65–92.

Stretton, Pat and Christine Finnimore, 'Black Fellow Citizens: Aborigines and the Commonwealth Franchise', *Australian Historical Studies* 25, 101 (1993): 521–35.

Sullivan, Zohreh T., 'Eluding the Feminist, Overthrowing the Modern? Transformations in Twentieth-Century Iran', in *Remaking Women: Feminism and Modernity in the Middle East*, ed. Lila Abu-Lughod (Princeton: Princeton University Press, 1998).

Talwar, Vir Bharat, 'Feminist Consciousness in Women's Journals in Hindi, 1910–1920', in *Recasting Women: Essays in Indian Colonial History*, ed.

Kumkum Sangari and Sudesh Vaid (New Brunswick: Rutgers University Press, 1990), 204–32.

Tata, Herabai, 'A Short Sketch of Indian Women's Franchise Work' (n.d.), in *Women's Voices: Selections from Nineteenth and Early-Twentieth Century Indian Writing in English*, ed. Eunice de Souza and Lindsay Pereira, 127–34 (Delhi: Oxford University Press, 2002).

Tinker, Hugh, *Separate and Unequal: India and the Indians in the British Commonwealth 1920–1950* (London: C. Hurst & Co., 1976).

Tusan, Michelle Elizabeth, 'Writing Stri Dharma: International Feminism, Nationalist Politics, and Women's Press Advocacy in Late Colonial India', *Women's History Review* 12, 4 (2003): 623–49.

Tyrrell, Ian, *Woman's World Woman's Empire: The Woman's Christian Temperance Union in International Perspective, 1880–1930* (Chapel Hill: The University of North Carolina Press, 1991).

Vahed, Goolam, 'Race, Empire and Citizenship: Sarojini Naidu's 1924 Visit to South Africa', *South African Historical Journal* 64, 2 (2012): 319–42.

Visram, Rozina, *Asians in Britain: 400 Years of History* (London: Pluto Press, 2002).

———, *Women in India and Pakistan: The Struggle for Independence from British Rule* (Cambridge: Cambridge University Press, 1992).

Visweswaran, Kamala, 'Small Speeches, Subaltern Gender: Nationalist Ideology and Its Historiography', in *Subaltern Studies IX: Writings on South Asian History and Society*, ed. Shahid Amin and Dipesh Chakrabarty, 83–125 (New Delhi: Oxford University Press, 1996).

Vyawahare, Malavika, 'Rhetoric about Women's Issues Outpaces Political Progress', *The New York Times*, 9 May 2014, available at http://india.blogs.nytimes.com/2014/05/09/rhetoric-about-womens-issues-outpaces-political-progress/?_r=0.

Wadia, Avabai B., *The Light Is Ours: Memoirs and Movements* (London: International Planned Parenthood Federation, 2001).

Waiz, S. A., ed., *Indians Abroad* (Bombay: Imperial Indian Citizenship Association, 1927).

Walker, Cherryl, *Women and Resistance in South Africa* (London: Onyx Press, 1982).

Weber, Charlotte, 'Unveiling Scheherazade: Feminist Orientalism in the International Alliance of Women, 1911–1950', *Feminist Studies* 27, 1 (2001): 125–57.

Whitehead, Kay and Lynne Tretheway, 'Aging and Activism in the Context of the British Dominions Woman Suffrage Union, 1914–1922', *Women's Studies International Forum* 31 (2008): 30–41.

Woodsmall, Ruth Frances, *Eastern Women Today and Tomorrow* (Boston: The Central Committee on the United Study of Foreign Missions, 1933).

———, *Moslem Women Enter a New World* (London: George Allen and Unwin, 1936).

Woollacott, Angela, 'Australian Women's Metropolitan Activism: From Suffrage, to Imperial Vanguard, to Commonwealth Feminism', in *Women's Suffrage in the British Empire: Citizenship, Nation and Race*, ed. Ian Christopher Fletcher, Laura E. Nym Mayhall, and Philippa Levine, 207–23 (London: Routledge, 2000).

———, 'Inventing Commonwealth and Pan-Pacific Feminisms: Australian Women's Internationalist Activism in the 1920s–30s', *Gender & History* 10, 3 (November 1998): 425–48.

———, *To Try Her Fortune in London: Australian Women, Colonialism, and Modernity* (Oxford: Oxford University Press, 2001).

Yasutake, Rumi, 'The Rise of Women's Internationalism in the Countries of the Asia-Pacific Region during the Interwar Years, from a Japanese Perspective', *Women's History Review* 20, 4 (2011): 521–32.

Zöllner, Hans-Bernd, ed., *Myanmar Literature Project. Working Paper No. 10:18. Two Books on Sex and Gender* (Druck: Universität Passau, 2011).

Index

About the Author

Sumita Mukherjee teaches history at the University of Bristol, UK, where she presently holds the position of senior lecturer in history. Her research mainly focuses on the movement of men and women from the Indian subcontinent to other parts of the world, and their return again to India. Her interests lie in the effects travel and migration had on a range of social and political identities during the time of the British Empire. She has published widely in this area, including the book *Nationalism, Education and Migrant Identities: The England-Returned* (2009).